Healthy Urban Environments

T0298382

Set in the 'human–environment' interaction space, this book applies new theoretical and practical insights to understanding what makes healthy urban environments. It stems from recognition that the world is rapidly urbanising and the international concern with how to create healthy settings and liveable cities in the context of a rapidly changing planet. A key argument is that usual attempts to make healthy cities are limited by human-centrism and bifurcated, western thinking about cities, health and nature. Drawing on the innovative 'more-than-human' scholarship from a range of disciplines, it presents a synthesis of the main contributions, and how they can be used to rethink what healthy urban environments are, and who they are for. In particular, the book turns its attention to urban biodiversity and the many non-human species that live in, make and share cities with humans.

The book will be of interest to scholars and students in human geography, health sociology, environmental humanities, public health, health promotion, planning and urban design, as well as policymakers and professionals working in these fields.

Cecily Maller is a Vice Chancellor's Senior Research Fellow and Co-leader of the Beyond Behaviour Change Research Program – Centre for Urban Research, School of Global, Urban and Social Studies, RMIT University, Australia.

Routledge Studies in Environment and Health

For more information about this series, please visit: https://www.routledge.com/Routledge-Studies-in-Environment-and-Health/book-series/RSEH

The study of the impact of environmental change on human health has rapidly gained momentum in recent years, and an increasing number of scholars are now turning their attention to this issue. Reflecting the development of this emerging body of work, the *Routledge Studies in Environment and Health* series is dedicated to supporting this growing area with cutting-edge inter-disciplinary research targeted at a global audience. The books in this series cover key issues such as climate change, urbanisation, waste management, water quality, environmental degradation and pollution, and examine the ways in which these factors impact human health from a social, economic and political perspective.

Comprising edited collections, co-authored volumes and single-author monographs, this innovative series provides an invaluable resource for advanced undergraduate and postgraduate students, scholars, policymakers and practitioners with an interest in this new and important field of study.

Ethics of Environmental Health
Edited by Friedo Zölzer and Gaston Meskens

Healthy Urban Environments
More-Than-Human Theories
Cecily Maller

Healthy Urban Environments

More-than-Human Theories

Cecily Maller

LONDON AND NEW YORK

First published 2018
by Routledge
2 Park Square, Milton Park, Abingdon, Oxon OX14 4RN

and by Routledge
711 Third Avenue, New York, NY 10017

Routledge is an imprint of the Taylor & Francis Group, an informa business

© 2018 Cecily Maller

British Library Cataloguing in Publication Data
A catalogue record for this book is available from the British Library

Library of Congress Cataloging-in-Publication Data
Names: Maller, Cecily, author.
Title: Healthy urban environments : more-than-human theories / Cecily Maller.
Description: Abingdon, Oxon ; New York, NY : Routledge, 2018. |
Series: Routledge studies in environment and health | Includes bibliographical references.
Identifiers: LCCN 2017060244 | ISBN 9781138658851 (hbk) | ISBN 9781315620534 (ebk)
Subjects: LCSH: Urban ecology (Sociology) | City planning—Health aspects. | City planning—Environmental aspects.
Classification: LCC HT241.M356 2018 | DDC 304.2/091732—dc23
LC record available at https://lccn.loc.gov/2017060244

ISBN: 978-1-138-65885-1 (hbk)
ISBN: 978-1-315-62053-4 (ebk)
ISBN: 9780367459031

Typeset in Sabon
by Keystroke, Neville Lodge, Tettenhall, Wolverhampton

To Gershon Maller and Christina Kerwin for teaching me the power of ideas

Contents

Acknowledgements   xi

1   Redefining healthy urban environments   1

PART I
Understanding more-than-human theories   21

2   The Affective Turn: non-representational theories,
    affect and emotions   23
3   The New Materialisms Turn: materiality, vital
    materialism and assemblages   47
4   The Practice Turn: social practices, performance
    and routine   71

PART II
Making more-than-human healthy urban environments   91

5   Understanding health as more-than-human   93
6   Cities as more-than-human habitat   109
7   Changing practices for understanding and making
    healthy urban environments   131
8   More-than-human healthy futures   151

Index   158

Acknowledgements

Like any long-term project, this book has percolated over several years and finally emerged in its current form thanks to many rewarding conversations with colleagues and thought-provoking encounters with the scholarship of others. I would like to acknowledge some of those to whom I feel particularly indebted. To Yolande Strengers; it is not easy to express gratitude to such a wonderful colleague and friend who inspired and encouraged so many rewarding scholarly and intellectual endeavours – not to mention many other types of adventures – that might never have been embarked upon, including this book, had we not had the chance to work together since 2011. It has been a privilege to join forces and weather the ups and downs of academia together. I particularly acknowledge Yolande's patience and perseverance in reading the dense drafts of the first chapters of this book, her insightful suggestions and our stimulating, and occasionally mischievous (but always productive), discussions as two self-confessed theory nerds. Having the freedom to lead our own research programme played no small part in our achievements, and I acknowledge the research leaders at RMIT University, particularly Ralph Horne and Jago Dodson, respectively, as directors of the Centre for Design and Centre for Urban Research, for their support of the Beyond Behaviour Change Research Programme.

The Beyond Behaviour Change Research Programme at RMIT University has provided fertile ground for the growing of ideas in various ways. First, the Social Practice Theory Reading Group has generated rich and provocative discussions about theories of social practice for several years. Second, the *Animals, Automated Devices and Ecosystems* symposium on the agencies of non-humans that Yolande Strengers and I chaired in Barcelona in October 2015 confirmed my interest in more-than-human theories and solidified my commitment to writing this book. The Centre for Urban Research and RMIT Europe were instrumental in enabling this event to occur. And third, the Beyond Behaviour Change Writing Retreats held in 2016 and 2017 were incredibly useful for producing several chapters in a condensed amount of time. I thank all those who attended for their scholarly companionship, and the Centre for Urban Research for supporting these events. Finally, this book would not have been written without the financial support received through an RMIT University Vice Chancellor's Senior Research Fellowship.

The ideas expressed in the book benefited enormously from other colleagues who read and provided incisive feedback, suggestions for chapters and general encouragement, including David Evans, Jean Hillier, Alan Latham, Russell Hitchings, Gordon Walker, Emma Power, Paula Arcari, Sarah Robertson and Martin Mulligan. I also thank audiences at the conferences of the Institute of Australian Geographers (2016, 2017), the Royal Geographical Society with the Institute of British Geographers (2017), and the Australian Sociological Association (2016), where I first aired some of the thinking that found its way into the book.

In producing this book, I am indebted to Dr Gershon Maller of Literati Academic and Literary Editors, Melbourne for his extensive structural edit that took the draft manuscript to another level. I also acknowledge the valuable support of the editorial and production teams at Routledge, particularly their patience.

On the home front, my heartfelt thanks to Dom Jurčec for his perceptive advice, astute editorial assistance and patience. I also acknowledge my two favourite 'non-humans', Si Si and Jack Maller, for their near-constant companionship during the writing process, and for getting me out walking our neighbourhood on a regular basis.

Finally, and in no small way, I acknowledge that I live and work on Country that belongs to the people of the Kulin Nation. I pay respect to all Elders past, present and future, and recognise that the lands and waters they care for were never ceded.

1 Redefining healthy urban environments

Introduction

Cities[1] may appear to be all about humans, but entangled relationships and encounters between people and innumerable 'non-humans' are at the heart of most urban challenges (Gandy 2002; Houston et al. 2017; Whatmore 2002; Wolch 1996). Despite its flaws, particularly the tendency towards homogenisation and human-centrism, I use 'non-humans' to describe any species, materials, matters, technologies or entities that can be artificially distinguished, partially or wholly, momentarily or more permanently, from humans. As Lulka (2009, p. 383) observes: 'nonhuman is an extremely impoverished term that cannot account for the multiplicitous ways of (non)life in the world'.[2] The world that humans share comprises various non-human animals, plants, fungi, microbes, atoms, molecules, energies and waters – something 'modern' humans often choose to selectively, and at times conveniently, forget. Most non-humans come under the problematic category of 'nature', seen as separate from, and opposed to 'culture' or 'society' (Cronon 1996a; Kaika 2005; Latour 2000). Furthermore, despite our best efforts to distance ourselves from it, humans need 'nature'. Due to industrialisation and the pursuit of 'progress', this truism is forgotten, even scoffed at in the drunken headiness of human technological advancement (Plumwood 2009; Wolch 1996). However, as we descend from our techno-induced high, humanity has returned to the idea that 'nature' (however defined) is important to many aspects of our lives. Moreover, in all but the most sceptical of circles, it is recognised that humans need nature to be healthy. Supported by a large body of established evidence (e.g., Egorov et al. 2016), and endorsed by organisations such as the World Health Organization (WHO), this notion cannot be dismissed. It also means that we can no longer ignore the fact that humans are *part of* nature. For example, there is increasing evidence that biodiversity is connected to human health and well-being, although how and in what ways these effects manifest is not entirely clear (Flies et al. 2017; Mills et al. 2017; Pett et al. 2016). Some studies show a positive relation between self-reported well-being and higher levels of neighbourhood biodiversity (e.g., Botzat et al. 2016;

Luck et al. 2011), while others indicate a link between biodiversity and the health of human gut flora (e.g., Flies et al. 2017; Mills et al. 2017).

It is an undeniably arrogant, but understandable, anthropocentric fallacy to assume that, in some circumstances, humans are separate from, above or in control of nature (Greenhough 2010; Haraway 2016; Pickering 2013; Plumwood 2009). Our lack of control is evidenced by the panic unleashed when viruses with pandemic potential arise due to increasing movement of humans and non-humans in the globalised world (Greenhough 2010). The default reaction is surprise when non-humans, like viruses, other species or natural disasters, disrupt human activity in urban environments because we conceptualise cities as human-centric. Many current global problems, such as climate change, pollution, habitat destruction and mass species extinctions can be attributed to western bifurcated thinking, or the 'hyper-separation' (Plumwood 2009, p. 116) that divides humans from nature (Kaika 2005; Wolch 1996). I argue that to improve human health and the health of the planet, we need to think differently about the world and our cities. Now more than ever before, we need to understand, see and treat cities as more-than-human.

> ## Box 1.1: The Healthy Cities Programme and the Ottawa Charter for Health Promotion
>
> The long history and widespread saliency of 'healthy cities' represents an opportunity to redefine the 'healthy' concept. Despite its versatility and widespread use, the idea of healthy cities is generally attributed to WHO's Healthy Cities Programme. WHO's Regional Office for Europe launched the programme in 1986 with various European cities as signatories (Ashton et al. 1986; Duhl & Hancock 1997). WHO defines a healthy city as 'one that continually creates and improves its physical and social environments and expands the community resources that enable people to mutually support each other in performing all the functions of life and developing to their maximum potential' (World Health Organization 1998, p. 13).
>
> The modern conception of the healthy city is principally attributed to Leonard Duhl and Trevor Hancock, who were involved at the outset of WHO's Healthy Cities Programme (Duhl & Hancock 1997). Duhl (1986) likened cities to organisms or ecosystems as a way of emphasising the interaction between the various parts, and their potential for self-regulation and adaptation to maximise functionality. However, this view has been criticised as mechanistic with no acknowledgement of conflict, social inequality or power (Petersen & Lupton 1996). Defining cities and other social arrangements as organic implies they are in some way 'natural'; this can mean inequalities between men and women, socio-economic groups, or cultures are either justified or ignored

(Petersen & Lupton 1996). In contrast, advocates of the Healthy Cities Programme would argue by working to reduce inequalities, distribute power and create health for all, this is what a healthy city does. This goal is said to be achieved through dynamic processes and relationships between citizens and governments and collective action from all sectors to work together for a common purpose (Duhl & Hancock 1997). The emphasis on processes is relevant to a more-than-human agenda, as this book will demonstrate.

Since its launch, thousands of cities have formally signed up to this global initiative. Several decades on, the term 'healthy city' arguably has its own currency. More recently, it has been replaced by similar efforts to achieve 'liveable', 'sustainable' or 'ethical' cities; yet, like healthy cities, each of these labels seeks to simply encapsulate the idea that cities can be substantially improved. Curiously, each term could be compressed in the others (e.g., a liveable city could be healthy, ethical and sustainable, or a sustainable city could be liveable, healthy and ethical, and so on).

In 1986, the same year the Healthy Cities Programme was launched, the first international conference on health promotion was held in Ottawa, Canada which culminated in the signing of the Ottawa Charter for Health Promotion (World Health Organization 1986). Health promotion conceives health as a resource for everyday life, not the objective of living or simply the absence of disease (World Health Organization 2012). The prerequisite conditions for health listed in the Ottawa Charter include peace, shelter, education, food, income, a stable ecosystem, sustainable resources and social justice and equity (World Health Organization 2012). A principle tenet of the Charter is that health promotion is not only the responsibility of the health sector, but encompasses all sectors of society (World Health Organization 2012). In other words, the achievement of health requires a multi-disciplinary approach. The Charter was designed to instigate actions required to achieve health for all by the year 2000, an outcome not yet achieved (Baum et al. 2006).

If the aims of the Ottawa Charter and the healthy cities ideal are still to be accomplished, 'far-reaching changes' are required to challenge the 'economic rationalism, individualism and professionalism' (Baum 1993, p. 38) dominating city and urban agendas, and an entrenched human-centrism regarding the way we conceptualise cities and who they are for.

The book aims to use more-than-human theories as a way to rethink and transform the idea of 'healthy cities' (see Box 1.1). The idea of making cities better places is not new; and although more evocative terms have, in some ways, superseded it, the notion of creating 'healthy cities' still resonates. Signed in the mid-1980s, the mandates of the WHO Healthy Cities Programme and the Ottawa Charter for Health Promotion have been a starting point (see Box 1.1). However, to date, notions of 'healthy' cities or 'healthy urban environments' are entirely human-centric, and their advocates have made little effort 'to *rethink* the concept of the city itself' (Petersen & Lupton 1996, p. 145; emphasis added). Whether we like it or not, cities will always be more-than-human and 'any presumed exclusive human "right to the city" . . . is increasingly untenable' (Houston et al. 2017, p. 2).

In this book, I present a definition of healthy urban environments to help reshape how we think about cities and who they are for. Premised by discussions about more-than-human relations and interactions, I argue that the concept of a 'healthy city' means a city designed and recognised as a place – or more accurately, a habitat – for more-than just humans. I therefore define 'healthy urban environments' as places that acknowledge, invite and actively encourage some living non-humans to flourish, and where humans and non-humans can productively co-exist and overall benefit from each other's presence.[3] Put simply, we need to surpass our entrenched speciesism regarding cities – that is, their design, governance and the ways we live in them. To reach the point where humans are no longer the only 'beings that count' in urban environments (Whatmore 2002, p. 155), we need to shift the dominant anthropocentric paradigm Pickering (2008) calls the 'terrible gravitational attraction' of 'human specialness' (p. 2) – a paradigm promoted and maintained by monotheist religions, politics, philosophies of humanism and ontologies of representationalism (Barad 2007; Cronon 1996a; Plumwood 2009).[4] Concepts and theories are required that decentre humans and embrace complexity, emergence and process, as well as those that overtly seek to cross or transcend disciplinary boundaries.

Why focus on cities and urban environments? As the next section explains, although they are not the only form of human settlement, urban living is now the prevailing mode of human habitation, and its impact is global.

The urban context

Most humans now live in cities, and urban populations are expected to double by 2050 (United Nations General Assembly 2016a). The impact of a large human population living in urban settings makes urbanisation 'one of the twenty-first century's most transformative trends' (United Nations General Assembly 2016a, p. 3). The magnitude of interest in cities and urbanisation was evident at *Habitat III*, the *United Nations Conference on Housing and Sustainable Urban Development*, held in Quito, Ecuador in October 2016. A main outcome of the event, signed by almost 170 nations, was the adoption of a New Urban Agenda[5] – a call to action that aims:

To set global standards of achievement in sustainable urban development, *rethinking* the way we build, manage, and live in cities through
drawing together cooperation with committed partners, relevant stake-
holders, and urban actors at all levels of government as well as the
private sector.

(United Nations General Assembly 2016b,
p. 1; emphasis added)

Although city living offers multiple benefits, urban life is not trouble-free,
and particularly the health and well-being of human occupants dominate
many national and international policy agendas. Urban human inhabitants
can experience a vast array of social and environmental problems, leading to
varying health and well-being outcomes, sometimes attributed to patterns
and distributions of wealth, injustice and inequality. Common environmental
problems faced by city residents include: pollution and accumulation of
waste, low-quality or poorly constructed housing, limited access to greenspaces, lack of transport options and reduced mobility, exposure to infectious
diseases and vulnerability to climate change impacts, heatwaves and natural
disasters. These problems are obvious, and pressing, areas for improvement
if cities are to become healthier and truly deserving of the moniker 'human
habitat' (United Nations General Assembly 2016b).

As well as habitat for humans, cities are increasingly recognised as
providing habitat for non-human animal and plant species (Hinchliffe &
Whatmore 2006; Jones 2018; Low 2003). For example, in Australia, regions
of Perth, Melbourne and Brisbane have been found to be 'biodiversity
hotspots' (Garrard & Bekessy 2014, p. 63). This challenges previous assumptions about urban environments and biodiversity being geographically
incompatible. Cities also form crucial habitats for threatened species,[6] where
urban areas are of greater importance for conservation than non-urban
areas (Ives et al. 2016). This contrasts with the dominant conservation
model being the designation of protected 'wilderness' areas, remote from
human settlements, which 'does not reflect ecological reality' (Ives et al.
2016, p. 118). Also problematic is that the term 'wilderness' is a modernist
social construction (Cronon 1996b) that ignores indigenous peoples'
relationship with, and care for, their lands (Instone 1998; Porter 2010; Rose
2012). Related to these developments are increasing calls to relinquish the
human-centricity of city planning, design and management and acknowledge,
accommodate, prioritise and foster biodiversity in cities (Franklin 2017;
Garrard et al. 2017; Hinchliffe & Whatmore 2006; Houston et al. 2017;
Wolch 1996).

Thinking of cities as being about, and for, creatures (or critters) other
than humans is congruent with 'more-than-human thinking'[7] (Abram 1997;
Head 2016; Whatmore 2002). The concept is advocated by many recent
works, including Haraway's (2016) *Staying with the Trouble: Making Kin
in the Chthulucene* and Bennett's (2010) *Vibrant Matter: A Political Ecology*

of Things. Even human bodies are now increasingly recognised as 'more-than-human', with the multitudes of organisms living in and on our bodies (Yong 2016). With scholars from diverse disciplines coming to similar conclusions, combined with calls from global organisations, such as the United Nations (United nations General Assembly 2016b), to urgently rethink how we understand cities, it is timely to consider what more-than-human approaches might offer in reimagining cities as dynamic habitats and as sites for change.

Theories and thinking about healthy urban environments

Aside from the concerns highlighted in Box 1.1, several problems arise from ideas about healthy cities and the UN's New Urban Agenda. Most thinking about healthy urban environments suffers from reductive understandings of dynamic urban interactions, experiences and encounters (Kaika 2017), and ideas about nature (Cronon 1996a). Standard approaches are informed by derivative models and indicators that comprise isolated levels or binary categories that either do not interact, or if they do, contain interactions that are vague or unclear. Despite a motivation to be comprehensive or emphasise process, layers such as 'individual', 'community' and 'environment' artificially divide subject from object, agency from structure, nature from culture and individuals from communities and societies. Correspondingly, this siloed thinking is replicated in policy and other interventions that seek to design 'solutions' to urban health and sustainability problems. For example, regarding the UN's New Urban Agenda, despite being positioned as a paradigm shift where cities are rightly recognised as processes, Kaika (2017) argues that 'the key questions posed, and the methodological tools and institutional frameworks proposed, thus far remain the same' (p. 93); hence, they 'cannot offer long-term solutions to local or global socio-environmental problems' (p. 98).

Traditional ways of understanding and creating healthy urban environments struggle to account for complexity, emergence, dynamic temporal and spatial processes, and the materiality and performativity of everyday life. These approaches exclude and ignore non-humans, place too much responsibility on individual humans (Ayo 2011; Lindsay 2010) and have too much faith in 'smart' or technological interventions (Kaika 2017; Strengers 2013). This contrasts with substantial work in a range of disciplines and theoretical approaches that describe more processual, complex and relational ways of understanding and being in the world that attempt to resolve these issues. Post-human or 'more-than-human'[8] theories are particularly relevant here (Abram 1997; Whatmore 2002).

However, at this point, I want to clarify why theory is important. As the philosopher Graham Priest (2002, p. xviii) argues, 'since "productive" research is ultimately dependent on more abstract research . . . [the latter is of] fundamental value to intellectual inquiry'. Theories are explanations that help us understand and know the world and its phenomena. The knowledge, ideas and ways of thinking derived from theories and the paradigms within which they are situated can be useful in planning and designing interventions for positive change. However, they do have limitations: theories are not necessarily prescriptions for action (Shove 2014), and not all theories have practical potential. Certain theories or their ideological derivatives occupy the zeitgeist in different political climates and are congruent with different disciplinary orientations, developments or fashions. Some theories become so normalised in everyday discourse and the media that other ways of knowing the world are routinely excluded, marginalised or ignored (Shove 2010; 2014). For example, two dominant ways of thinking about urban policymaking and programme design are rational choice theory (from economics) and behaviour change theories (from psychology) (Shove 2010; Strengers & Maller 2015; Strengers et al. 2015). Different modes of thinking and describing problems before designing potential solutions can come from unexpected quarters. These ideas might be viewed as risky or even dangerous at the time, but they can also productively disrupt the status quo when required. I place more-than-human theories in this category.

Some of the theories presented in this book have been called 'wild' (Thrift 2008), while others are 'subversive and innovative' (Nicolini 2012, p. 23). Together, more-than-human theories offer a range of tantalising prospects for thinking about new and exciting ways to do research, reframe current problems and experiment with potential solutions to urban challenges on the horizon. Concepts and theories are urgently needed that embrace complexity, emergence and process, and also those that seek to cross or transcend disciplinary boundaries. Crucially, there is a pressing need to contest dominant ways of seeing, knowing and making changes that detrimentally separate humans from non-humans (Haraway 2016; Head 2016; Houston et al. 2017; Plumwood 2009; Steele et al. 2015).

This book does not seek a definitive set of answers to create healthy cities. Instead, it has three inter-related objectives related to rethinking what healthy cities are and who they are for. First, it aims to foster a greater appreciation of the things, critters, artefacts and non-human publics that make the world more-than-human. Second, to open ways of thinking, knowing and understanding cities and urban environments as more-than-human habitat. Finally, it seeks to encourage experimentation with new concepts and ideas from a more-than-human perspective and think about different interventions for change, accepting that, due to the dynamic complexity of cities, there will be unpredictable or unforeseen outcomes. The remainder of this chapter outlines the book's structure and content.

Structure and overview

The book is divided into two parts. Part I, 'Understanding more-than-human theories', draws on philosophical and theoretical resources from three different bodies of related thinking, or 'turns', presented in Chapters 2, 3 and 4. Each chapter describes the main literature associated with each turn and, using key contributions from each, tackles the first aim of the book: to gain an appreciation of things that make the world more-than-human. Part II, 'Making more-than-human healthy urban environments', addresses the second and third aims of the book by discussing how the ideas presented in Part I can be applied in urban settings, including how they might be used to rethink urban environments and cities from a more-than-human stance.

Part I: Understanding more-than-human theories

Recent decades have witnessed a highly productive period for more-than-human thinking and theory, and they continue to grow in popularity. Yet these exciting ideas have rarely been translated for use in contexts such as urban planning, design or health promotion. What I refer to as more-than-human theories are sourced from a vast collection of inter-related works and 'relational ontologies' (Castree 2003) spanning disciplines including, but not limited to, human and cultural geography, environmental humanities, post-humanist sociology, feminist studies, science and technology studies (STS), urban political ecology and political science.[9] More-than-human theories have destabilised and opened ideas about knowledge, sociality, materiality, causality, agency, determinism and ethics. Considered as a broad category, they argue for approaches that seek to study, understand and experience the world in less human-centred and more material, performative, relational and dynamic ways. More-than-human approaches have much to offer those wanting to think about cities and health differently, including the dissolution of binary categories, decentring humans and recognising non-human actors such as plants, animals and technologies. Moreover, they bring everyday encounters and seemingly mundane social practices to the fore, such as gardening or cycling.[10]

Three 'turns'

To make sense of the main branches of thought, positions and concepts, I have grouped the work I draw on under the 'more-than-human' mantle according to three inter-related 'turns' in the social sciences and humanities that emerged in the 1990s to early 2000s (although each has a much longer history). These are: The Affective Turn, The New Materialisms Turn and The Practice Turn.[11] Describing these so-called 'turns'[12] is but one way to understand and translate this diverse and complex body of literature; others have used different labels, ways of grouping or describing these contributions according to their own particular objectives.[13] Each turn is briefly explained below before being more explicated in Chapters 2, 3 and 4 respectively.

What is known as 'The Affective Turn' occurred across a range of disciplines in the social sciences and humanities, including human geography (e.g., Thrift 2008; Whatmore 2006) and critical theory (e.g., Clough & Halley 2007; Gregg & Seigworth 2010). The idea was to move away from representational and linguistic (i.e., talk and text) understandings of the world that dominate many disciplines (Barad 2003) and turn to the 'dynamism immanent to bodily matter' and its capacity for self-organisation (Clough 2008, p. 1). According to Clough (2008, p. 1), this dynamism is 'the most provocative and enduring contribution of the affective turn'. Although 'there is no single, generalisable theory of affect' (Bennett 2010; Clough & Halley 2007; Seigworth & Gregg 2010, p. 3; Thrift 2008; Wetherell 2012), in more-than-human theories, 'affect' is usually referred to as the capacity or potential to affect and be affected by the world, largely through emotions and feelings.[14] This means that aside from humans, many more creatures, critters, devices, entities and things are perceived as active agents creating changes in, and being changed by, the world in ongoing ways. For example, cars affect the way that most cities are shaped by roads and other infrastructure to support their movement. While cars and roads can generate feelings of excitement or satisfaction, they can also create fear and stress. On the other hand, a river may have attracted human settlers because of its beauty and ability to support life, but the city that emerged on its banks caused it to become polluted; hence, the river no longer supports plant or animal life. Ironically, the humans it once attracted now feel it is dirty and unsafe.

Many scholars who write about affect draw on the work of Deleuze and Guattari (1987), who, in turn, were influenced by Spinoza and Bergson (Bennett 2010; Clough 2008). Work on affect is closely intertwined with non-representational theory (Kingsbury 2015), a British theoretical phenomenon most strongly developed in geography. It is perhaps less well known elsewhere (Cresswell 2012). I discuss non-representational theories, emotions and affect in Chapter 2. Non-representational thinking helps to identify various ways of understanding phenomena compared to mainstream social science. It is known for encouraging 'wild' thinking (Thrift 2008), useful for finding new ways of doing research in urban environments and designing interventions and solutions not reliant on quantification. In general, the main contributions of non-representational and affective approaches focus on: human-non-human relations, pre-cognitive affects and emotions (i.e., how cities are experienced and felt), and the consideration of phenomena through ideas of nonlinearity and emergence rather than representation and quantification. In these ways, these approaches are about understanding detailed, nuanced experiences that might reveal new insights that others would miss. For research and policymaking, these ideas are useful in understanding how the design, management and governance of cities impact humans and non-humans, how humans and non-humans interact and respond to each other in cities, and the affective nature of attempts to create change or intervene through politics, policies and planning. For example, a wide range of affects were manifest in the resistance from human citizens to a large, potentially disruptive 'sky-rail' project to remove level crossings in Melbourne, Australia (Stone & Woodcock 2016). Conversely, affects can generate hope and support for change, such as the contagious atmosphere of positivity arising from President Obama's inauguration speech in 2009 (Anderson 2014).

Chapter 3 discusses new materialism. Sometimes referred to as the 're-turn' to materialism (Greenhough 2010; Whatmore 2006) or the plural *materialisms* (Coole & Frost 2010), it encompasses an extensive body of literature found principally in strands of geography, STS and political theory.[15] The adjective 'New' indicates that there was an 'Old' Materialism, which indeed there was (Lemke 2015). The Old or Historical Materialists were (and are) concerned with 'Marxian critiques of idealism and continuing that tradition's humanist bent' (Washick & Wingrove 2015, p. 63) to focus on the impacts of economic and social structures (Bennett 2010, p. 62). New Materialisms draw on ideas pre-dating Marx and the 'Old Materialists', by incorporating the philosophies of Spinoza and Bergson to conceptualise the world – cities in particular – in less human-centred ways. As in The Affective Turn, there is no unifying theory or approach (Whatmore 2006), but instead a collection of related ideas that at heart share an interest in the vibrancy, agency and performativity of matter, materials and other non-humans (Braun 2005; Whatmore 2002). Chapter 3 elaborates that New Materialisms' contributions are to further decentre humans and move past the assumed passivity of 'the environment' – a crucial step if cities are conceptualised as more-than-human. These theories shift notions of human sovereignty and exceptionalism to thinking that conceives the world more clearly as more-than-human, where cities are filled with active and vibrant non-humans, such as the many plants and animals in cities, and digital assistants and smart technologies in homes and workplaces.

Various ways of conducting research to understand more-than-human worlds are required to decentre humans. New Materialisms encourage innovative concepts and methods from a range of resources to achieve this objective, including relational and democratic data-making techniques, often involving humans and non-humans. An example from conservation is enlisting the public to help collect data about the plants and animals they encounter in cities through citizen science, facilitated by social media and 'apps' (Dickinson et al. 2012). In adopting a relational and democratic stance, New Materialisms try to break down disciplinary boundaries and advocate paradigm changes to more-than-human ontologies and epistemologies. As a corollary, New Materialisms also call for new forms of politics that are relational and convivial, inclusive of non-humans in whatever ways that make sense and are ethical in different circumstances or conditions. In relational politics, solutions are less certain and there is an emphasis on political processes and collective efforts to find pathways rather than following standard bureaucratic conventions. Like non-representational approaches, the new materialist world view accepts that outcomes are never certain in a changing world. This position means embracing decision-making with uncertainty and flexibility (Kareiva & Fuller 2016) – conditions that are not straightforward to accept or comforting when complex judgements about cities need to be made. However, as is true of more-than-human theories more generally, the value of New Materialisms is that they provoke new and exciting ways of thinking and path-finding rather than presenting ready-made, one-size-fits all solutions or 'top-down recipes' (Kareiva & Fuller 2016, p. 107).

The Practice Turn (Chapter 4) arguably has a broader and even more dispersed history than the other turns, located in disciplines including philosophy, cultural theory, history, geography, sociology, anthropology and STS (Schatzki et al. 2001). The work of Bourdieu (1990), Giddens (1984) and Pickering (1995) in particular set the scene in the late twentieth century, providing fertile ground for an expansive literature on practice to develop. Shared with the previous turns, there is no single unified or unifying theory of practice, but rather a collection of closely related theories and conceptualisations (Warde 2005). However, in the 2000s, what could be argued is that a post-humanist subset of The Practice Turn has emerged. Described in detail by Schatzki (2002), Reckwitz (2002) and Shove, Pantzar and Watson (Shove et al. 2012) among others, these works clearly define what social practices are and what a social practice ontology might mean for research as well as for policymaking.

Theories of social practice decentre human cognitive thought and rational decision-making. Instead, they foreground the act of doing rather than cognition, together with the competences, meanings and materials involved in performance (Shove et al. 2012). Practices are considered recognisable activities or entities regularly and routinely performed over time and space, connected to other practices. For example, practices of shopping for food are likely connected with other practices of cooking and eating. In The Practice Turn, there is also a focus on human bodies, as well as non-human materials, technologies and things that comprise and participate in social practices. Although practices usually rely on the existence of a human practitioner, they remain more-than-human because of their inclusion of various materials, matters and technologies that necessarily 'co-perform' practices or facilitate their performance. Hence consistent with the other more-than-human theories discussed so far, practices are about human–non-human relations and entanglements. However, practice theories differ in their concern with repeated or regular activities rather than the events or potentially singular entanglements of interest to non-representational theories or New Materialisms.

There is a well-developed body of literature on practices that is mostly empirically based and has clear implications for policymakers in a range of fields that connect to a healthy cities agenda. Work with theories of practice can be seen in organisation studies (Nicolini 2012), domestic energy and water consumption (Browne et al. 2013; Shove et al. 2014; Strengers 2012;

Walker et al. 2014), food consumption (Halkier & Jensen 2011; Warde et al. 2007), housing (Horne et al. 2011; Maller et al. 2012), transport and mobility (Spurling & McMeekin 2015; Watson 2012), digital technologies (Ropke & Christensen 2012; Strengers 2013) and human health (Blue et al. 2016; Maller et al. 2016; Supski et al. 2016). Theories of social practice are therefore incredibly useful for applying more-than-human thinking to a healthy cities agenda. Because practice theories are used extensively in applied projects, have a long genealogy and are referred to by most other more-than-human theories, Chapter 4 makes the case that practices are useful as a 'lead theory' to rethink 'healthy cities'. For example, because of their focus on regular performances, practice theories can be used to understand how different forms of more-than-human action in cities are connected across time and space, and where it might be productive to intervene.

Part II: Making more-than-human healthy urban environments

Part II tackles the second and third aims of the book. Taking the key ideas, provocations and inspirations from theories discussed in Part I, it explores how they can help shift existing paradigms about healthy cities and reconceptualise cities as more-than-human habitat. It then seeks to encourage experimentation with new concepts and ideas from a more-than-human perspective and to think about intervening for change differently from past approaches. It has three key chapters focused on these tasks.

Chapter 5, the first of Part II, is 'Understanding health as more-than-human'. The aim is to recast health using the more-than-human thinking developed in Part I as the first step towards rethinking healthy cities. It begins by reviewing current ways of thinking about health, drawing on work in public health and health promotion, namely the social determinants approach (Wilkinson & Marmot 2003) and socio-ecological models of health (Hancock 1993). These ways of understanding health are often used in policymaking, planning and urban design; moreover, they advocate for multisectoral collaboration beyond the health sector. The chapter then discusses some of the problems with how health is conceived in these frameworks, particularly the perpetuation of binaries such as healthy/unhealthy, nature/culture and agency/structure. Drawing on theories of practice outlined in Chapter 4 and enriched by the other theories in Part I, the second section of the chapter reframes health in urban environments by taking activities usually considered as behaviours, such as physical activity, and reconceptualising them as practices. In this way, the many non-humans that comprise everyday life and affect health outcomes in significant ways are brought to the fore. Using a more-than-human health framing, the concluding section discusses ways urban health might be improved, consistent with multisectoral approaches encouraged by the social determinants of health and similar framings.

Chapter 6, 'Cities as more-than-human habitat', concerns urban interactions and entanglements between humans and living non-humans, such as plants and animals. Drawing on literature from conservation, urban ecology, public health and human geography, the chapter examines the way cities provide habitat for humans and non-human species. However, rather than seeing non-human species as passive recipients of urban habitat, this chapter explores how animals and plants actively make habitat in urban environments, sometimes taking advantage of human activities and places intended for human use – for example, domestic gardens. Through these ideas, the chapter shows how cities are made and remade by both humans and non-humans, and can therefore be conceptualised as more-than-human habitat. As well as non-human species, Chapter 6 also looks at how multispecies encounters, such as human–plant and human–animal interactions, can be beneficial (and sometimes harmful) to their human and non-human participants. Gardening and wildlife feeding practices are used to argue that seeing, knowing and living with the animals and plants in cities is a key means to make cities healthier places for both humans and other species.

Chapter 7, 'Changing practices for understanding and making healthy urban environments', focuses on experimentation and intervention in practices. To achieve this, it draws the ideas together from previous chapters to discuss how to make cities healthy from a more-than-human perspective. It applies some of the innovative more-than-human methods and ideas presented earlier in the book to discuss how to change social practices in the domains of research, and policy and practice. These two domains are highlighted because practice changes in research and policy can extend to other domains, such as everyday life; they are therefore a good place to start in rethinking and changing cities. This chapter particularly argues for a breakdown in the siloed thinking reflected in disciplinary-based research and sectorial policymaking. The first part of the chapter discusses how practices of research and policymaking could be changed by reframing problems and doing research differently by bringing in relational perspectives. The latter part of the chapter discusses how to redesign interventions for healthy cities as shared habitats for non-humans and humans using innovative more-than-human thinking. For example, the chapter introduces the notion that interveners are not necessarily always human; methods, policies and living non-humans like rivers can be agents of change, create political acts and be active members of the political realm.

Chapter 8, 'More-than-human healthy futures', offers a brief conclusion, reaffirms the book's main argument, discusses remaining gaps in the approach to provide direction for where researchers and practitioners might go next with these ideas, and provides a final call to action.

Conclusion

As the urban footprint extends across the globe and more people call cities home, non-human species extinctions and habitat loss are occurring on an unprecedented scale. Due to the irreversible damage to the earth's ecosystems caused by urbanisation, this book argues that there is an urgent need to *rethink* cities and reconceptualise healthy urban environments as more-than-human habitat. Despite what we might ordinarily think, cities are already made and remade habitat for, and by, humans and non-humans; they therefore always have been, and always will be, more-than-human in a myriad of ways.

As noted, there has been significant activity regarding more-than-human thinking. In recent decades, both as theory and as a broadly defined body of work, it is continuing to gain popularity. However, the rich and stimulating ideas more-than-human theories generate remain largely in academic circles, almost held captive as the subject of rigorous debates and discussion. Without being overly instrumental, this book attempts to take more-than-human thinking from theory into practice by doing the work of translation in the context of rethinking healthy cities. In interpreting and summarising some key contributions of more-than-human thought, the book is aimed at applied researchers, scholars and students in a range of fields, including health sociology, public health, human geography and urban planning and design. It is also aimed at professionals and policymakers interested in innovative ideas and concepts, especially those willing to go beyond the status quo. The first two aims of the book are designed to help readers appreciate, understand, perceive and know cities as more-than-human. The third is designed to encourage practitioners of all kinds to experiment and make cities healthy for more-than just humans. At the risk of temporarily perpetuating a human/nature binary, I close this introduction with the thought that, as a motivation to keep reading, we already know 'nature' is healthy for cities; now cities need to be healthy for 'nature'.

Notes

1 In this book, although I refer to cities in general, of course no two cities are alike and I want to avoid universalising them. However, for the sake of argument, as urban places, most cities share many similar characteristics and suffer from similar challenges of sustainability, equity and environmental and social justice. In nearly all cities, the long 'naturecultures' (Haraway 2003) and histories of indigenous peoples, and the violence they have been subjected to under colonialism, have been systematically obscured and denied (Porter 2010).
2 See Stengers (2010) for further in-depth discussion of the inadequacy of the term 'non-human'.
3 The book is focused on living non-humans rather than non-living or inanimate ones, although they do get a mention in some passages.
4 These ideas resonate with the concept of the 'state apparatus' referred to by Deleuze and Guattari (1987) and the 'shadow of the linguistic turn' highlighted by Pickering (2008, p. 2).
5 In addition to the Sustainable Development Goals: http://unhabitat.org/un-habitat-for-the-sustainable-development-goals/ (accessed 22 January 2018).
6 That is, either those considered at risk of extinction according to the International Union for Conservation of Nature's (IUCN) Red List of Threatened Species or those considered to be of national significance by other criteria (e.g., in Australia,

the Environment Protection and Biodiversity Conservation Act (EPBC) Act 1999) (Ives et al. 2016).

7 'More-than-human' is a more encompassing and inclusive, if clumsy, term to designate human–non-human relations and entanglements (Head 2016).

8 I deliberately avoid using acronyms or abbreviations to resist collapsing diverse entities into one homogenous abbreviation, acknowledging that terms like 'more-than-human' also do this in part.

9 See Bennett (2010) and Deleuze and Guattari (1987) for the philosophical origins of more-than-human thought.

10 The boundaries around this grouping of theory are relatively open and ill-defined, generally consistent with the described ontological stances. There are numerous intersections, crossovers and dialogues, and possible points of tension or dissonances between theories I associate with the category of more-than-human.

11 Although 'turn' is said to be somewhat overused (Whatmore 2006), it is useful here to mark the confluence of related ideas that indicated a shift or trend in thinking that identifies or characterises scholarship in one or more disciplines.

12 See Whatmore (2006) for a critique of the New Materialist Turn in geography.

13 For other examples, see Anderson and Harrison (2010) and Whatmore (2006).

14 Wetherell, although defining affect similarly to other recent scholars, including Thrift (2008), Bennett (2010) and Seigworth and Gregg (2010), is not interested in non-human affect: 'Research on affect in cultural studies (e.g., Thrift, 2008a) is often obfuscating when it elides together affect as topic (the study of emotion) with affect defined as becoming and intensity so that sunsets, iron filings, talking parrots, financial meltdowns, earthquakes, sobbing Englishmen, angry Libyans, etc., are studied under the same rubric. By affect, I will mean embodied meaning-making. Mostly, this will be something that could be understood as human emotion' (Wetherell 2012, p. 4).

15 New Materialism is also found in philosophy, feminist theory, anthropology, archaeology and the visual arts.

References

Abram, D 1997, *The Spell of the Sensuous: Perception and Language in a More-than-human World*, Vintage Books.

Anderson, B 2014, *Encountering Affect: Capacities, Apparatuses, Conditions*, Ashgate.

Anderson, B & Harrison, P 2010, 'The promise of non-representational theories', in B Anderson & P Harrison (eds), *Taking-place: Non-representational Theories and Geography*, Ashgate, pp. 1–34.

Ashton, J, Grey, P & Barnard, K 1986, 'Healthy Cities – WHO's new public health initiative', *Health Promotion International*, vol. 1, no. 3, pp. 319–324.

Ayo, N 2011, 'Understanding health promotion in a neoliberal climate and the making of health conscious citizens', *Critical Public Health*, vol. 22, no. 1, pp. 99–105.

Barad, K 2003, 'Posthumanist performativity: toward an understanding of how matter comes to matter', *Signs*, vol. 28, no. 3, pp. 801–831.

Barad, K 2007, *Meeting the Universe Halfway: Quantum Physics and the Entanglement of Matter and Meaning*, Duke University Press.

Baum, F 1993, 'Healthy Cities and change: social movement or bureaucratic tool?', *Health Promotion International*, vol. 8, no. 1, pp. 31–40.

Baum, F, Jolley, G, Hicks, R, Saint, K & Parker, S 2006, 'What makes for sustainable Healthy Cities initiatives? A review of the evidence from Noarlunga, Australia after 18 years', *Health Promotion International*, vol. 21, no. 4, pp. 259–265.

Bennett, J 2010, *Vibrant Matter: A Political Ecology of Things*, Duke University Press.

Blue, S, Shove, E, Carmona, C & Kelly, MP 2016, 'Theories of practice and public health: understanding (un)healthy practices', *Critical Public Health*, vol. 26, no. 1, pp. 36–50.

Botzat, A, Fischer, LK & Kowarik, I 2016, 'Unexploited opportunities in understanding liveable and biodiverse cities: a review on urban biodiversity perception and valuation', *Global Environmental Change*, vol. 39, Supplement C, pp. 220–233.

Bourdieu, P 1990, *The Logic of Practice*, Polity Press.

Braun, B 2005, 'Environmental issues: writing a more-than-human urban geography', *Progress in Human Geography*, vol. 29, no. 5, pp. 635–650.

Browne, AL, Medd, W & Anderson, B 2013, 'Developing novel approaches to tracking domestic water demand under uncertainty: a reflection on the "up scaling" of social science approaches in the United Kingdom', *Water Resources Management*, vol. 27, no. 4, pp. 1013–1035.

Castree, N 2003, 'Environmental issues: relational ontologies and hybrid politics', *Progress in Human Geography*, vol. 27, no. 2, pp. 203–211.

Clough, PT 2008, 'The Affective Turn: political economy, biomedia and bodies', *Theory, Culture & Society*, vol. 25, no. 1, pp. 1–22.

Clough, PT & Halley, JOM 2007, *The Affective Turn: Theorizing the Social*, Duke University Press.

Coole, D & Frost, S 2010, 'Introducing the new materialisms', in D Coole, S Frost & J Bennett (eds), *New Materialisms: Ontology, Agency, and Politics*, Duke University Press, pp. 1–43.

Cresswell, T 2012, 'Nonrepresentational theory and me: notes of an interested sceptic', *Environment and Planning D: Society and Space*, vol. 30, no. 1, pp. 96–105.

Cronon, W 1996a, 'Introduction: in search of nature', in W Cronon (ed.), *Uncommon Ground: Rethinking the Human Place in Nature*, WW Norton, pp. 23–56.

Cronon, W 1996b, 'The trouble with wilderness; or, getting back to the wrong nature', in W Cronon (ed.), *Uncommon Ground: Rethinking the Human Place in Nature*, WW Norton, pp. 69–90.

Deleuze, G & Guattari, F 1987, *Thousand Plateaus: Capitalism and Schizophrenia*, (translated by Brian Massumi), University of Minnesota Press.

Dickinson, JL, Shirk, J, Bonter, D, Bonney, R, Crain, RL, Martin, J, Phillips, T & Purcell, K 2012, 'The current state of citizen science as a tool for ecological research and public engagement', *Frontiers in Ecology and the Environment*, vol. 10, no. 6, pp. 291–297.

Duhl, L 1986, 'The healthy city: its function and its future', *Health Promotion*, vol. 1, no. 1, pp. 55–60.

Duhl, L & Hancock, T 1997, 'Industrialized countries: healthy cities, healthy children', in *The Progress of Nations*, UNICEF, pp. 59–61.

Egorov, AI, Mudu, P, Braubach, M & Martuzzi, M 2016, *Urban Green Spaces and Health*, WHO Regional Office for Europe, Copenhagen.

Flies, EJ, Skelly, C, Negi, SS, Prabhakaran, P, Liu, Q, Liu, K, Goldizen, FC, Lease, C & Weinstein, P 2017, 'Biodiverse green spaces: a prescription for global urban health', *Frontiers in Ecology and the Environment*, pp. 510–516.

Franklin, A 2017, 'The more-than-human city', *Sociological Review*, vol. 65, no. 2, pp. 202–217.

Gandy, M 2002, *Concrete and Clay: Reworking Nature in New York City*, MIT Press.

Garrard, GE & Bekessy, SA 2014, 'Land use and land management', in J Byrne, N Sipe & J Dodson (eds), *Australian Environmental Planning: Challenges and Future Prospects*, Routledge, pp. 61–72.

Garrard, GE, Williams, NSG, Mata, L, Thomas, J & Bekessy, SA 2017, 'Biodiversity sensitive urban design', *Conservation Letters*, doi:10.1111/conl.12411.

Giddens, A 1984, *The Constitution of Society: Outline of the Theory of Structuration*, Polity Press.

Greenhough, B 2010, 'Vitalist geographies: life and the more-than-human', in B Anderson & P Harrison (eds), *Taking-place: Non-representational Theories and Geography*, Ashgate, pp. 37–54.

Gregg, M & Seigworth, GJ 2010, *The Affect Theory Reader*, E-Duke Books Scholarly Collection, Duke University Press.

Halkier, B & Jensen, I 2011, 'Methodological challenges in using practice theory in consumption research: examples from a study on handling nutritional contestations of food consumption', *Journal of Consumer Culture*, vol. 11, no. 1, pp. 101–123.

Hancock, T 1993, 'Health, human development and the community ecosystem: three ecological models', *Health Promotion International*, vol. 8, no. 1, pp. 41–47.

Haraway, DJ 2003, *The Companion Species Manifesto: Dogs, People, and Significant Otherness*, Prickly Paradigm Press.

Haraway, DJ 2016, *Staying with the Trouble: Making Kin in the Chthulucene*, Duke University Press.

Head, L 2016, *Hope and Grief in the Anthropocene: Re-conceptualising Human–nature Relations*, Routledge.

Hinchliffe, S & Whatmore, S 2006, 'Living cities: towards a politics of conviviality', *Science as Culture*, vol. 15, no. 2, pp. 123–138.

Horne, R, Maller, C & Lane, R 2011, 'Remaking home: the reuse of goods and materials in Australian households', in R Lane & A Gorman-Murray (eds), *Material Geographies of Household Sustainability*, Ashgate, pp. 89–111.

Houston, D, Hillier, J, MacCallum, D, Steele, W & Byrne, J 2017, 'Make kin, not cities! Multispecies entanglements and "becoming-world" in planning theory', *Planning Theory*, doi:10.1177/1473095216688042.

Instone, L 1998, 'The coyote's at the door: revisioning human–environment relations in the Australian context', *Ecumene*, vol. 5, no. 4, pp. 452–467.

Ives, CD, Lentini, PE, Threlfall, CG, Ikin, K, Shanahan, DF, Garrard, GE, Bekessy, SA, Fuller, RA, Mumaw, L, Rayner, L, Rowe, R, Valentine, LE & Kendal, D 2016, 'Cities are hotspots for threatened species', *Global Ecology and Biogeography*, vol. 25, no. 1, pp. 117–126.

Jones, DN 2018, *The Birds at My Table: Why We Feed Wild Birds and Why It Matters*, Cornell University Press.

Kaika, M 2005, *City of Flows: Modernity, Nature, and the City*, Routledge.

Kaika, M 2017, '"Don't call me resilient again!": the New Urban Agenda as immunology . . . or . . . what happens when communities refuse to be vaccinated with "smart cities" and indicators', *Environment and Urbanization*, vol. 29, no. 1, pp. 89–102.

Kareiva, P & Fuller, E 2016, 'Beyond resilience: how to better prepare for the profound disruption of the Anthropocene', *Global Policy*, vol. 7, pp. 107–118.

Kingsbury, P 2015, 'Book review: *Encountering Affect: Capacities, Apparatuses, Conditions*', *Antipode*, https://radicalantipode.files.wordpress.com/2015/08/book-review_kingsbury-on-anderson.pdf, accessed 22 January 2018.

Latour, B 2000, 'When things strike back: a possible contribution of "science studies" to the social sciences', *British Journal of Sociology*, vol. 51, no. 1, pp. 107–123.

Lemke, T 2015, 'New materialisms: Foucault and the "Government of Things"', *Theory, Culture & Society*, vol. 32, no. 4, pp. 3–25.

Lindsay, J 2010, 'Healthy living guidelines and the disconnect with everyday life', *Critical Public Health*, vol. 20, no. 4, pp. 475–487.

Low, T 2003, *The New Nature*, Penguin Books.

Luck, GW, Davidson, P, Boxall, D & Smallbone, L 2011, 'Relations between urban bird and plant communities and human well-being and connection to nature', *Conservation Biology*, vol. 25, no. 4, pp. 816–826.

Lulka, D 2009, 'The residual humanism of hybridity: retaining a sense of the earth', *Transactions of the Institute of British Geographers*, vol. 34, no. 3, pp. 378–393.

Maller, C, Horne, R & Dalton, T 2012, 'Green renovations: intersections of daily routines, housing aspirations and narratives of environmental sustainability', *Housing, Theory and Society*, vol. 29, no. 3, pp. 255–275.

Maller, C, Nicholls, L & Strengers, Y 2016, 'Understanding the materiality of neighbourhoods in "healthy practices": outdoor exercise practices in a new master-planned estate', *Urban Policy and Research: Special Issue on Health*, vol. 34, pp. 55–72.

Mills, JG, Weinstein, P, Gellie, NJC, Weyrich, LS, Lowe, AJ & Breed, MF 2017, 'Urban habitat restoration provides a human health benefit through microbiome rewilding: the Microbiome Rewilding Hypothesis', *Restoration Ecology*, vol. 25, no. 6, pp. 866–872.

Nicolini, D 2012, *Practice Theory, Work, and Organization: An Introduction*, Oxford University Press.

Petersen, A & Lupton, D 1996, *The New Public Health: Health and Self in the Age of Risk*, SAGE Publications.

Pett, TJ, Shwartz, A, Irvine, KN, Dallimer, M & Davies, ZG 2016, 'Unpacking the people–biodiversity paradox: a conceptual framework', *BioScience*, vol. 66, no. 7, pp. 576–583.

Pickering, A 1995, *The Mangle of Practice: Time, Agency and Science*, University of Chicago Press.

Pickering, A 2008, 'Against human exceptionalism', paper presented at a workshop: *What Does It Mean to Be Human?*, 25 January, https://ore.exeter.ac.uk/repository/bitstream/handle/10036/18873/XTRwrkshp-250108.pdf?sequence=1, accessed 30 May 2016.

Pickering, A 2013, 'Being in an environment: a performative perspective', *Natures Sciences Sociétés*, vol. 21, no. 1, pp. 77–83.

Plumwood, V 2009, 'Nature in the active voice', *Australian Humanities Review*, vol. 46, pp. 113–129.

Porter, L 2010, *Unlearning the Colonial Cultures of Planning*, Ashgate.

Priest, G 2002, *Beyond the Limits of Thought*, Oxford University Press.

Reckwitz, A 2002, 'Toward a theory of social practices: a development in culturalist theorizing', *European Journal of Social Theory*, vol. 5, no. 2, pp. 243–263.

Ropke, I & Christensen, TH 2012, 'Energy impacts of ICT – insights from an everyday life perspective', *Telematics and Informatics*, vol. 29, pp. 348–361.

Rose, DB 2012, 'Why I don't speak of wilderness', *EarthSong Journal: Perspectives in Ecology, Spirituality and Education*, vol. 2, no. 4, pp. 9–11.

Schatzki, TR 2002, *The Site of the Social: A Philosophical Account of the Constitution of Social Life and Change*, Pennsylvania State University Press.

Schatzki, TR, Knorr Cetina, K & Von Savigny, E 2001, *The Practice Turn in Contemporary Theory*, Routledge.

Seigworth, GJ & Gregg, M 2010, 'An inventory of shimmers', in M Gregg & GJ Seigworth (eds), *The Affect Theory Reader*, Duke University Press, pp. 1–25.

Shove, E 2010, 'Beyond the ABC: climate change policy and theories of social change', *Environment and Planning A*, vol. 42, pp. 1273–1285.

Shove, E 2014, 'Putting practice into policy: reconfiguring questions of consumption and climate change', *Contemporary Social Science*, vol. 9, no. 4, pp. 415–429.

Shove, E, Pantzar, M & Watson, M 2012, *The Dynamics of Social Practice: Everyday Life and How It Changes*, SAGE Publications.

Shove, E, Walker, G & Brown, S 2014, 'Transnational transitions: the diffusion and integration of mechanical cooling', *Urban Studies*, vol. 51, no. 7, pp. 1506–1519.

Spurling, N & McMeekin, A 2015, 'Sustainable mobility policies in England', in Y Strengers & C Maller (eds), *Social Practices, Intervention and Sustainability: Beyond Behaviour Change*, Routledge, pp. 78–94.

Steele, W, Mata, L & Fünfgeld, H 2015, 'Urban climate justice: creating sustainable pathways for humans and other species', *Current Opinion in Environmental Sustainability*, vol. 14, pp. 121–126.

Stengers, I 2010, 'Including nonhumans in political theory: opening Pandora's Box?', in B Braun & S Whatmore (eds), *Political Matter: Technoscience, Democracy, and Public Life*, University of Minnesota Press, pp. 3–34.

Stone, J & Woodcock, I 2016, 'The "sky rail" saga: can big new transport projects ever run smoothly?', *The Conversation Australia*, https://theconversation.com/the-sky-rail-saga-can-big-new-transport-projects-ever-run-smoothly-54383, accessed 19 May 2017.

Strengers, Y 2012, 'Peak electricity demand and social practice theories: reframing the role of change agents in the energy sector', *Energy Policy*, vol. 44, no. 226–234.

Strengers, Y 2013, *Smart Energy Technologies in Everyday Life: Smart Utopia?*, Palgrave Macmillan.

Strengers, Y & Maller, C 2015, 'Introduction: social practices, intervention and sustainability, beyond behaviour change', in Y Strengers & C Maller (eds), *Social Practices, Intervention and Sustainability: Beyond Behaviour Change*, Routledge, pp. 1–12.

Strengers, Y, Moloney, S, Maller, C & Horne, R 2015, 'Beyond behaviour change', in Y Strengers & C Maller (eds), *Social Practices, Intervention and Sustainability: Beyond Behaviour Change*, Routledge, pp. 63–77.

Supski, S, Lindsay, J & Tanner, C 2016, 'University students' drinking as a social practice and the challenge for public health', *Critical Public Health*, pp. 1–10.

Thrift, N 2008, *Non-representational Theory: Space, Politics, Affect*, Taylor & Francis.

United Nations General Assembly 2016a, *Draft Outcome Document of the United Nations Conference on Housing and Sustainable Urban Development (Habitat III): Item 10 of the Provisional Agenda, 17–20 October*, United Nations.

United Nations General Assembly 2016b, 'The New Urban Agenda explainer', paper presented to *United Nations Conference on Housing and Sustainable Urban Development (Habitat III)*, 17–20 October, Quito, Ecuador, http://resilientneighbors. com/wp-content/uploads/2016/12/NUA-explained.pdf, accessed 22 January 2018.

Walker, G, Shove, E & Brown, S 2014, 'How does air conditioning become "needed"? A case study of routes, rationales and dynamics', *Energy Research & Social Science*, vol. 4, pp. 1–9.

Warde, A 2005, 'Consumption and theories of practice', *Journal of Consumer Culture*, vol. 5, no. 2, pp. 131–153.

Warde, A, Cheng, S-L, Olsen, W & Southerton, D 2007, 'Changes in the practice of eating: a comparative analysis of time-use', *Acta Sociologica*, vol. 50, no. 4, pp. 363–385.

Washick, B & Wingrove, E 2015, 'Politics that matter: thinking about power and justice with the new materialists', *Contemporary Political Theory*, vol. 14, no. 1, pp. 63–79.

Watson, M 2012, 'How theories of practice can inform transition to a decarbonised transport system', *Journal of Transport Geography*, vol. 24, pp. 488–496.

Wetherell, M 2012, *Affect and Emotion: A New Social Science Understanding*, SAGE Publications.

Whatmore, S 2002, *Hybrid Geographies: Natures Cultures Spaces*, SAGE Publications.

Whatmore, S 2006, 'Materialist returns: practising cultural geography in and for a more-than-human world', *Cultural Geographies*, vol. 13, no. 4, pp. 600–609.

Wilkinson, R & Marmot, M (eds) 2003, *Social Determinants of Health: The Solid Facts*, World Health Organization.

Wolch, J 1996, 'Zoöpolis', *Capitalism Nature Socialism*, vol. 7, no. 2, pp. 21–47.

World Health Organization 1986, *The Ottawa Charter for Health Promotion*, World Health Organization, Health and Welfare Canada, and Canadian Public Health Association.

World Health Organization 1998, *Health Promotion Glossary*, World Health Organization.

World Health Organization 2012, *The Ottawa Charter for Health Promotion*, World Health Organization, www.who.int/healthpromotion/conferences/previous/ottawa/ en/, accessed 1 August 2012.

Yong, E 2016, *I Contain Multitudes: The Microbes within Us and a Grander View of Life*, Bodley Head.

Part I
Understanding more-than-human theories

This part of the book presents the theoretical foundations of more-than-human theories, presented across three 'turns': The Affective Turn (Chapter 2), The New Materialisms Turn (Chapter 3) and The Practice Turn (Chapter 4). In doing so, it draws on philosophical and theoretical resources from three different but related bodies of theory to address the book's first aim: to foster a greater appreciation of the things, critters, artefacts and non-human publics that make the world more-than-human. Each chapter in this part describes the main literature associated with each turn and discusses the key contributions from each. As well as covering The Practice Turn, Chapter 4 discusses how the three turns fit together. This part of the book also starts to introduce ideas that correspond to the second aim: to open ways of thinking, knowing and understanding cities and urban environments as more-than-human habitat, dealt with in more detail in Part II.

2 The Affective Turn

Non-representational theories, affect and emotions

Introduction

This chapter reviews the main contributions from The Affective Turn in the social sciences relevant to more-than-human thinking about healthy urban environments. Its principal interest is in non-representational and affective approaches (affect and emotions) that emerged in several disciplines in the late 1990s and early 2000s. Work on emotions and affect is recognised more broadly than non-representational theories, which have tended to be confined to geography and are less widely known, both within geography and elsewhere (Cresswell 2012; Kingsbury 2015; Lorimer 2005). The chapter aims to cover ideas from scholarly work most relevant to this book rather than a comprehensive coverage of scholarship and criticism.

As indicated by the prefix, *non*-representational thinking differentiates itself from representational thought. Like affective approaches and other more-than-human theories, non-representational theories present alternative accounts of being or becoming in the world (ontology) as well as other means and methods of knowing and explaining it (epistemology), compared to mainstream social science. The chapter explains how these approaches turn our attention to things that challenge representation, such as affects, emotions and nonlinear notions of time and temporality. These concepts can be used to think differently about the impacts of cities on humans and non-humans, and change the way we conduct research and undertake policymaking in urban environments (discussed further in Chapter 7). They also help policymakers and researchers to be more comfortable with the idea that the outcomes of interventions can be unpredictable, also shown in Chapters 3 and 4.

Non-representational and affective theories are closely inter-related (Kingsbury 2015), often interwoven (e.g., Anderson 2014; Anderson & Harrison 2010a; Buser 2014; Lorimer 2008; McCormack 2003; Thrift 2004; Wetherell 2012), and are both critical of representation.[1] Before a section each dedicated to non-representational theories and affect and emotions, the chapter begins with an explanation and brief critique of representation.

What is representation?

The idea of representation underpins traditional science and informs how most research is carried out: 'Science provides us with representations of atoms, elementary particles, polymers, populations, genetic trees, economies, rational decisions, aeroplanes, earthquakes, forest fires, irrigation systems, and the world's climate. It's through these representations that we learn about the world' (Frigg & Nguyen 2016, p. 1).

Representation in social science is associated mostly with positivism, post-positivism and social constructivism (Anderson & Harrison 2010b; Barad 2003),[2] where knowledge is created through accurate 're-presentations' (subjective, textual or linguistic) of the (objective, material) world. Significantly, representationalism separates language and text from materials and materiality, and discounts dynamic relations between subjects and objects – something more-than-human theories aim to resolve. Representations take many forms, including surveys, descriptions, photographs, maps, digital material, models and theories (Frigg & Nguyen 2016). They comprise the 'hard' evidence or 'representative' data to support 'evidence-based' decision-making in policy settings, for example census data, or national surveys about physical activity. Typically, representation deals with two distinct kinds of separated entities: representations themselves and entities represented (subjective and objective knowledges). Sometimes a third entity is included, 'the existence of a [human] knower' who uses language to represent the entity phenomena in question (Barad 2003 p. 804).[3]

Dewsbury (2003, p. 1908) argues that there is a 'general overdependence that social science has on the representational setup and the interpretation of empiricism to facilitate knowledge production'. Capturing its main weaknesses, Barad (2003) presents a twofold critique of representation. First, she argues language has been given too much power at the expense of performativity and materiality: 'Language matters. Discourse matters. Culture matters . . . the only thing that does not seem to matter anymore is matter' (Barad 2003, p. 801). The backgrounding of the material world in favour of essentialising language in representational accounts is widely noted (Anderson & Harrison 2010a; Barad 2003; Bennett 2010; Dewsbury 2003; Latham & Conradson 2003; Thrift 2008). However, foregrounding materiality is one of the tenets of The Affective Turn and the non-representational approaches discussed shortly in this chapter. Second, like Pickering (1993), Barad (2003, p. 804) is critical of the processes of making representations and their accuracy regarding 'that which they purport to represent'. In other words, she problematises the lack of reflection, awareness or investigation of specific representational practices upon which representational research is based. For example, large national surveys produce one way of understanding an issue (Law 2009), but there are often unexpected or unexplainable outcomes because survey questions with a limited set of multiple-choice answers cannot capture the complexity of everyday lives. Nevertheless, the epistemological limitations of this way of producing knowledge are often ignored in the rush to intervene or make policy. A related reproach is the assumed fidelity of representations when they are reproduced and replicated – a fidelity assumed to occur reliably 'without deviation or departure' from the original (Doel 2010, p. 117). Dewsbury (2003) finds further inadequacies with representationalist research, noting a lack of attention to affects and emotions, important aspects of social life that are traditionally considered to be irrelevant to or too difficult to capture through representation. These include passions and desires and matters of belief and faith, 'all forces that move beyond our familiar, (because) denoted, world. These are not light matters for they forge the weight of our meaningful relation with the world' (Dewsbury 2003, pp. 1907–1908).

In sum, the main weaknesses of representative approaches are an over-reliance on text and language (with its inherent human-centrism); the bypassing or backgrounding of materiality and material relations, perpetuating the divide between subject and object; a limited ability to account for emergence and change; a lack of reflexiveness towards the making of representations; an overestimation of the capacity for faithful repetition and reproduction; and failing to include affect and emotions. These weaknesses are accompanied by a sense that representational work often leaves something out – that it can only ever provide a limited understanding and way of knowing the world. In seeking to find ways to make cities more-than-human habitat, it is worth exploring other ways that might fruitfully change the way we conceptualise, organise, care for and modify urban environments.

There are numerous alternatives to representation, with most originating from the premise that producing knowledge about and knowing the world is more complex, material, relational, embodied, intangible and un-predictable than the binary model representation implies and demands. Many alternatives are covered in this book, such as affective, non-representational and assemblage thinking[4] and theories of social practice, among others. The former are the focus of this chapter, while the latter are covered in Chapters 3 and 4.[5] Although these approaches may still be considered 'fringe', they offer ways to overcome the limitations of representational thinking and extend the palette of concepts, paradigms and tools applied to complex, trans-disciplinary problems such as those posed by climate change. Continuing to rely on divided, human-centric representational knowledge, common to many traditional academic or applied disciplines like planning and health, is unlikely to produce the required innovative and ethical solutions.

Non-representational thought

Like many more-than-human theories, non-representational theories and approaches cover a diverse body of work seeking alternatives to representation in understanding, intervening in and changing social life (Anderson & Harrison 2010b; Lorimer 2008). Theorists, including Nigel Thrift, view the non-representational project as 'avowedly unmappable' and to have 'its own logic of radical revisionism' (Lorimer 2007, p. 90). Accepting this inherent variability, I extract key ideas from the literature on non-representational theories that distinguish it from representationalism and connect it with more-than-human theories. More specifically, there is a concentration of non-representational theory development applied to human geography in the UK (Cresswell 2012), largely characterised by the work of Thrift (2008; Thrift et al. 2010; Thrift & Dewsbury 2000), Dewsbury (2003; 2010), Anderson and Harrison (2010a), Lorimer (2005; 2007; 2008; 2010) and Latham and McCormack (Latham & McCormack 2004; McCormack 2003). Anderson and Harrison (2010b) link non-representational theories with various traditions in human geography. However, extending beyond human geography, non-representational theories share ideas and orientation with theories of practice in sociology, work on affect, actor–network theory and assemblage thinking. Other scholars whose work can be grouped with or has informed non-representational thinking include Barad (2007), Pickering (1995), Deleuze and Guattari (1987), Bennett (2010) and Latour (2005).[6]

'Non-representational' considered as a category deals with practices and doing, post-humanist accounts of life and an orientation towards an open-ended future (Anderson & Harrison 2010b; Latham & Conradson 2003).[7] It seeks, among other things, 'to find new ways of engaging space, landscape, the social, the cultural and the political' (Anderson & Harrison 2010a, p. 3). What makes non-representational theories distinctive, however, is their unabashed commitment to improvisation, uncertainty and openness – a feature which has proved to upset the status quo (Thrift et al. 2010). Using the example of human movement and dancing, Thrift (2008) describes non-representational understandings as capturing the ongoing improvisations of social life that resist neat, discrete or measurable categories typically found in a survey on physical activity (Thrift et al. 2010). Cresswell (2012, p. 97) explains the 'fuzzy' offerings of non-representational thinking in this way:

> the heart of [non-representational theory can be identified] through its insistence on the following: on the practical and processual fluidity of things (rather than the finished and fixed); on the production of meaning in action (rather than through preestablished systems and structures); on an ontology that is relational (rather than essentialist); on habitual interaction with the world (rather than 'consciousness' of it); on the possibilities of things emerging surprisingly (rather than being predetermined); on a wide definition of Life as humans/with/plus (rather than strictly humanistic); and on all-inclusive materiality where everything produces the 'social' constantly (rather than an already achieved 'social' constructing everything else).

Despite its inherent indeterminacy, three inter-related features summarise non-representational thinking: materiality, performativity and affect.

I examine each in turn, while cognisant of the diversity of scholarship and criticism applied to each that cannot be fully dealt with here. The main point is that non-representational thought as a body of theory can contribute to our understanding of more-than-human cities because it attempts to surpass simplistic binary approaches and embrace the inherent complexity of life.

First, common to broader post-humanist social thought, non-representational theories are '*thoroughly* materialist' (Anderson & Harrison 2010b, p. 14; original emphasis), and in their attempt to give equal weight to non-humans, they form 'a warp and weft of inhuman traffic with its own indifferent geographies' (Thrift 2008, p. 10). This broader non-exclusive materialist approach is made evident by an interest in more-than-human bodies, senses, affects and relations as social phenomena: '[non-representational theories do] not limit *a priori* what kind of beings make up the social. Rather everything takes-part and in taking-part, takes-place: everything happens, everything acts' (Anderson & Harrison 2010b, p. 14). In thinking about cities and complex urban environments inhabited and made by people and living non-humans, the idea of dynamic inclusivity is relevant and has considerable appeal.

However, despite these evocative proclamations, and Thrift's insistence on 'fading, fading, fading' the subject (cited in Thrift et al. 2010, p. 188), non-representational theories do not entirely lose their humanist mantle. For example, empirical work from a non-representational perspective retains an element of human focus compared to vitalist or assemblage traditions[8] more attuned to the 'liveliness of the world' (Greenhough 2010, p. 38).[9] Furthermore, Thrift (2008, p. 13) admits that his treatment of non-representational theories retains a 'certain humanism' as he declares 'dropping the human subject entirely seems . . . to be a step too far'. This is evident in many examples he works through, from dancing to driving cars and grieving the loss of his father. However, views vary among representational theorists concerning the extent to which the human subject can be removed (e.g., Anderson & Harrison 2010b; 2010a), and because work is ongoing in this area, the issue remains open.

The second distinguishing feature of non-representational theories is their roots in performativity, practice and the detailed examination of routine activities that takes 'some of the small signs of everyday life for wonders' (Thrift 2008, p. 2). For example, a rainbow witnessed during lunch hour or a rare animal sighted on a walk through a park. Anderson and Harrison (2010b, p. 7) describe this as a keen interest in the 'background "hum" of on-going activity' in places such as cities that may be overlooked by representational approaches. As discussed in detail in Chapter 4, this overt interest in everyday life and 'practices' has clear parallels with social practice theories.

However, in non-representational thinking, practices are understood as performances reproduced over time through 'the establishment of corporeal routines and specialised devices' (Thrift 2008, p. 8). Practices are quotidian activities that make up routines, such as driving a car or catching public transport to work, cooking, cleaning, caring for pets, working, taking children to school and so on. Despite the emphasis on routine, activity in non-representational accounts is characterised by openness, invention and the possibility of something different occurring in each moment of performance: 'an affirmation of life, of existence as such, as precarious, as active, and unforeseeable' (Anderson & Harrison 2010b, p. 1). This indeterminancy presents a micro-perspective of action and doing, one rooted in very specific moments, where despite the routinisation and familiarity of practices, the future holds endless possibilities. For example, a child walking to school each day might follow a familiar route, yet each walk has the potential for adjustments, such as stopping to observe an unfamiliar animal or bird, or seeking shelter when there is an expected downpour or weather event. In other words, careful attention is paid to the unpredictability of practice performances; their assumed reproducibility is rendered less secure and resolves the critique of over-reliance on faithful reproduction directed at representational approaches (Doel 2010).

The inherent unpredictability of practice captured by non-representationalism is significant because it questions assumed replication and acknowledges dynamic interactions between the human and non-human world. Anderson and Harrison (2010b, p. 7) describe the capacity for improvisation and uncertainty between repeated performances of practices:

> humans are envisioned in constant relations of modification and reciprocity with their environs, action being understood not as a one way street running from the actor to the acted upon, from the active to the passive or mind to matter, but as relational phenomena incessantly looping back and regulating itself through feedback phenomena.

The description of 'constant relations' and 'relational phenomena incessantly looping back' foreground the movement and action involved in every instance of practice performance that Thrift (2008) also seeks to emphasise. Each moment of performance presents an opportunity for innovation and change, but also disruption. A broken cleaning appliance, a power blackout during cooking or a cancelled bus service necessitate solutions to immediate problems, but these events may also redirect the course of future practice performance. In highlighting the potential for mutations or coding errors in the carrying out of practices, Thrift (2008, p. 21) specifies that non-representational theories are seeking to underline 'the ceaseless work of transmutation which drives the "social"'. A partial explanation of why transmutation is apparent in non-representational accounts of practice is related to the third distinguishing feature of the theory: a commitment to events or encounters as the primary vehicle for understanding social relations. Thrift (2008, p. 2) is adamant on this point: 'encounters are all that there is, and their results are not pre-given'.

Events and encounters can be variously defined, but they mean something specific to non-representational theorists.[10] Events and encounters concern nonlinear or emergent temporalities. In one sense, they are 'a continual differing, if only in modest ways, that takes place in relation to an ever-changing complex of other events' – such as how a rock or statue may be slowly weathered over time (Anderson & Harrison 2010b, p. 20). An event can also be understood as a 'rare' or 'absolute' surprise, something unexpected that instantly changes future possibilities (Anderson & Harrison 2010b, p. 21). The 9/11 terrorist attacks on the World Trade Centre in New York are an obvious example. Common to both concepts is the premise that an 'event does not resemble, conform, or reproduce a set of *a priori* conditions . . . rather [events] break with their extant conditions, forcing or inviting us to think and act differently' (Anderson & Harrison 2010b, p. 22). Breaking with earlier declarations of being 'thoroughly materialist' and more-than-human (Anderson & Harrison 2010b), the potential for events to surprise and to create different futures hints again at human-centrism, or at the very least inherent subjective leanings – just who is surprised and whose future might be different?

This problematisation of the concept of events in non-representationalism warrants further, albeit brief, investigation here because it raises and resolves issues regarding temporality as replication that representational theories cannot accommodate. That discussion is followed by the role of affect in non-representational theories before explicating affect and emotion per se.

Regarding the attention given to events and encounters in non-representational thinking, and maintaining the humanist perspective raised by Anderson and Harrison (2010a) for the moment, these concepts have been criticised as a reification of the present while devaluing memories and the past (Jones 2011). This critique could arise from the fact that non-representational thinking adopts a nonlinear approach to time. Jones (2011, p. 876) specifies that non-representational theories focus on the 'present moment of practice', and hence it tends towards 'a form of "presentism" . . . due to [the] relative neglect of the trajectories of the past-into-present . . . always in place through various interconnecting ecological, corporeal, material, cultural, economic and memorial flows'.

Jones (2011, p. 879) qualifies his critique by noting it is only when 'the event is taken as pure – in isolation from temporal trajectories' that non-representational thinking strays to a reified version of the present. As a solution, he makes the case for greater inclusion of memory in non-representational accounts. Like others, he is quick to point out that memories do not only pertain to individual human bodies, but are 'public, social, shared, collective memories' (Jones 2011, p. 878; Maller & Strengers 2013; 2015). However, a closer reading of Dewsbury's (2003) and other non-representational work reveals that the charge of being 'present-ist' cannot so easily be directed towards non-representational thinking. As Dewsbury (2003, p. 1918) explains, it works with '"concrete multiplicities" where a whole host of processes are bringing the present moment about . . . . It is not that origins are removed altogether: it is just that they have durations that make them less grand and nontotalizing'.

Similarly, Anderson and Harrison (2010b, p. 16) argue that non-representational scholarship accounts for entities and timespaces that are simultaneously both present and absent, as opposed to linear; 'it has drawn attention to the role "objects" such as affects, virtual memories, hauntings and atmospheres in the enactment, composition and durability of the social'. This way of thinking about time is nonlinear; it means that past, present, future are folded in on one another during the moment of performance or a single event, rather than treated discretely or sequentially. As Bissell (2014, p. 1950) observes: 'the experience of tomorrow's commute will be different from today's, not just because other things might be encountered, but because each experience in time alters the constitution of bodies and milieus'.

An outcome of how events are conceptualised in non-representational theories is that they provide a way to reconnect with representation and resolve some of its problems. Despite their position as being something other than representational, non-representational theories do not 'refuse representation *per se*, only representation as the repetition of the same or representation as a mediation' (Anderson & Harrison 2010b, p. 25). In this way, embodied gestures, sequences of actions and 'certain turns of phrase and idiomatic expressions, certain organisations of objects in space, do not "express" or "stand-for" [i.e., represent] certain cultural meanings, values and models . . . Rather they are enactments' (Anderson & Harrison 2010b, p. 9).

In other words, representations are treated by non-representational theories as events, as specific happenings or activities (Cresswell 2012).[11] Rather than the meaning or significance of events, the focus is on their material compositions and how they are made (Anderson & Harrison 2010b; Cresswell 2012). Such 'wild ideas' (Thrift 2008, p. 18) cast representations as open-ended and full of possibility. As Dewsbury (2003, p. 1911) states, the representational view is not wrong, but limited:

> The nonrepresentational argument comes into its own in asking us to revisit the performative space of representation in a manner that is more attuned to its fragile constitution . . . the representational system is not wrong: rather, it is the belief that it offers complete understanding – and that only it offers any sensible understanding at all – that is critically flawed.

A last point about non-representational theories is their attempt to incorporate affect. Affect is the capacity to create and experience or absorb change in the world. Events and encounters take place between multiple non-human participants where each has the capacity to affect and be affected by others in unfolding of events as they take place – through their materiality, their presence/absence, performances, practices and capacities to act (Anderson & Harrison 2010b; Latham & Conradson 2003; Thrift

2008). Returning to the example of a child walking to school, an encounter with an unfamiliar bird might produce delight or surprise, or if the bird attacks, as Australian magpies do during nesting season, fear or anger. For its part, the bird may express curiosity or wariness as it considers the child and whether it is perceived as a threat worthy of attack. During the encounter, each participant produces or create affects in the other. Acknowledging the centrality of affect to more-than-human approaches and to social life more generally, Anderson and Harrison (2010b, pp. 16–17) declare 'the social is affected and it is often through affect that relations are interrupted, changed or solidified'.

Thrift (2008) presents a thorough account of the affective dimensions of non-representational thinking in his influential *Non-representational Theory: Space, Politics, Affect*, particularly when discussing its application to empirical work. In contrast to more formal instances of data collection through interviews, for example, he explains how there should be a focus on precognitive experiences and modes of play; furthermore, that mistakes and clumsiness should be privileged as non-representational approaches trade 'in modes of perception that are not subject based' (Thrift 2008, p. 7). Often drawing on dance and performance arts as examples of affect in everyday life (revealing his 'minimal humanism'), Thrift (2008, pp. 12–13) argues that both affect and sensation are 'as fully important as signs and significations but . . . only recently have begun to receive their due'. In relation to the difficulty with which affect and non-representational thinking may be applied empirically, he replies, somewhat evasively – although admittedly accurately – that 'it seems to me to be of the greatest methodological importance to acknowledge that this is a world which we can only partially understand' (Thrift 2008, pp. 18–19).[12] For these and other reasons, the non-representational approach to affect has been criticised by others also seeking to weave notions of affect into social enquiry. For example, Wetherell (2012, pp. 19–20) declares:

> The large initial claims made for the non-representational, for un-mediated, pre-social body tracks, and for direct connections between the social and the somatic are radically misleading. They are incoherent as a social psychology of affect. Worse, I think, these approaches block useful and pragmatic empirical work on affect and the building of inter-disciplinary foundations for the sake of what is largely a chimera. They place some of the most random and least important affective phenomena on a pedestal and take them as generic.

In looking for 'a social psychology' (representational) explanation of affect, Wetherell's (2012) critique is understandable. However, as Thrift (2008, p. 18) explains:

> In recent years there has been an equal tendency to argue that social science must be more practical, policy-oriented, and so on, a tendency

which risks losing touch with wild ideas completely; it is the kind of social science that does not understand the basic point that it is producing a form of intelligibility [that maintains the status quo].

This retort is consistent with other scholars located in or near the non-representational camp, including Dewsbury (2003), Massumi (1987; 2002) and Deleuze and Guattari (1987).

Studying affects taking a non-representational approach openly challenges traditional modes of empirical enquiry; yet it is the point of non-representational thinking to embrace uncertainty in research, to centre moments of delight or distress, to see the world as open, and to experiment with different ways of understanding it. In this way, non-representational thinking brings to our attention to the detailed moments that make up everyday life in cities that present opportunities for innovation of, or disruption to, practice. For example, Latham and McCormack (2017) discuss how the affective materialities of human bodies and the built form of cities interact to generate new practices such as Parkour. Using examples of 'prosaic activities such as running, and walking', they show how it is possible 'to experience a kind of "focused intensity", a state which 'encompasses not just the ability to exclude a multiplicity of potential distractions but also a concentrated openness' for the unexpected (Latham & McCormack 2017, p. 375).

Leaving debates aside for now, non-representational thinking can contribute to research and policymaking because it brings our attention to things that might be overlooked in representational, bifurcated and typically human-centric approaches. With its focus on affects and events, non-representational thinking presents a different way to understand cities and the sorts of more-than-human entanglements, relations and encounters generated by daily routines, creating peaks and troughs of activity, such as rush-hour. Examples include the way city design and planning choreographs atmospheres of movement that might encourage physical activity (Barnfield 2016; Latham & McCormack 2017), the stresses caused by traffic in work commutes (Wener & Evans 2011) or the anxiety caused by rare events such as thunderstorm asthma (Forouzan et al. 2014).

The remainder of this chapter returns to a gap in representational approaches highlighted above concerning affect and emotion. As will be discussed, interest in affect and emotion has grown in recent decades as a response to prioritising rationality, thought and text over feelings, movement and actions. Building on the ideas introduced above, the following section explains how understanding emotions and affect has great potential for more-than-human interventions to create healthy urban environments.

Affect and emotions

Affect and emotions are ignored or suppressed in the bulk of representational social science (Dewsbury 2003). However, there is a growing body of work that shows they have much to offer those seeking new and innovative ways to understand current and future social, environmental and political challenges facing cities; consequently, as outlined in this chapter, there is a broad and growing interest in emotions and affect. Affect and emotions are differentiated by some and not by others. In my view, and explained in more detail below, there are significant differences, but I see them as inter-related and closely intertwined. As affect is less well known, I begin this section with a brief introduction, building on the description of affect provided in the previous discussion of non-representational theories.

As mentioned in the previous section, in its most simplistic form, affect is the recognition of the capacity for agency arising from relations between entities, or after the philosopher Baruch Spinoza, simply 'an ability to affect and be affected' (Anderson 2014; Massumi 1987, p. xvi).[13] However, in common with non-representational theories, the simplicity of this statement hides myriad complex arguments and variations that surface when reading about affect. This complexity has prompted several authors to endorse its indeterminacy (Anderson 2014; Bondi & Davidson 2011; Davidson et al. 2007; McCormack 2006; Thrift 2008): 'there is no single, generalisable theory of affect: not yet, and (thankfully) there never will be' (Seigworth & Gregg 2010, p. 3). As well as recent interest, questions concerning affect extend back several centuries (Thien 2005; Thrift 2008). Tolia-Kelly (2006, p. 451) proclaims '"affect" is a term with a distinctly psychological pedigree', while Thrift (2008) cites its philosophical and evolutionary foundations; however, Anderson (2014, p. 6) asserts: 'the genealogy of affect remains to be written'. Regardless of its precise historical roots, contemporary interest in affect emerged as a correction to the over-prioritisation of rationality, and in conjunction with increasing attention paid to bodies, feelings and movement (Clough 2007; Dewsbury 2003; Leys 2011; Reckwitz 2017; Thien 2005). Calls for a 'Turn to Affect' in theory cite its neglect as 'criminal' (Thrift 2008, p. 172), or just as dramatically, 'that we ignore . . . affective intensities and resonances at our peril' (Leys 2011, p. 436).

The recent flurry of activity on affect is associated with its political and ethical potential arising from 'a long tradition of feminist scholarship on emotional life' that, among other contributions, has destabilised thought linking emotions with femininity (Anderson 2014, p. 6; Bondi 2005; Pile 2010).[14] Affect scholarship is popular in a range of theories and disciplines, each varying in how it is defined and perceived and also regarding its political potential (Anderson 2014). Comprising something significantly more than emotion or emotional states, as a concept, affect is not easy to grasp (Lorimer 2008). Lorimer's (2008, p. 552) attempt at a comprehensive definition, 'by the theoretician's longhand', is: '[the] properties, competencies, modalities, energies, attunements, arrangements and intensities of differing texture, temporality, velocity and spatiality, that act on bodies, are produced through bodies and transmitted by bodies'. As noted in this definition, affect[15] can be attached to, and produced by, human bodies, but also to an almost endless list of other more-than-human entities, including practices, discourses and institutions, among others. Often multiple entities are involved, such as the previously mentioned policies and decision-making that led to the construction of an elevated railway line, or 'sky-rail', in Melbourne, Australia. Although many benefits were expected from the project, such as improved safety, economic development and better travel times, the negative affects generated by this project meant locals became angry about potential property impacts and, due to a long history of poor public consultation, became highly distrustful of the government's intentions (Stone & Woodcock 2016). This outcome was a surprise to the government in power, who were not expecting this response because they did not consider the affective dimensions of the project. Opposing political parties and the tabloid newspapers had a field day; for weeks, they circulated images of giant machines and imposing concrete pylons overshadowing residents' backyards. As Anderson (2014, p. 6) explains: 'Affects are constantly infusing embodied practices, resonating with discourses, coalescing around images, becoming part of institutions, animating political violences, catalysing political communities, and being known and intervened in, amongst much else.'

In his book-length study *Encountering Affect: Capacities, Apparatuses, Conditions*, Anderson (2014) exemplifies affects pertaining to disasters portrayed in the media, macroeconomic policies and inspirational speeches by politicians, such as US President Obama's 2009 inauguration speech. In short, affect thinking is distinguished by its attentiveness to the shared corporality of bodies and what they do rather than the rationality of minds – in other words, feelings and *precognitive actions* rather than thoughts – and like non-representational theories, the capacity or potential of affect to create ripples in social worlds (Reckwitz 2017). However, questions concerning affect are not so easily resolved; they become incredibly more complex regarding their relations to emotions – whether emotions are captured by and are part of affect, or whether they stand apart as something different. Recent work turning to affect is entangled with a corollary of interest in emotions by diverse disciplines including human geography, media studies and history (Leys 2011), philosophy, neurobiology and political science (Bondi 2005), and sociology and psychology (Thien 2005), among others. For example, Ginn's (2014, p. 534) work in geography discusses how relations between slugs and gardeners 'are "sticky": joined together by shared histories, curiosity and disgust', while in psychiatry, Albrecht et al. (2007, p. S96) conceptualise the negative emotions caused by drought and a large open-cut coal mine as 'solastalgia': 'the pain or distress caused by the loss of, or inability to derive, solace connected to the negatively perceived state of one's home environment'.

Many authors draw on research from neuroscience, psychoanalysis and psychotherapy (Pile 2010), reflecting a general inclination that increasingly sees a convergence between the natural and social sciences. Although convergence can be productive, and is in fact increasingly encouraged (Bondi 2005;

Thrift 2008), it can also be empirically problematic and theoretically fraught. More particularly, it risks reversing several progressive ontological and epistemological gains in the social sciences. For example, in scholarship drawing on the dominant paradigm of emotions from neuroscience, emotions belong to bodies as 'bodily responses' and are considered entirely independent from cognition and intention (Leys 2011, p. 463). This bifurcation of body and mind reinstates a previously outdated dualism (Leys 2011). In other work on neuro- and related sciences, such dualisms are called into question, prompting Leys (2011, p. 440) to assert that 'a new scientific paradigm for research on the emotions is needed'.

Moving on from general concerns pertaining to the study of emotions, I now turn to a more focused discussion of affect and emotion framed by this book's core interest in more-than-human theories. Substantial deliberations about the differences and similarities between affect and emotions occur in human geography (Bondi 2005), where detailed engagements, provocations and responses are played out in the literature: for example, between Thien (2005), Tolia-Kelly (2006) and McCormack (2006; 2007) and between Bondi (2005), Pile (2010) and Bondi and Davidson (2011).[16] Like discussions of affect in general, there are also a variety of stances on affect and emotions in human geography (Bondi & Davidson 2011), despite 'sympathies of approach and subject matter' (Pile 2010, p. 10). To understand how these ideas can most usefully be applied in rethinking healthy urban environments, awareness of these differences and debates is useful because each approach has different conceptual and practical implications. I find two general positions reflected in the literature:[17] first, a choice between one approach or the other, where affect and emotion are seen to fundamentally differ and proponents privilege one over the other, and; second, an ambiguous stance that resists drawing clear boundaries between affect and emotion, without elevation; one that acknowledges each perspective has its strengths and weaknesses. I consider the latter position more useful, as it means that rather seeking a definitive position on affect and emotions (and therefore resisting entanglement in debates), it provides an inherent flexibility responsive to the empirical or practical context at hand. The remainder of this chapter examines each of these positions to create a more comprehensive overview of the issues at hand.

In the first position, which considers affect and emotion as different, contributions have diverged into what are often termed 'emotional' versus 'affective/affectual' geographies (Pile 2010; Tolia-Kelly 2006). These two inter-related fields of research are quite distinctive, but each has its own quirks and contradictions. As Tolia-Kelly (2006, p. 213) observes: 'The value of an "affectual" approach over an "emotional geographies" approach is often intangible and immeasurable, yet these two fields are simultaneously conjoined and separate because of their subject matter, language, their political vision and genealogies.'

In general, scholars supporting affective or emotional approaches agree that both affects and emotions are socially shared (Bondi 2005; Wetherell

2012), but for many, this is where the agreement ends. From an ontological point of view, the main differences are explained by the alignment of affective geographies with non-representational theories, while feminist theories underpin emotional geographies (e.g., Bondi & Davidson 2011; Thien 2005). The following discussion shows how the different ontologies underpinning affect and emotion manifest themselves regarding the different critiques of affective and emotional geographies.

As Anderson (2014, p. 12) comments, when affect and emotion are bifurcated, it is usually 'affect with the impersonal, life and the objective; emotion with the personal, identity and the subjective'; however, 'every theory of affect and emotion makes some form of implicit or explicit distinction'. He rightly observes that we need to think about 'what sort of definition is offered and the work definitions do' (Anderson 2014, p. 12). In affective geographies, related as they are to non-representational theories,[18] affect is often considered: 'a quality of life that is beyond cognition and always interpersonal. It is, moreover, inexpressible: unable to be brought into representation. Affect, in these terms, has consequently become (albeit unwittingly) a key testing, and proving, ground for non-representational theory' (Pile 2010, p. 8).

Furthermore, work in affective geographies has made deliberate attempts to distinguish itself from emotional geographies, marking 'a conceptual break with emotions, producing a distinctive affectual geography' (Pile 2010, p. 8). Moreover, 'while it is implicated in corporeal sensibility, affect is never reducible to the personal quality of emotion' (McCormack 2003, p. 501). Nevertheless, emotions are still present in affective geographies, but in a reduced capacity – collapsed under an encompassing concept of affect (see Thrift 2008). As Tolia-Kelly (2006, p. 213) writes: 'Emotion in "affectual geographies" is relegated to immediacy, immanence and the virtual in the everyday lived environment, intrinsically embedded in universalist thought rather than the geopolitical landscape that constitutes our universal political life.'

By way of contrast, Thien (2005, pp. 450-451) states the case for emotional geographies: 'Emotional geographies encompasses a growing interdisciplinary scholarship that combines the insights of geography, gender studies, cultural studies, sociology, anthropology and other disciplines to understand how the world is mediated by feeling.'

As well as doing the 'recovery work that embraces embodied experience' (Tolia-Kelly 2006, p. 213), Thien (2005, p. 451) argues that 'placing emotion in the context of our always intersubjective relations offers more promise for politically relevant, emphatically [more-than-] human, geographies'. She suggests that 'affect is the how of emotion. That is, affect is used to describe (in both the communicative and literal sense) the motion of emotion' (Thien 2005, p. 451). However, those privileging affective geographies find various weaknesses in the concept of emotions in emotional geography. These include: making assumptions about the nature of emotions, objectifying them, reifying expressed emotional accounts over those that cannot or are unable to be expressed, and not engaging with political attempts to manipulate or mobilise emotions or 'non-cognitive and/or precognitive emotional life' (Pile 2010, p. 8). A further criticism is that emotional geographies can be 'exclusively human-centred' (McCormack 2006, p. 330): that is, 'insufficiently 'transhuman'' (Bondi 2005, p. 438), leaving little room for more-than-human emotion.

Furthermore, affective geographies more readily connect with a more-than-human agenda than work done to date in emotional geographies because they have 'a distinctive, intentional bent' towards more-than-human (Thien 2005, p. 450). As Lorimer (2008, p. 552) argues:

> Affect is distributed between, and can happen outside, bodies which are not exclusively human, and might incorporate technologies, things, non-human living matter, discourses or even, say, a swathe of noise or swarm of creatures. Such recombinant, process-based thinking expands a field of ethological study to take in hybrids, composites and virtual states.

While those aligned with affective geographies see decentring humans as a key step in acknowledging more-than-human affects and emotions, those aligned with emotional geographies argue that by decentring humans, the resulting depersonalised and abstracted form of affect is wanting in various aspects. One often-cited criticism is that affective geographies are 'inattentive to issues of power' (Tolia-Kelly 2006, p. 213). Moreover, it is not that one perspective attends to these issues more successfully than the other, because each is concerned with different concepts of politics, ethics and power. For example, emotional geographies pay attention to the agency of differently produced and differently abled human bodies, acknowledging that some bodies have greater capacity to create affects than others:

> Various bodies through their racialized, gendered and sexualized markedness, magnetize various capacities for being affected; a slave and holocaust victim do not necessarily experience pain, suffering, anomie, in the same way due to their social positioning and 'enforced' capacities of (im)mobility, experience and affecting the social space around them.
>
> (Tolia-Kelly 2006, p. 215)

Furthermore, Tolia-Kelly (2006, p. 215) writes that affective geographies as described by Thrift (2004) and others are universalising, normalising, singular and textual, and have a 'Westnocentric literary and sensory palette'. Affective geographies are 'accused of producing a depersonalised politics incapable of resonating with people's actual experiences' (Pile 2010, p. 13) and being 'ironically, disembodied' (Bondi 2005, p. 438). This position is supported by Thien (2005, p. 452), who writes: "'affect" as a term and a concept is employed here in masculinist, technocratic and distancing ways'. She argues that the abstraction of affect deliberately distances itself from emotions which are labelled as soft or feminine. On this point, Thien (2005, p. 452) emphasises that affective geographies reinstate masculine/feminine, rational/emotional and other dualisms: 'In this conceptual positioning, these transhuman geographies re-draw yet again not only the demarcation between masculinist reason and feminized emotion, but also the false distinction between "personal" and "political" which feminist scholars have extensively critiqued'.

Conversely, one of the main weaknesses directed at emotional geographies is their nominal 'return to the subject as the subject of emotion' (Clough 2008, p. 1). This seemingly 'backwards' step in view of contemporary advances made against subject/object dualisms in the social sciences – usually associated with representational approaches – has been noted and criticised (Clough 2008; Thrift 2008). As Pile (2010, p. 12) declares: 'affectual geography views the psychological subject with enduring suspicion.' Some argue it is precisely the return to the felt and personalised aspects of emotion that have enabled emotional geographies to more easily embrace (and be associated with) progressive political agendas (e.g., Tolia-Kelly 2006). However, returning to subjects not only might bifurcate them from objects, and thus return to the problems of representation, but simultaneously recentralises humans as the epicentre of all social and emotional life in cities. This position overlooks the many non-humans that have begun to make their presence felt in accounts of the social, as well as in practical contexts such as biodiversity in urban planning, and 'it foregoes the possibility of cultivating ethical sensibilities attuned to non-human affective energies and agencies, including, for instance, those involving animals' (McCormack 2006, p. 331).

A consideration of the divisions between affective and emotional geographies motivates the question of why it must be a unilateral choice. Is it possible that emotional and affective geographies or individual/subjective affects could be combined with more abstract, socially shared human and more-than-human affective states? Although the answer to this question is dependent on particular research questions, practical contexts or interests, the proposition leads to the second, less antagonistic, position observed in the literature, where the boundaries between affect and emotional geographies are blurred.

Beyond and within human geography, some researchers liberally allow affect to be interpreted widely and include emotional subjective states as permissible definitions or components (e.g., Davidson et al. 2007; Gregg & Seigworth 2010). This diversity naturally occurs when concepts with loose boundaries have broad appeal in scholarly literature. Bondi and Davidson (2011, p. 596) 'welcome the diverse range of borrowings that inform contributions to this (and closely related) fields of research'. Other scholars see affect and emotion as necessary, neither being satisfactory on their own (Bondi 2005; Simonsen 2007). Some rejoice in the blurriness of the boundaries: 'emotions and affects might thus be considered disagreeable in many ways, but their rough edges, the very wildness that frustrates domestication is precisely what gives them such power' (Bondi & Davidson 2011, p. 595).

Anderson (2014, p. 163) offers a flexible and balanced approach for working with affect and emotions, although he acknowledges that his is only one (limited) version. Commencing with the vagueness often associated with terminology in general, he argues that use of affect and emotion 'is too reliant on unspecified social and cultural assumptions about what specific terms mean and do. It is presumed everyone will know exactly what the word "emotion" is being used to name, for example' (Anderson 2014, p. 11). This is a significant observation, because definitions matter, even more so when a variety of uses and interpretations are suggested. Rather than an all-encompassing theory or definition, what Anderson (2014, p. 13) proposes is a 'analytics of affect'. This approach comprises three translations or types of affects and a series of propositions that centre on understanding processes of mediation. These in turn are loosely defined as 'the array of processes that shape affective life and result in temporary orderings of affect' (Anderson 2014, p. 168).

The three translations of affect proposed by Anderson (2014, p. 164) are: 'an object-target of apparatuses; a bodily capacity emergent from encounters; and a collective condition that mediates how life is lived and felt'. The latter two translations are almost self-explanatory, but what I interpret as an 'object-target of apparatuses' (Anderson 2014, p. 164), after Reckwitz (2017), could be a particular happening, issue or collection of entities that produces a response or physical arousal. Furthermore, affect can be, and usually is, two or more of these translations occurring simultaneously. One example is the protest march, where large numbers of people come together to voice concerns about the lack of government action on issues such as global capitalism, immigration or climate change. A march is motivated by certain affects and emotions, such as concern, but through its enactment and performance, a protest march can also *generate* affects, such as excitement or anticipation.

The three translations of affect described by Anderson (2014) combined with the emphasis on processes of mediation (or how particular affects come to be) are an attempt to resolve some of the criticisms directed at early work on affective geographies as universalising and depoliticised (Tolia-Kelly 2006), depersonalised (Pile 2010), disembodied (Bondi 2005), masculine and guilty of perpetuating binaries (Thien 2005). Also, instead of either marginalising or privileging subjectivities, as found in affective and emotional geographies, Anderson (2014, p. 12) aims to: 'Make terms such as feeling, mood, atmosphere, and so on, into sensitising devices designed to attend to and reveal specific types of relational configurations, rather than unproblematic claims about what affect really is "out there" in the world.'

Anderson's (2014) approach to affect, although it presents solutions to the divisions between, and weak points of, affective and emotional geographies, may still default to a reliance on language and text, depending on the way his analytics are operationalised. In this way, it may share in some of the critique directed at representational approaches discussed at the beginning of this chapter. Also problematic is that relying on language means that humans again become centralised and prioritised over more-than-humans. Reprioritising humans and their talk and text, however, is a perennial trap for any research, including that drawing on more-than-human theories. It is therefore important to reiterate that affects and emotions may attach to, and by implication be generated by, anything, including a wide array of non-humans (Lorimer 2008); these include a sky-rail project, a cute endangered mammal, or the 'spatial atmosphere' of cities that may be awe-inspiring, pleasurable or fearful (Reckwitz 2017, p. 122). However, the arrays of affects produced and how they may or may not change over time is difficult to predict and control.

The relational propensity of affect, with its implied agency and capacity to create effects, can lead to comparisons with assemblage thinking and the distributed agency created by and shared in assemblages. Except that affect and assemblage both share origins in the work of Deleuze and Guattari (1987),[19] there has been little exploration of the intersections between these bodies of theories and what each might offer the other – unlike their acknowledgement and presence in non-representational theories (e.g., Thrift 2008). However, Bennett's (2010, p. 61) discussions of affective bodies (pp. 21–23), including ideas such as the 'geoaffect' and her advocacy to elevate vibrant (more-than-human) matter in social life, politics and ethics, are a notable exception. The next chapter explores assemblage thinking in the work of Bennett (2010) and others, and how this theoretical work assists in recognising the significance of non-humans.

Conclusion

Current ideas about cities and how to make them healthy are hindered by reductive approaches to the quotidian but manifold dynamic experiences, encounters, affects and practices that characterise urban environments. The interactive flow of humans, animals, plants, materials, weather systems, infrastructures, technologies and other non-humans that form a vast array of modalities, weave through cities to create recognisable peaks and troughs of activity, various positive and negative affects and emotions over multiple timescales. These are typified by the morning and evening rush-hour, day, night, seasonal changes and one-off events. The repetitive and frequent nature of many of these flows often renders them mundane and without significance. The only way non-human agents come to the attention of human inhabitants, scholars, planners and policymakers is when things are perceived to go wrong: a cancelled bus service, a flu epidemic, an insect or rodent infestation, a severe weather event. This chapter draws attention to these complex interactions by showing how different ideas about knowledge, sociality, affects and emotions can change the way cities are understood.

The increased global circulation and movement of practices, human bodies, artefacts and other non-humans from one place to many others has intensified the number and type of encounters, relations and events on a scale unique to the current era (Bennett 2010, p. 108). With a 24-hour global news cycle and the proliferation of social media platforms, affects and emotions created by and attached to global events such as cyclones, war, famine and mass habitat destruction have greater reach and impact than ever before. However, it is often difficult to connect this myriad of phenomena to the daily lives and rhythms that comprise the relative safety of cities. Part of the reason for this lacuna is that cities are conceptualised in human-centric terms – environments made for and controlled by (certain) humans to the exclusion of other agents. Cities are also conceptualised as discrete entities, often seen to subsist self-sufficiently and autonomously, when in fact they are nodes of intense, interconnected events and the nexus of vast flows of activity, bodies and things from everywhere. The many worlds we inhabit are ubiquitous.

To move beyond simplistic notions of cities as discrete and for humans only, new and different conceptual tools are needed to make sense of happenings and connections over a range of distances and various timescales. A key part of this endeavour is to challenge dominant ways of seeing, knowing and describing the world that harmfully bifurcate humans from non-humans and artificially disrupt one place from another. Ideas that embrace complexity, emergence, affect and process will transcend the current disciplinary limitations of representation, space and time. There is a need to disrupt the status quo. The Affective Turn presents various ways to tackle this task and destabilise thinking about everyday life in cities.

This first chapter in Part I on The Affective Turn has launched our journey into the world of more-than-human thinking and its potential to change the way we think about and know cities. It introduced and discussed work in non-representational and affective theories advocating processual, complex and relational ways of understanding and being. The chapter began by introducing some of the limitations of representational approaches that currently characterise the social sciences and limit thinking about cities. These included privileging text and language rather than materials, affects and emotions; ignoring relations between subjects and objects and their changing dynamics over space and time; and reifying representations as the ultimate form of knowledge. This led to a discussion of non-representational theories premised on the idea that precognitive affects and emotions are important in understanding how practices, or action and doing, unfold. Furthermore, these typically neglected aspects of being in the world have significant capacity to create change. Non-representational thought also argues for nonlinear ideas of time, and places value on emergence in moments conceptualised by the notion of events. It encourages experimentation rather than assuming events will unfold predictably, and being alert for affects that may lead to unexpected encounters. It can also help explain unanticipated outcomes such as resistance to major urban infrastructure projects like elevated railways.

The Affective Turn helps reconceptualise how to think about cities differently – and importantly, how the effects or impacts of change might be differently understood and experienced. Thinking non-representationally and with affect encourages us to see how cities are experienced and felt, and motivates the study of detailed, nuanced experiences that other approaches may overlook. These ways of thinking encourage us to design research and policies that consider in detail, and in a more inclusive way, human–non-human interactions expressed through encounters, affects and emotions, as well as notions of nonlinearity and emergence in urban environments. The challenge is to develop these understandings, not just from a human-centric position, but from a more-than-human one. Nevertheless, despite their theoretical advances and acknowledging that 'everything acts' (Anderson & Harrison 2010b, p. 14), affective and non-representational thinking struggle to relinquish human-centrism, and only partially realise the potential of non-human agency and materialism. I argue that in themselves, these theories are not sufficient to fully achieve the potential of more-than-human theories.

To shift dominant anthropocentric ontologies that elevate and maintain human specialness, there is a need to go further than current work in The Affective Turn. This is where new materialisms come to the fore. For example, Chapter 3 considers whether it is possible and permissible to extend ideas of affect and emotions to non-human species when discussing everyday life by introducing the idea of critical anthropomorphism. It expands some of the ideas already introduced and how they can be more effectively employed to rethink healthy cities.

Notes

1 See Anderson (2014), particularly pp. 12–14 and 84–93, and Thrift (2008), pp. 172–182 for discussions of how affect is non-representational.
2 Anderson and Harrison (2010b, p. 3) argue that social constructivism was 'distinguished by a preoccupation with representation; specifically, by a focus on the structure of symbolic meaning (cultural representation)'.
3 Similarly, Deleuze and Guattari describe the three prongs of representation as subject, concept, being (Massumi 1987).
4 Assemblage thinking is based on ideas of distributed agency and the work of Deleuze and Guattari (1987). See Chapter 3 for further explanation.
5 Aside from their disciplinary roots, the lines differentiating these theories can become somewhat blurry and are drawn here loosely.
6 Anderson and Harrison (2010b) and Thrift (2008), among others, cite the work of Latour and Deleuze as influential in the development of non-representational theories. See also Dewsbury (2003).
7 See Anderson and Harrison (2010b; 2010a) for a genealogy of non-representational thinking, as well as Thrift (2008).

8 For example, Haraway (2008) and Whatmore (2002).
9 See Chapter 3 for a more detailed discussion of liveliness and vibrancy.
10 Derived from Delueze and Guattari (1987).
11 With non-representational thinking therefore not necessarily *anti*-representational but instead differently positioned in regard to its treatment of representation, some have questioned the suitability of the name 'non-representational' (Anderson & Harrison 2010b). In its place 'more-than-representational' has been proposed (Lorimer 2005), but to date it has not taken hold.
12 This argument has also been made by Cronon (1996) in regard to understanding nature.
13 Anderson (2014, p. 9) states this is the 'vaguest and most general definition'.
14 See Bondi (2005) for the detailed contributions of feminist geography.
15 Some scholars prefer the use of 'affects' in the plural rather than 'affect', as noted by Anderson (2014). I alternate between the two.
16 See Bondi (2005) for an overview of the study of emotions in human geography.
17 These 'positions' are really points on a spectrum, although a few scholars would align themselves purely with one stance.
18 Closely aligned to the work of Deleuze and Guattari, Spinoza and Bergson (Clough 2008; Thrift 2008).
19 And by default, Spinoza and Bergson.

References

Albrecht, G, Sartore, G-M, Connor, L, Higginbotham, N, Freeman, S, Kelly, B, Stain, H, Tonna, A & Pollard, G 2007, 'Solastalgia: the distress caused by environmental change', *Australasian Psychiatry*, vol. 15, no. 1, Supplement 1, pp. 95–98.
Anderson, B 2014, *Encountering Affect: Capacities, Apparatuses, Conditions*, Ashgate.
Anderson, B & Harrison, P 2010a, *Taking-place: Non-representational Theories and Geography*, Ashgate.
Anderson, B & Harrison, P 2010b, 'The promise of non-representational theories', in B Anderson & P Harrison (eds), *Taking-place: Non-representational Theories and Geography*, Ashgate, pp. 1–34.
Barad, K 2003, 'Posthumanist performativity: toward an understanding of how matter comes to matter', *Signs*, vol. 28, no. 3, pp. 801–831.
Barad, K 2007, *Meeting the Universe Halfway: Quantum Physics and the Entanglement of Matter and Meaning*, Duke University Press.
Barnfield, A 2016, 'Affect and public health – choreographing atmospheres of movement and participation', *Emotion, Space and Society*, vol. 20, pp. 1–9.
Bennett, J 2010, *Vibrant Matter: A Political Ecology of Things*, Duke University Press.
Bissell, D 2014, 'Transforming commuting mobilities: the memory of practice', *Environment and Planning A*, vol. 46, no. 8, pp. 1946–1965.
Bondi, L 2005, 'Making connections and thinking through emotions: between geography and psychotherapy', *Transactions of the Institute of British Geographers*, vol. 30, no. 4, pp. 433–448.
Bondi, L & Davidson, J 2011, 'Lost in translation', *Transactions of the Institute of British Geographers*, vol. 36, no. 4, pp. 595–598.
Buser, M 2014, 'Thinking through non-representational and affective atmospheres in planning theory and practice', *Planning Theory*, vol. 13, no. 3, pp. 227–243.

Clough, PT 2007, 'Introduction', in PT Clough & JOM Halley (eds), *The Affective Turn: Theorizing the Social*, Duke University Press, pp. 2–33.

Clough, PT 2008, 'The Affective Turn: political economy, biomedia and bodies', *Theory, Culture & Society*, vol. 25, no. 1, pp. 1–22.

Cresswell, T 2012, 'Nonrepresentational theory and me: notes of an interested sceptic', *Environment and Planning D: Society and Space*, vol. 30, no. 1, pp. 96–105.

Cronon, W 1996, 'Introduction: In search of nature', in W Cronon (ed.), *Uncommon Ground: Rethinking the Human Place in Nature*, WW Norton, pp. 23–56.

Davidson, J, Bondi, L & Smith, M (eds) 2007, *Emotional Geographies*, Ashgate.

Deleuze, G & Guattari, F 1987, *Thousand Plateaus: Capitalism and Schizophrenia*, (translated by Brian Massumi), University of Minnesota Press.

Dewsbury, J-D 2003, 'Witnessing space: "knowledge without contemplation"', *Environment and Planning A*, vol. 35, no. 11, pp. 1907–1932.

Dewsbury, J-D 2010, 'Language and the event: the unthought of appearing worlds', in B Anderson & P Harrison (eds), *Taking-place: Non-representational Theories and Geography*, Ashgate, pp. 148–160.

Doel, M 2010, 'Representation and difference', in B Anderson & P Harrison (eds), *Taking-place: Non-representational Theories and Geography*, Ashgate, pp. 117–130.

Forouzan, A, Masoumi, K, Haddadzadeh Shoushtari, M, Idani, E, Tirandaz, F, Feli, M, Assarehzadegan, MA & Asgari Darian, A 2014, 'An overview of thunderstorm-associated asthma outbreak in southwest of Iran', *Journal of Environmental and Public Health*, vol. 2014, p. 4.

Frigg, R & Nguyen, J 2016, 'Scientific representation', *Stanford Encyclopedia of Philosophy Archive* (Winter), https://plato.stanford.edu/archives/win2016/entries/scientific-representation/, accessed 5 May 2017.

Ginn, F 2014, 'Sticky lives: slugs, detachment and more-than-human ethics in the garden', *Transactions of the Institute of British Geographers*, vol. 39, no. 4, pp. 532–544.

Greenhough, B 2010, 'Vitalist geographies: Life and the more-than-human', in B Anderson & P Harrison (eds), *Taking-place: Non-representational Theories and Geography*, Ashgate, pp. 37–54.

Gregg, M & Seigworth, GJ 2010, *The Affect Theory Reader*, E-Duke Books Scholarly Collection, Duke University Press.

Haraway, DJ 2008, *When Species Meet*, University of Minnesota Press.

Jones, O 2011, 'Geography, memory and non-representational geographies', *Geography Compass*, vol. 5, no. 12, pp. 875–885.

Kingsbury, P 2015, 'Book review: *Encountering Affect: Capacities, Apparatuses, Conditions*', *Antipode*, https://radicalantipode.files.wordpress.com/2015/08/book-review_kingsbury-on-anderson.pdf, accessed 22 January 2018.

Latham, A & Conradson, D 2003, 'The possibilities of performance', *Environment and Planning A*, vol. 35, no. 11, pp. 1901–1906.

Latham, A & McCormack, DP 2004, 'Moving cities: rethinking the materialities of urban geographies', *Progress in Human Geography*, vol. 28, no. 6, pp. 701–724.

Latham, A & McCormack, DP 2017, 'Affective cities', in ML Silk, DL Andrews & H Thorpe (eds), *Routledge Handbook of Physical Cultural Studies*, Routledge, pp. 369–377.

Latour, B 2005, *Reassembling the Social: An Introduction to Actor-Network-Theory*, Oxford University Press.

Law, J 2009, 'Seeing like a survey', *Cultural sociology*, vol. 3, no. 2, pp. 239–256.

Leys, R 2011, 'The Turn to Affect: a critique', *Critical Inquiry*, vol. 37, no. 3, pp. 434–472.

Lorimer, H 2005, 'Cultural geography: the busyness of being "more-than-representational"', *Progress in Human Geography*, vol. 29, no. 1, pp. 83–94.

Lorimer, H 2007, 'Cultural geography: worldly shapes, differently arranged', *Progress in Human Geography*, vol. 31, no. 1, pp. 89–100.

Lorimer, H 2008, 'Cultural geography: non-representational conditions and concerns', *Progress in Human Geography*, vol. 32, no. 4, pp. 551–559.

Lorimer, H 2010, 'Forces of nature, forms of life: calibrating ethology and phenomenology', in B Anderson & P Harrison (eds), *Taking-place: Non-representational Theories and Geography*, Ashgate, pp. 56–78.

Maller, C & Strengers, Y 2013, 'The global migration of everyday life: investigating the practice memories of Australian migrants', *Geoforum*, vol. 44, pp. 243–252.

Maller, C & Strengers, Y 2015, 'Resurrecting sustainable practices: using memories of the past to intervene in the future', in Y Strengers & C Maller (eds), *Social Practices, Intervention and Sustainability: Beyond Behaviour Change*, Routledge, pp. 147–162.

Massumi, B 1987, 'Translator's foreword: pleasures of philosophy', in G Deleuze & F Guattari (eds), *Thousand Plateaus: Capitalism and Schizophrenia*, University of Minnesota Press, pp. ix–xv.

Massumi, B 2002, *Parables for the Virtual: Movement, Affect, Sensation*, Duke University Press.

McCormack, DP 2003, 'An event of geographical ethics in spaces of affect', *Transactions of the Institute of British Geographers*, vol. 28, no. 4, pp. 488–507.

McCormack, DP 2006, 'For the love of pipes and cables: a response to Deborah Thien', *Area*, vol. 38, no. 3, pp. 330–332.

McCormack, DP 2007, 'Molecular affects in human geographies', *Environment and Planning A*, vol. 39, no. 2, pp. 359–377.

Pickering, A 1993, 'The mangle of practice: agency and emergence in the sociology of science', *American Journal of Sociology*, vol. 99, no. 3, pp. 559–589.

Pickering, A 1995, *The Mangle of Practice: Time, Agency and Science*, University of Chicago Press.

Pile, S 2010, 'Emotions and affect in recent human geography', *Transactions of the Institute of British Geographers*, vol. 35, no. 1, pp. 5–20.

Reckwitz, A 2017, 'Practices and their affects', in A Hui, TR Schatzki & E Shove (eds), *The Nexus of Practices: Connections, Constellations, Practitioners*, Routledge, pp. 114–125.

Seigworth, GJ & Gregg, M 2010, 'An inventory of shimmers', in M Gregg & GJ Seigworth (eds), *The Affect Theory Reader*, Duke University Press, pp. 1–25.

Simonsen, K 2007, 'Practice, spatiality and embodied emotions: an outline of a geography of practice', *Human Affairs*, vol. 17, no. 2, doi:10.2478/v10023-007-0015-8, www.degruyter.com/view/j/humaff.2007.17.issue-2/v10023-007-0015-8/v10023-007-0015-8.xml.

Stone, J & Woodcock, I 2016, 'The "sky rail" saga: can big new transport projects ever run smoothly?', *The Conversation Australia*, https://theconversation.com/the-sky-rail-saga-can-big-new-transport-projects-ever-run-smoothly-54383, accessed 19 May 2017.

Thien, D 2005, 'After or beyond feeling? A consideration of affect and emotion in geography', *Area*, vol. 37, no. 4, pp. 450–454.

Thrift, N 2004, 'Intensities of feeling: towards a spatial politics of affect', *Geografiska Annaler: Series B, Human Geography*, vol. 86, no. 1, pp. 57–78.

Thrift, N 2008, *Non-representational Theory: Space, Politics, Affect*, Taylor & Francis.

Thrift, N & Dewsbury, J-D 2000, 'Dead geographies – and how to make them live', *Environment and Planning D: Society and Space*, vol. 18, no. 4, pp. 411–432.

Thrift, N, Anderson, B & Harrison, P 2010, '"The 27th letter": an interview with Nigel Thrift', in B Anderson & P Harrison (eds), *Taking-place: Non-representational Theories and Geography*, Ashgate, pp. 183–198.

Tolia-Kelly, DP 2006, 'Affect – an ethnocentric encounter? Exploring the "universalist" imperative of emotional/affectual geographies', *Area*, vol. 38, no. 2, pp. 213–217.

Wener, RE & Evans, GW 2011, 'Comparing stress of car and train commuters', *Transportation Research Part F: Traffic Psychology and Behaviour*, vol. 14, no. 2, pp. 111–116.

Wetherell, M 2012, *Affect and Emotion: A New Social Science Understanding*, SAGE Publications.

Whatmore, S 2002, *Hybrid Geographies: Natures Cultures Spaces*, SAGE Publications.

3 The New Materialisms Turn

Materiality, vital materialism and assemblages

Introduction

The previous chapter introduced non-representational theories, thinking with affect and emotions, and nonlinear notions of time and temporality that challenge ideas and methods of representation used in research and policymaking. What was less clear in the more-than-human theories of The Affective Turn is their treatment of matter and materiality. Although theorists working with non-representational and affective approaches declare interests in, and orientation to, the material world, this stance is muted compared to other more-than-human theories. Homing in on materiality, this chapter specifically discusses the so-named turn to new materialism – or materialisms.[1]

'New materialisms' is a catchphrase for the recent materialist turn across the social sciences. The more-than-human theories I place in this category orient themselves around the physical affects, liveliness and agency of living and non-living matter at various scales and forms, from the micro of sub-atomic particles to bodies and complex urban assemblages such as cities. The chapter shows how new materialisms pay detailed attention to the different forms of agency and 'thing power' (Bennett 2010)[2] possessed by non-humans relevant to understanding complex environmental or socio-material problems found in urban environments. Acknowledging that there is some overlap with the theories of affect and non-representation introduced in Chapter 2, this chapter attempts to cover the work of theorists 'happy to fly under the new materialist flag' (Coole 2013, p. 2). Building on the ideas introduced in The Affective Turn, new materialisms bring various other contributions that are useful in rethinking healthy cities, and here I highlight two.

First, the chapter argues for giving non-human actors and agents more equal status with humans, while simultaneously decentring humans. This is a necessary step to move away from ideas of human sovereignty (Washick & Wingrove 2015), essentialism (Bennett 2010) and exceptionalism (Pickering 2008; Stengers 2010) to demonstrate the active and vibrant nature of non-humans, often considered simply as backdrops to human activity (Appadurai 1988; Bennett 2010; Cronon 1996; Latour 2005; Pickering 2013; Plumwood 2009). For example, parks and gardens are usually valued for the relaxation and physical activity opportunities they provide humans, rather than as part of ecosystems and providing habitat for a range of non-human species. In this way, I argue new materialisms allow us to see non-humans and their activities extant in cities, and set the scene for making cities more biodiverse.

Although they are decentred, new materialisms include humans as part of nature. Including humans in nature instead of setting them apart from or above nature ('the nature/culture divide') (Kaika 2005; Latour 2000) is important because it has implications for how human health and well-being are conceived, and for thinking about how to make cities healthy urban environments.[3] The concept of biophilia (Wilson 1984)[4] explains the range of health and well-being benefits arising from activities such watching wild-life, views of vegetation and parks from windows, and caring for pets and plants (Maller et al. 2006).[5]

Second, decentring humans and using more open and dynamic methods also leads squarely to numerous questions of ethics, politics and policy-making such that politics becomes 'a more-than-human affair' (Hinchliffe & Whatmore 2006, p. 124). Of course, there are a wide range of possible political agendas to pursue. Regarding healthy cities as more-than-human habitat, this would carve out a political agenda that essentially encourages and brings animals and plants back to urban environments, reduces the environmental impact and damage caused by humans living in cities, and makes cities more equitable not only for disadvantaged human populations, but non-human, native and endemic species that arguably have rights to city habitats (Houston et al. 2017).

In rethinking what healthy cities are and how to create them, new material-ists argue for a different type of politics – that is, relational or convivial politics (Bennett 2010; Castree 2003; Hinchliffe & Whatmore 2006; Latour 2005; Mol 1999) – instead of adopting the usual human-centric, formalised political processes. In this way, they embrace experimentation and unpredictability and accept that the outcomes of interventions are always unpredictable, like the affective and non-representational theories outlined in Chapter 2. New materialisms do not seek to devise sure-fire political solutions, but instead emphasise processes, pathways and possibilities, accepting that the world is constantly changing; 'such reconceptualisations can clarify our ethical imperatives and political possibilities' (Washick & Wingrove 2015, p. 63). This uncertainty can be challenging for those wanting to make quick deci-sions about how to improve cities or be guaranteed that the outcomes of interventions will be those that are desired.

There are many debates about materiality and materialism that surpass the capacity of a single book, let alone a single chapter. The chapter therefore presents a streamlined account drawing out key highlights that complement the other chapters in Part I of this book.[6] It is structured as follows. First, it reviews the origins of new materialisms and situates them regarding previous materialist thought. Second, it explains what characterises and distinguishes new materialisms in the context of other more-than-human theories and conventional approaches. Third, it distils key insights important for under-standing healthy urban environments to be carried forward from this to the later parts of this book. Principally, this concerns the political and ethi-cal implications of a new materialist world view and what they imply for attempts to create healthy cities.

Before discussing how new materialisms came about, I briefly introduce assemblage thinking and how I see it as linked to new materialisms more closely than other more-than-human theories (evident in the title of this chapter). It is useful to understand assemblage thinking because it is increasingly written about and used to apply more-than-human thinking to urban settings and challenges – for example, community management of forests (Li 2007) and energy consumption in households (Strengers et al. 2016).

Assemblage thinking has grown in popularity since first characterised by Deleuze and Guattari (1987) (Anderson & McFarlane 2011)[7]; however, it has long-standing use in a range of disciplines, including ecology, archaeo-logy and art history (Anderson & McFarlane 2011). More recently, it has become prominent in human geography, where it is used to think about spatial and temporal formations and processes (Anderson & McFarlane 2011). Like other more-than-human theories, it comes in many shapes and forms without a single correct use or description (Marcus & Saka 2006). Similar to new materialisms, ideas of assemblage are used to focus on pro-cesses of becoming and decay, and the relations and distributed agencies between multiple entities, emphasising emergence, multiplicity and indeter-minacy rather than end products or states (Anderson & McFarlane 2011; DeLanda 2006). Assemblage thinking particularly centres on ideas of distributed agency, originated by Deleuze and Guattari (1987) and developed later by others, including Bennett (2010). As Li (2007, p. 264) explains, assemblage thinking is premised on agency and requires 'hard work . . . to draw heterogeneous elements together' inviting analysis of how elements in different assemblages cohere or break apart. Explained further in the following section, heterogeneous elements are what link assemblage thinking most closely with new materialisms as there is an orientation to the relations between and produced by multiple matters and entities, both human and non-human, and their various agencies.

The origins of new materialisms

'New materialism' is a term found in various disciplines, including human geography, science and technology studies and political theory, and is also associated with theories such as Barad's (2003) agential realism, actor–network, assemblage thinking and non-representational and feminist theories (Anderson & Tolia-Kelly 2004; Fox 2016; Hein 2016; Latham & McCormack 2004; St. Pierre et al. 2016; Whatmore 2006). Each theory or approach has its own peculiarities regarding materiality according to respective disciplinary or theoretical concerns. There is no consistent stance or position for what is now known as 'The Material Turn'. For example, as Anderson and Tolia-Kelly (2004, p. 673) argue, 'despite having numerous points of entry and departure it is held together only by a sensitivity, and responsiveness, to diverse (im)material matters'. In common, however, new materialisms 'challenge the latent humanism of much social science, political theory and everyday actions' (Hinchliffe 2011, p. 398), while 'in the process absolving matter from its long history of attachment to automatism or mechanism'(Bennett 2010, p. 3).

Stepping away from any single disciplinary lens, interest in matter and materiality has waxed and waned during different periods of scholarship according to what has been fashionable at the time. Reflecting on recent neglect, Hinchliffe (2011, p. 396) asserts, in a similar vein to proponents like Bennett (2010) and Latour (1992; 2000; 2005), that materiality has not 'been given much more than lip service in most social sciences'. He further explains that this malaise may be due to 'the world and its things are just too lively to follow the script. Command and control of humans and non-humans is not so much the answer, but the problem' (Hinchliffe 2011, p. 397). Pickering (2013, p. 25) agrees, but argues that more to the point is the assumed passivity of matter, reflected by the 'fabulous range of resources for thinking about autonomous active human beings as if they were masters of a passive universe' and the dearth of similar resources for thinking about matter. A good example of this is how urban environments, and all they contain, are usually clumped together and classified as passive backgrounds for human activity rather than being comprised of heterogeneous agents and materials of all kinds. Latour (2005, p. 69) has commented extensively on the dematerialised nature of the social sciences, particularly sociology[8], stating that non-humans have been 'explicitly excluded from collective existence by more than one hundred years of social explanation'.

After its general demise in the 1970s and early 1980s (Lemke 2015),[9] 'materialism is once more on the move' (Coole & Frost 2010a, p. 2). There are a range of reasons for the renewed interest in material worlds; here I highlight some predominant, related explanations while bypassing more complex theoretical assertions and histories less likely to be of interest to readers of this book. First, interest in materialism is a reaction to the overemphasis on language and text attributed by many to the cultural turn[10] (Barad 2003; Coole & Frost 2010b; Lemke 2015). This point also featured in Chapter 2 when introducing affect and non-representational theories. Historically, particularly in westernised thinking, matter has been classified as the inferior half of a binary that prioritises language, consciousness, emotions and subjectivity that are arguably 'superior to the baser desires of biological material or the inertia of physical stuff' (Coole & Frost 2010a, p. 2). Although this distinction may be perceived as recycled dualism, it remains evident in many disciplines and, according to new materialists, a significant paradigm shift remains warranted (Pickering 2013).

Second, new materialisms represent an important corrective step towards the dismissal of interests in materiality as 'naively representational' (Lemke 2015, p. 4). This claim is hotly contested by new materialists and in assemblage thinking (Deleuze & Guattari 1987). Coole and Frost (2010a, p. 10) assert that 'matter is no longer imagined here as a massive, opaque plenitude but . . . recognised instead as indeterminate, constantly forming and reforming in unexpected ways. One could conclude, accordingly, that "matter becomes" rather than that "matter is".'

In seeing matter as dynamic and ever-changing, new materialist thinking challenges some conventional conceptualisations of urban environments in two ways. First, that the materialities of cities are generally considered fixed and unchanging, and simply part of the passive backdrop to humans and their doings and concerns; and second, that the material features of urban environments somehow determine, or script, human activity. For example, pathways are often built according to designers' or engineers' ideas about how people move through a place; yet such infrastructure is often underutilised or ignored if it is not the shortest or most easily navigated route. In its place, 'desire lines' or informal paths are made by people (Bates 2017), and sometimes animals.

Reflecting on the discussions in Chapter 2, there are many more similarities than differences between non-representational theories, ideas of assemblage and new materialisms. However, in my view, work under the banner of new materialisms arguably goes a lot further in the decentralisation of human subjects compared to affective and non-representational theories. This is particularly evident in scholarship by Barad (2003), Bennett (2010), Coole and Frost (2010b), DeLanda (1997; 2006), Latour (1992; 2005), Stengers (2010) and Pickering (2013), along with numerous others. For instance, some in the new materialisms camp hold a monist[11] stance by not differentiating between sentient beings and non-sentient entities or forms of matter (i.e., they do not distinguish between things that are non-living and those that are alive). Although not all authors contributing to new materialisms scholarship might agree, many sympathise with this position.

In the introduction to their edited collection, Coole and Frost (2010a) make a compelling case for The New Materialisms Turn. Rather than relying simply on the neglect or absence of matter and materiality to explain its current resurgence, they develop their reasoning based on ground-breaking developments in the natural sciences, particularly in biology and postclassical physics, where:

> unprecedented things are currently being done with and to matter, nature, life, production, and reproduction. [In this] context . . . theorists are compelled to rediscover older materialist traditions while pushing them in novel, and sometimes experimental, directions or . . . fresh applications.
>
> (Coole & Frost 2010a, p. 4)

They further explain how the natural sciences are pushing our understanding of matter in new directions, 'thus undermining classical ontologies while inspiring the sort of radical reconceptions of matter we associate with new materialisms' (Coole & Frost 2010a, p. 10). This thinking is echoed by Whatmore (2006), Barad (2003; 2007), Coole (2013) and Pickering (2013), together with Latour (2000; 2005) and others who consistently argue that the mainstream social sciences cannot continue to carry on as if the natural sciences do not matter, or more worryingly, do not exist – and vice versa. Global deaths and illnesses arising from lifestyle diseases are one area where despite decades of intervention from medicine and public health, rates of ill-health are escalating (Daar et al. 2007). To redirect this trend, new contextualised, materialised and processual understandings of health and disease are needed that bring together the latest thinking in the natural and social sciences (Maller 2017).

However, what the new materialists are arguing for is a greater crossover between the social and natural sciences and respective disciplines, while at the same time dissolving binaries between what is considered 'social' and 'natural' (Haraway 2008; Latour 2000). This type of thinking is evident in work on the materiality of human bodies where theories of epigenetics have been brought together with social practices to understand obesity (Maller 2017). Another novel example is interest in the 'social life' of trees, where mature trees in established forests have been found to support other trees, including their offspring, but also other unrelated individuals of various species, through mycorrhizal networks[12] via which they share nutrients and information by sending signals about environmental conditions (Gorzelak et al. 2015; Simard 2009; Simard et al. 1997; Wohlleben 2016). Once thought of as individual competitors, trees are now considered social beings. Such ground-breaking explorations have the potential to generate transformative ideas about how to achieve healthy urban environments from a more-than-human perspective attuned to multispecies relations.[13]

The use of the adjective 'new' in new materialisms hints at the presence of materialism in previous scholarship. Like authors who have similarly commented on the 're'turn (e.g., Greenhough 2010; Whatmore 2006), Coole and Frost (2010a, p. 4) use the term 'renewed materialisms' to acknowledge that many new materialists draw on the work of 'materialist traditions developed prior to modernity'.[14] Before discussing some of the features of new materialisms in more detail, I briefly consider the 'old' materialisms – why they are distinguished from newer forms, and the genealogy of these ideas.

The so-called 'old materialisms' largely relate to the work of critical theory and Marx in the nineteenth century regarding concerns about power and the material effects of social and economic structures, particularly on those people at the lower end of the socio-economic spectrum (Bennett 2010; St. Pierre et al. 2016). Regarding a more-than-human agenda, old materialisms are, above all, overtly humanist, and have been criticised for being deterministic and lopsidedly structural and fixed rather than dynamic, reflexive or reciprocal (Bennett 2010; Coole & Frost 2010a). To complicate the issue further, what are referred to as 'new' materialisms have much older roots, stretching back to work in philosophy by Spinoza and Bergson on vitalism (Bennett 2010; Deleuze & Guattari 1987). Dismissed by some circles, and viewed as controversial in others, vitalism has been revisited by various scholars, including Bennett (2010), and before her, Deleuze and Guattari (1987) (Coole & Frost 2010a).

Vitalism is based on the idea that living matter possesses a special kind of force that differentiates it from non-living or inorganic matter (Bennett 2010; Coole & Frost 2010a). Related to a kind of 'life-force', vitalism appealed to those interested in health and well-being, where ill-health was thought to result from an imbalance in the matter of human bodies (Williams 2003). Vitalism and new materialisms are therefore related but historically different movements distinguished by how they position themselves in relation to matter. In short, vitalism is concerned only with living things or organic matter, whereas new materialisms envelop organic and inorganic matter, and in fact aim to dissolve these and similar binaries. New materialisms, therefore, go beyond vitalism as well as earlier or 'old' forms of materialisms through their progression of the mechanism of early materialists and the preclusion of non-living matter by the vitalists (Coole & Frost 2010a). However, in this complex field, there are also 'new' or critical vitalists who moved on from the former preoccupation solely with living matter to encompass all material forms, blurring the distinction between neo-vitalism and new materialisms. For example, in her 'partial genealogy' of vitalism (Abrahamsson 2011, p. 400), Bennett (2010, p. 10) highlights the blurring of boundaries between these two camps, extending the ideas of the critical vitalists in her conception of 'vital materialism'. Significantly, Abrahamsson (2011) sounds a note of warning regarding the revival of earlier materialist and/or vitalist thinkers. He states that a return to these ideas can be problematic because they are transposed from the earlier political and social contexts in which they were developed.

Moreover, this is exactly where the work of new materialisms can add value without any historical or conceptual baggage. New materialisms capture an interest in all material forms, processes and agencies of the world; they embrace materiality in all its guises, eschewing binaries such as living/dead, human/non-human and organic/inorganic true to an 'antipathy toward oppositional ways of thinking' (Coole & Frost 2010a, p. 8). Therefore, unlike older forms of materialisms, they cannot be mistaken for a 'dead' materiality (Coole & Frost 2010a) that views materials as objects fixed in time and space, non-dynamic, static/inert, unchanged, unmoving and only capable of simplistic representation. The following sections describe some of the key characteristics of the new materialisms, including an introduction to the political implications relevant to a healthy urban environments agenda.

Characterising new materialisms

What is new or different about new materialisms, and how are they useful for rethinking healthy urban environments? Although new materialisms defy categorisation (and even labelling) (Coole 2013; Lemke 2015; St. Pierre et al. 2016), to sum up some of what has already been covered in this chapter, work in the new materialisms sphere moves away from linguistic and textual (human) representations of the world (Coole & Frost 2010a; Lemke 2015) to more reflexive, expansive materialist ontologies and epistemologies which increasingly cross the boundaries of social and natural or physical sciences. This might explain why there has been a recent fixation on new materialisms and assemblages in geography (see Anderson & Wylie 2009; Latham & McCormack 2004), where the natural and the human or social sciences meet.[15] In the main, however, the turn to materialism has also come from fields outside of geography, particularly science and technology studies and urban political ecology. There are three features of new materialisms that comprise their chief identifying characteristics: (1) new materialisms are about processes of becoming, (2) matter is always considered vital and (3) material agency is not predictable, predetermined or prefigured.[16]

Processes of becoming

First, as alluded to earlier in the chapter, new materialisms emphasise process and activity, and therefore are about becoming, as opposed to simply being. For example, 'what is invoked is a process not a state, a process of materialisation in which matter literally matters itself' (Coole 2013, p. 3), and this orientation does not preclude humans. As Coole and Frost (2010a, p. 8) argue, the active processes of materialisation described by new materialists embrace 'embodied humans . . . [as] an integral part, rather than the monotonous repetitions of dead matter from which human subjects are apart'. This is a very different stance to previous ideas about matter and materiality that saw them as separate from humans and inert, passive and void of value – unless assigned value by people. As Bennett (2010, pp. 57–58) explains, objects previously thought of inert or fixed are simply 'materials whose rate of speed and pace of change are slow compared to the duration and velocity of the human bodies participating in and perceiving them'.

A recognition of the multiple, intricate and complex nature of becoming (Coole 2013) means that matter comes in many forms and substances (Anderson & Wylie 2009; Latham & McCormack 2004); it is interconnected on multiple dimensions and scales that 'move with variable speeds and manifest themselves with variable intensity' (Coole 2013, p. 5). The point being that entities, structures and things that appear stable 'emerge as unstable, indeterminate assemblages that are composed of and folded into manifold smaller and larger assemblages' (Coole 2013, p. 5). An urban forest or parkland is a classic example of what might appear to be a stable assemblage, but in fact is in a constant state of dynamism (Cronon 1996). Apart from the change of seasons, numerous other processes and ecosystem activities among trees and plants are imperceptible to humans, such as communication via electrical impulses that travel one third of an inch per minute (Wohlleben 2016). In commenting on the different rates of activity between the lives of humans and trees, Wohlleben (2016) observes that, from a human perspective, trees live their lives in the 'slow lane'.

Another way to register the significance of a shift towards new materialist thinking is to (re)consider the bodies of humans and other animals. No longer satisfied with regarding bodies as harbouring a single living being, new materialists increasingly acknowledge that bodies comprise a multitude of micro- and other organisms, materials and matters (Bennett 2010; Coole & Frost 2010b; Fox 2016; Haraway 2008). This is most evident in work about microbiomes, the millions of bacteria living in human (and other animal) digestive systems (Yong 2016). Microbiomes are being recognised as essential to many aspects of human health in the assemblage of more-than-human bodies. Hence, 'in a world of vibrant matter, it is thus not enough to say that we are "embodied." We are, rather, an array of bodies, many different kinds of them in a set of nested microbiomes' (Bennett 2010, pp. 112–113). Coole and Frost (2010a, p. 19) consequently describe (human and other) bodies as open systems because 'complexity theories and developing technologies are rendering bodies less discrete qua organic entities distinct from physical, environmental, or technologically refabricated matter'. Significantly, this dynamic and fluid form of human embodiment is a point that feminists and class theorists have frequently stressed (Anderson & Tolia-Kelly 2004; Coole & Frost 2010a).

Arising from new knowledge generated across the natural sciences, 'the interactions between human, viral, animal, and technological bodies are becoming more and more intense' (Bennett 2010, p. 108). Bennett (2010) states that one of the advantages of seeing the world as vital rather than passive is that 'vital materiality better captures an "alien" quality of our own flesh, and in so doing reminds humans of the very *radical* character of the (fractious) kinship between the human and the nonhuman' (p. 112; original emphasis). This is most evident in the pandemic outbreaks of zoonoses such as bird or swine flu, where viruses can be transferred from animals to humans (Greenhough 2010; Herring 2008). Rates of transmission are intensified through factory farming practices, global commodity chains, globalised human travel patterns and increasing urbanisation bringing more animals and people in contact with each other more frequently. In 'the current scientific climate it is becoming increasing hard to hold human life apart from materiality and to deny agency to all forms of life except humans' (Greenhough 2010, p. 37).

Sometimes evident in new materialist scholarship is avoidance of the term 'object'. This term reflects old, inert materialist thinking, and continues to prop up (one half of) the subject/object divide. Perhaps because it conjures up greater agency and less determinacy, the term 'thing' is often used in its place. For example, Bennett (2010, p. 3) writes of 'thing power' to describe when objects become 'The Other', asserting that 'the notion of thing-power aims instead to attend to the it as actant'. Here Bennett (2010, p. 20) refers to the capacity to act and affect in a Latourian sense of the word 'actant',[17] or similarly, referring to the affective bodies described by Spinoza that can intervene, she writes 'thing-power ... draws attention to an efficacy of objects in excess of the human meanings, designs, or purposes . . .. [It] may thus be a good starting point for thinking beyond the life–matter binary.' The capacity to intervene is distinct from having conscious intentions; however, as Latour (2005, p. 72) writes, 'things might authorize, allow, afford, encourage, permit, suggest, influence, block, render possible, forbid, and so on'.

A corollary to the complex processes of becoming outlined above is the second characteristic of new materialisms: vibrancy. As advocated by Bennett (2010), Latour (2005) and others, new materialisms involve a 'materialisation that contains its own energies and forces of transformation' (Coole 2013, p. 13).

Matter is vibrant

New materialisms are predicated on notions of agency and the capacity for matter and materials to create effects in the world. Agency in a new materialisms sense is quite different to human-centric interpretations. At the outset, new materialisms recognise 'agency as being distributed across a far greater range of entities and processes than had formerly been imagined' (Coole 2013, p. 7). It follows that non-humans – and not just humans – have agency, and in fact that it is not a uniquely human trait. Coole (2013) describes agency in terms other than the capacity for self-reflection, rationality, cognition and action.[18] Instead, in new materialisms, agency is thought to comprise 'shifting associations . . . that are incessantly engendering new assemblages [that have] . . . porous membranes, rather than fixed boundaries, allow[ing] such systems to interact with and transform one another' (Coole 2013, p. 6).

Furthermore, this extended notion of agency implies that there are no sole actors acting on behalf of themselves or others.[19] As Bennett (2010, p. 37) explains, 'humans and their intentions participate but they are not the sole or always the most profound actant in the assemblage'. However, rather than absolving humans entirely from the results of their actions, this stance broadens the sources of harmful and helpful effects, agents and actants in the world from humans to non-humans. Bennett's (2010) analysis of an electricity blackout in Canada and the United States in 2003 exemplifies this point. In her account, she explains how agencies shared by multiple actants created the events, where large tracts of North America were without electricity for 24 hours with over 100 power plants shut down and 50 million people over 24,000 square kilometres affected (2010 p. 25). Actants included transmission lines, electrons, trees, wind, substations, electromagnetic fields, economic theory, legislation and humans, among many others. In this scenario, arguing for confederate or distributed agencies rather than assigning blame to one or a few things or people effectively absolved humans from the bulk of the accountability while highlighting the collective power of a larger assemblage of people and things (Bennett 2010). Although this example illustrates the complex entanglements and relations of non-humans with humans, as well as dispelling lingering doubts about their passivity, this reasoning could be problematic when applied to events in which humans play a more defining and morally culpable role. This is particularly problematic when such events result in large-scale losses or displacement of human (and other) lives or deprivation of human or more-than-human rights – for example, racial vilification, war and extinction of species due to habitat fragmentation and urbanisation. In these cases, reasoning that human actors were not to blame will be politically, morally and ethically unpalatable. However, Bennett (2010, p. 38) criticises tendencies for moral condemnation, arguing that they are unethical due to their divisiveness and legitimisation of violence: 'a moralized politics of good and evil, of singular agents who must be made to pay for their sins . . . legitimates vengeance and elevates violence to the tool of first resort'.

She usefully proposes that accepting 'agency as distributive and confederate thus reinvokes the need to detach ethics from moralism' (Bennett 2010, p. 38). This broader concept of accountability means considering action as always produced by multiple agents and actants, and reorients attention to *doing* and the various relations and materialities involved, rather than being limited to the intentions, behaviours or motivations of a single (human) actor. As Bennett (2010, p. 28) shows in the example of the North American blackout of 2003, there is not so much an agent or a doer, but a 'doing' – 'a doing and an affecting by a human-non-human assemblage'.

In sum, new materialisms have an overt relational stance where 'if matters act, they never act alone' (Abrahamsson et al. 2015, p. 15).[20] If we accept that actors (human or non-human) never act, or cannot act, alone, the assignation of responsibility and culpability for unfortunate or harmful events will need to be rethought. This connects with ideas about toppling human sovereignty to admit that humans are not always in control and not always the most powerful actant in any given assemblage (Bennett 2010). Events and disasters that affect cities, like widespread energy blackouts, suburban bushfires or pandemic diseases, illustrate that, despite what we may believe, humans are not always in command of the various goings-on in urban environments.

Material agency is not predictable

The third feature is that new materialisms recognise and embrace unpredictability and do not accept that material life is always predetermined or prefigured. This means that the emergent processes and dynamism characterising new materialisms as described by the first two features develop in a nonlinear fashion, invoking 'swerves and swarms, the event, rather than causal chains or laws' (Coole 2013, p. 3). Importantly, this fluidity does not imply the absence of inertia, 'turgidity' or 'congealing' of material processes which are important in analysing power dynamics. However, instead of being considered as fixed, these apparently more enduring forms are not considered to be impenetrable or permanent (Latham & McCormack 2004; Latour 2005).

As a direct result of taking matter to be vital and unpredictable, there are implications for how the 'environment' is conceptualised and engaged; questions arise about the boundaries that exist, if any, between humans and non-humans – the latter usually considered pacified and backgrounded as mere settings or surrounds (Coole & Frost 2010a; Cronon 1996; Washick & Wingrove 2015). The removal of these boundaries underlies one of the political aims of the new materialists, where concerns for and treatment of 'the environment' and the many non-humans that make up 'nature' feature in the work of Latour, Stengers, Mol, Whatmore, Bennett, Haraway and many others. As Washick and Wingrove (2015, p. 64) write: 'the appeal of a posthumanist materialism . . . underscore[s] a need to challenge the human of traditional humanism: the knowing subject whose capacities of mind impose meaningful form on a passive object-world'.

Motivated by and premised on new developments in science technology and neurobiology, new materialists argue for a reduction in the human impact on earth's ecosystems, including the way we produce, reproduce and consume materials (Coole & Frost 2010a).[21] As Coole and Frost (2010a, p. 13) explain further, like Cronon (1996) before them, developments in physics such as chaos and complexity theory are 'undermining the idea of stable and predictable material substance, hastening a realization that our natural environment is far more complex, unstable, fragile, and interactive than earlier models allowed'. This fragility and 'a recognition that matter is not the passive receptacle or recipient of human agency' has further ethical and political imperatives and possibilities for making healthy urban environments (Washick & Wingrove 2015, p. 63), the most relevant of which are discussed in the following section.

The politics of new materialisms

The characteristics of new materialisms mean there are decidedly political implications arising from this scholarship; in fact, it is the political and ethical potential of a new materialist world view that attracts most criticism (e.g., Abrahamsson 2011; Abrahamsson et al. 2015; Washick & Wingrove 2015). New materialisms' political potential has been framed by Washick and Wingrove (2015, p. 63) as a radical stance 'to promote generosity, responsibility, and/or receptiveness to difference'. This implies, correctly, that there are a wide range of possible political agendas to pursue, but the dimensions covered here are limited to those most relevant to the book's theme. The main political aspect I want to cover concerns relaxing human exceptionalism and human-centrism to see, acknowledge and know non-humans in urban environments as companions and fellow agents.

Transcending human-centrism, Bennett (2010, p. 108) declares 'a vital materialist theory of democracy seeks to transform the divide between speaking subjects and mute objects into a set of differential tendencies and variable capacities'.[22] A range of non-humans – animals, plants, minerals – can disrupt and create political acts and events to 'catalyze a public' (Bennett 2010, p. 107) or 'force thought' (Stengers 2010). In sum, in moving on from human-centrism, new materialists argue for non-human publics to be elevated to valued members of the political realm (Bennett 2010; Braun & Whatmore 2010; Coole & Frost 2010a; Latour 1992; 2005; Stengers 2010). However, Bennett (2010) and others writing in a similar vein carefully qualify this political aim in several ways. First, as Coole and Frost (2010a, p. 18) argue, the aim is to redefine politics in a way that is less about 'a merely formal constitutional, institutional, or normative edifice' and is more of 'an ongoing process of negotiating power relations'. This elevates the role of communication while representing a subtle shift in thinking towards a relational politics rather than one reliant on formal democratic or other political processes. Hinchliffe and Whatmore (2006, p. 125) summarise new materialist approaches to politics as 'politics of conviviality' that are 'better attuned to the comings and goings of the multiplicity of more-than-human inhabitants that make themselves at home in the city than conventional political accounts.'

As Bennett (2010, p. 104) maintains, this means 'the political goal of a vital materialism is not the perfect equality of actants, but a polity with more channels of communication between members'. She believes that politics is about conjoint action between humans and non-humans that:

> Paves the way for a theory of action that more explicitly accepts non-human bodies as members of a public, more explicitly attends to how they, too, participate in conjoint action and more clearly discerns instances of harm to the (affective) bodies of animals, minerals, vegetables and their ecocultures.
>
> (Bennett 2010, p. 103)

However, critics argue that what is made evident by an approach that politically elevates non-humans is that, as well as enchantment, new materialist encounters can be ambiguous, ambivalent and harmful, with the potential to cause conflict (Ginn 2014) or 'pain, distress, illbeing, and many terminate life' (Gregson 2011, p. 403). This potential for encountering conflict and harm may explain why some critics have argued that the political aims of new materialisms are naïve (Abrahamsson 2011). Principally directed at Bennett (2010) and other work in new materialisms are accusations that pragmatically, it amounts to nothing more than a metaphysical and rhetorical aesthetic, with little substance or capacity to effect real political and ethical change (Gregson 2011; Washick & Wingrove 2015).

These critiques come from valid concerns about inequality, exclusion and injustice towards humans, particularly around issues of class, gender and power (e.g., Washick & Wingrove 2015). However, such concerns fail to move beyond a human-centric perspective. These critiques assume that by foregrounding non-humans, marginalised humans will be further diminished, harmed or ignored. This type of reasoning is not particularly sound nor justified (Ferguson 2015). In their defence, the work of the new materialists may have been misinterpreted or misread (Bennett 2015; Ferguson 2015), particularly if one has more-than-human leanings. In Bennett's (2015, p. 83) response to some of her critics, she states that rather than focusing on 'the trappings of the system', new materialisms offer a first step, 'the possibility of "laying down a path by walking" out from it'. This is an important point regarding the current volume, which does not seek to provide all the answers, but suggests ways of moving forward to create healthy cities that are more-than-human habitat.

Similarly, Ferguson (2015, p. 81) remarks that 'some new materialist adventures work to bring enduring structures into conversation with surprising, open-ended potentialities'. It could also be argued that new materialisms do not attempt to engage in all kinds of politics, and in fact, as indicated in the above extract, the politics they propose is of a different kind. By definition, to be political implies that not everyone will be served or pleased by processes and outcomes. Instead, the political work of new materialisms aims to serve a specific purpose – to bring non-humans into human-centric worlds and see and know those that are already there, such as the many plants and animals that live in and make cities.

To achieve this, some of the ways forward suggested by work in new materialisms include turning to what might be regarded as everyday actions or practices of curiosity, care and empathy towards non-humans (Bawaka Country et al. 2013; Bennett 2010; Haraway 2008; 2016). Being curious and caring towards non-humans means taking on different ways of seeing, knowing and doing. These actions are consistent with new materialisms' orientation towards various processes of becoming shared between multiple entities (Coole 2013), including 'becoming with' (Haraway 2008, p. 244)[2] or 'co-becoming' (Bawaka Country et al. 2013, p. 195). Similarly, Bell et al. (2017) argue for 'engaged witnessing' and the deep listening practice of 'Dadirri' carried out by Indigenous Australians to give full consideration to all human and non-human members of a community. They propose that practising Dadirri is a way of learning about, and learning from, both humans and non-humans.

A fine example of this way of thinking in a research context comes from a highly innovative project from north east Arnhem Land in Northern

Australia. This long-term collaborative research project with the Indigenous Yolŋu people aimed to inform the theory and practice of natural resource management. To decentre their western privilege, the human researchers acknowledge the land ('Country') in their work through attribution as lead author on a series of publications (see Bawaka Country et al. 2013; Bawaka Country et al. 2015; Bawaka Country et al. 2016).[24] They describe their approach to working as more-than-human in this context as follows:

> In discussing what it means to see humans as one small part of a broader cosmos populated by diverse beings and diverse ways of being, including animals, winds, dirt, sunsets, songs and troop carriers, we argue for a way of knowing/doing which recognises that 'things' can only come into 'being' through an ongoing process of be(com)ing together. They are never static, fixed, complete, but are continually emerging in an entangled togetherness.
>
> (Bawaka Country et al. 2013, pp. 185–186)

This example should inspire other similar approaches that acknowledge non-humans as participants in, and potential recipients of, the benefits (or harms) arising from research (also argued by Haraway 2008).[25] In other cases where non-humans will benefit, such as greening initiatives to encourage biodiversity in cities, or be harmed, such as land clearing, it would, from this perspective, be a significant oversight to not include non-humans as research participants and authors. Of course, these ideas fly in the face of the established orthodoxy of the scientific method and bring accusations of anthropomorphism to mind.[26] However, these initiatives to foreground non-humans involve subtle, but powerful, changes to the way that research is designed, carried out and disseminated by using notions of seeing, knowing and doing differently; these involve curiosity, care and empathy (Bell et al. 2017; Bennett 2010; Haraway 2008), for example by acknowledging non-humans as participants and authors in research as highlighted above in work by Bawaka Country et al. (2013), or changing text and language that depersonalises non-humans by referring to them as 'it'. As Kimmerer (2013, p. 49) argues, constituted in English, 'science can be a language of distance which reduces a being to its working parts; it is a language of objects'. Conversely, in the languages of indigenous peoples of North America, living beings are referred to in the same way as family members, to recognise their vitality, agency and relationality, in what Kimmerer (2013, p. 48) calls the 'grammar of animacy'.

There is evidence that these and other more-than-human approaches are already happening in some research arenas. In animal cognition and behaviour research, for example, it is becoming accepted to use what is known as 'critical anthropomorphism' (Burghardt 2007) to understand how animals experience and know the world, and to explain more complex aspects of their behaviour such as tool use and emotions (e.g., Konok et al. 2015).

Explaining what critical anthropomorphism means in practice, Burghardt (2004, p. 15) states that it 'involves not only careful replicable observation, but also knowledge of the natural history, ecology, and sensory and neural systems of animals as well'. He writes:

> We need to use all our scientific and natural history knowledge about a species, including its physiology, ecology, and sensory abilities to develop testable hypotheses, which may indeed be based on 'hmm, what would I do if I were in a similar situation to the other species?'
>
> (Burghardt 2007, p. 137)

Consistent with arguments made by the new materialists, Burghardt (2007, p. 137) states that human-centrism or anthropocentrism can only be overcome 'through a critical anthropomorphism'. Burghardt is starting to lean towards what Despret (2004, p. 130) articulates as knowing becoming a practice of caring where 'the experimenter, far from keeping himself [or herself] in the background, involves himself: he involves his body, he involves his knowledge, his responsibility and his future.' As well as the work by Bawaka Country et al. (2013; 2015; 2016), there are many examples of rich empirical studies that employ this type of thinking. This includes multispecies ethnographies (Fuentes & Baynes-Rock 2017; Kirksey & Helmreich 2010; Van Dooren et al. 2016); the 'engaged witnessing' and practice of Dadirri to engage with, and learn from, angophora trees and lace monitors in Ku-ring-gai Chase National Park, New South Wales (Bell et al. 2017); fatty acid omega-3's entanglement with human bodies and other non-humans outlined by Abrahamsson et al. (2015);[27] Hillier's (2013) 'ghostly cows' on their way to auction and slaughter in Melbourne; and to the 'planty capacities' described by Head et al. (2015) and Cloke and Jones (2004). These examples demonstrate how curiosity, caring and empathy can produce different sensitivities to and ways of seeing and knowing the multitudes of non-humans who comprise cities and ecosystems.

Bennett (2015, p. 86) emphasises the importance of these sensitivities in her 'vital materialism', but that there is no one answer or perfect approach:

> All anyone has is a set of imperfect tactics: appeal to shared (win-win) interests, evoke sympathy for the suffering of other bodies, call to replace narrow self-interest with enlightened understandings of it that highlight our status as Earthlings or materialities profoundly intertwined with the lives and continued flourishing of other (organic and inorganic) bodies.

As well as encouraging experimentation to 'alter or derail the machine so as to minimize its harms and distribute more equally its costs and benefits', Bennett (2015, p. 86) describes how one might intervene in or 'reverse engineer' environmental problems – conceptualised as urban assemblages –

in four steps: (1) determine the various functioning parts; (2) decide which parts are currently key 'operators' of the assemblage's effects; (3) determine which parts are likely to be most susceptible to 'tinkering, re-purposing or destruction'; and (4) decide what are the 'best ways to forge or cobble together a different machinic assemblage'. These steps could be applied to a range of urban problems, from consumption, pollution and traffic to habitat loss, and although highly theoretical, at least present a clear strategic path forward.

To see, know and work with some of the non-humans present in cities requires cooperation and collaboration among scientists of various disciplines and likeminded people (including citizen scientists and those who identify as multi-disciplinary) and some of the many non-humans implicated in these endeavours (see Chapter 7 for further elaboration). The combined effect of this productive relational activity would likely result in the fruitful transcendence of disciplinary and academic boundaries and potentially deliver the emergence of ground-breaking new disciplines and sub-disciplines. However, following the claims of the non-representational and new materialist literature covered in this chapter and Chapter 2, herein lies a paradox. These approaches to knowing and changing the world rely on performativity and the process of doing policymaking and research, with less of a focus on achieving predetermined outcomes. Accepting this inherent indeterminism means that outcomes in this context will always be of an emergent nature and unpredictable. As Thrift (2008) points out, despite our cleverest efforts, humans can only ever attain partial understandings of the world. However, in the face of these uncertainties, I concur with Bennett (2011, p. 405) in adopting 'the encouragement model of political and ethical action'. Taking a positive stance remains the most useful and practical way forward. In other words, there is value in the idea of path-laying towards a better, optimistic, more hopeful future that 'seeks to inject, into a mediatised public culture of crass alarmism and cynical stupidity, a mood of wonder at the creativity of life' (Bennett 2011, p. 405).

Conclusion

Work in new materialisms has richly theorised the material nature of life previously considered missing from the social sciences, and goes further than related endeavours such as The Affective Turn and non-representational thinking (Chapter 2). As an umbrella term, there have been various strands of materialism whose origins can be traced to different philosophical roots. Although having 'new' and 'old' labels may appear unnecessary, important distinctions discussed in the chapter explain the use of these tags and why new materialisms are differentiated and have value for thinking about healthy urban environments. New materialisms firmly advocate for a more-than-human position that recognises non-humans in all aspects of the everydayness of urban environments, even in institutions and processes usually considered the domain of humans alone, such as politics and research. In these contexts, new materialisms seek to understand the way multiple beings and matters make their way in, connect to, take part in, comprise and affect the world. All matter and non-humans are therefore seen as 'vital' rather than 'environmental', or merely passive.

These ideas of relationality, vibrancy and politics that characterise new materialisms present several challenges and opportunities for designing interventions and doing research on healthy urban environments, starting with the decentring of western and human-centric ideas about knowledge and privilege to see other ways of knowing, and other beings that count and act. Opportunities arise from the fact that new materialisms connect with indigenous approaches to understanding and living with animals, plants and Country, and draw on paradigm-changing ideas crossing disciplinary boundaries such as critical anthropomorphism. Taking these ideas forward means that cities are conceptualised and recognised as shared habitat – that is, habitat for other species as well as humans (discussed in detail in Chapter 6). Another challenge is that new materialisms contest ideas of sociality, extending them beyond humans and other animals to plants and trees. If this is the case, then there is a need to better understand the complex relations and multispecies entanglements that make cities as they are, as well the environmental impacts arising from human and non-human actors.

New materialisms encourage relational thinking at multiple scales simultaneously, from multispecies assemblages in parks and remnant ecosystems to microbiomes inside human bodies. Understanding the links between these scales would be useful in events such as thunderstorm asthma or viral pandemics that cross species' divides. This shift in perspective creates different understandings of time and space so that the lives of non-humans, like microbes living life in the fast lane or trees living life in the slow lane, can be understood beyond limited human conceptions. Finally, it means going forward and being comfortable with producing decision-making and interventions where outcomes are uncertain or unpredictable. This entails embracing hope and recognising that the infrastructural materialities and vibrant matters of cities are active, ever-changing and not necessarily prescriptive or directive of the actions of humans and other species. Relatedly, to move past human sovereignty, action must be considered the product of multiple agents and actants with multiple relations and materialities at play, and not restricted to the intentions of a singular, human player. Although this can appear to devolve responsibility for harm, what it does in effect is accept that humans are not always in command and control of the events and happenings that make up and befall cities.

With The Affective Turn covered in Chapter 2 and The New Materialisms Turn covered in the present chapter, Chapter 4 covers the third 'turn', The Practice Turn. This chapter continues our journey into more-than-human thinking and offers further ideas that resolve or attend to some of the challenges presented by new materialisms in thinking about and intervening in urban environments.

Notes

1 Although somewhat clumsy, the use of the plural 'materialisms' follows Coole and Frost (2010a) and others' (e.g., Lemke 2015; Coole 2013) who recognise a range of divergent interests in new materialism(s), and not a single approach or theory.
2 Or 'thingification', after Barad (2003, p. 812).
3 See Chapters 5 and 6 for discussion of 'human–nature' relationships.
4 Biophilia is a theory that posits that humans benefit from contact with nature and knowing about plants, animals and landscapes because we needed them to survive early in our history (Wilson 1984).
5 Discussed further in Chapters 5 and 6.
6 For further reading, see Coole and Frost (2010b), Latham and McCormack (2004), Anderson and Wylie (2009), Hein (2016) and a series of debates in *Contemporary Political Theory* (2015, vol. 14, no. 1) and also *Dialogues in Human Geography* (2011, vol. 1, no. 3). DeLanda (2006) argues that although the theory is attributed to Deleuze and Guattari, it was not fully articulated in their original work from 1987. Instead he states it is connected to other concepts throughout Deleuze's work.
7 Although their original term was *agencement* (Deleuze & Guattari 1987), it was first translated from French to 'assemblage' in English by Paul Foss and Paul Patton in 1981 (Phillips 2006).
8 See also Latour (1992; 2000).
9 Some researchers in human geography argue that it never really went away; for example, Anderson and Tolia-Kelly (2004, p. 670) state: 'the teleological nature of this tale of "de-materialisation" and "re-materialisation" has, we would argue, also functioned to write out the presence of specific figures of matter in the multi-faceted cultural turn'.
10 Which itself was a correction to positivism and its emphasis on empiricism and rationality.
11 Monism refers to the idea that everything is made up of the same stuff (Bennett 2010).
12 'A mutualistic symbiosis between a fungus and a plant root, where fungal-foraged soil nutrients are exchanged for plant-derived photosynthate' (Smith and Read 2008, in Gorzelak et al. 2015, p. 1).
13 Of course such ideas come with a warning to check for incommensurability (Kuhn 1970).
14 This is way new materialist scholarship is often more accurately referred to as the (re)turn to materialism (Greenhough 2010; Whatmore 2006).
15 Although not always harmoniously or unproblematically. See Abrahamsson (2011) and Whatmore (2006).
16 These are condensed from a useful summary provided by Coole (2013).
17 Latour (2005, p. 71) explains that 'any thing that does modify a state of affairs by making a difference is an actor – or, if it has no figuration yet, an actant'.
18 This idea originates from Kantian ideas about autonomous free will, as opposed to some neo-Kantian ideas about intentionality (Bennett 2010).
19 This point is consistent with ideas of relationality in non-representational theories as well as assemblage thinking.
20 See also Bennett (2010, p. 21): '[their] efficacy or agency always depends on the collaboration, cooperation, or interactive interference of many bodies and forces'.
21 Lemke (2015, p. 4) concurs: 'the "material turn" criticizes the idea of the natural world and technical artifacts as a mere resource or raw material for technological progress, economic production or social construction'.

22 See Bennett (2010, Chapters 7 and 8) for a full account of the political dimensions of her work.
23 After Despret (2004).
24 Aside from its rich content, this project is an impressive example of acknowledging more-than-humans in research. As the authors explain: 'This is a co-authored paper, driven, shaped and conceived through a collaborative effort between four humans – three academics from south-eastern Australia and one Yolŋu elder from Bawaka. However, it is much more than that, too, with authorship attributed to Bawaka Country, with explicit acknowledgement that Bawaka Country includes the aforementioned human authors. Country is a proper noun in Aboriginal English where "People talk about country in the same way that they would talk about a person: they speak to country, sing to country, visit country, worry about country, feel sorry for country, and long for country. People say that country knows, hears, smells, takes notice, takes care, is sorry or happy . . .. Rather, country is a living entity with a yesterday, today and tomorrow, with a consciousness, and a will toward life"' (Rose 1996, p. 7).
25 See Chapter 7 for other examples, and also Bell et al. (2017) for an in-depth discussion of more-than-human methods.
26 As Daston and Mitman (2005, p. 2) explain: 'Anthropomorphism is . . . used to describe the belief that animals are essentially like humans, and is usually applied as a term of reproach, both intellectually and morally.'
27 Bennett (2007; 2010) also partially addresses this phenomenon.

References

Abrahamsson, C 2011, 'Book review forum: *Vibrant Matter: A Political Ecology of Things*', *Dialogues in Human Geography*, vol. 1, no. 3, pp. 399–402.
Abrahamsson, S, Bertoni, F, Mol, A & Martín, RI 2015, 'Living with omega-3: new materialism and enduring concerns', *Environment and Planning D: Society and Space*, vol. 33, no. 1, pp. 4–19.
Anderson, B & McFarlane, C 2011, 'Assemblage and geography', *Area*, vol. 43, no. 2, pp. 124–127.
Anderson, B & Tolia-Kelly, D 2004, 'Matter(s) in social and cultural geography', *Geoforum*, vol. 35, no. 6, pp. 669–674.
Anderson, B & Wylie, J 2009, 'On geography and materiality', *Environment and Planning A*, vol. 41, no. 2, pp. 318–335.
Appadurai, A 1988, 'Toward an anthropology of things', in A Appadurai (ed.), *The Social Life of Things: Commodities in Cultural Perspective*, Cambridge University Press, pp. 3–63.
Barad, K 2003, 'Posthumanist performativity: toward an understanding of how matter comes to matter', *Signs*, vol. 28, no. 3, pp. 801–831.
Barad, K 2007, *Meeting the Universe Halfway: Quantum Physics and the Entanglement of Matter and Meaning*, Duke University Press.
Bates, C 2017, 'Desire lines: walking in Woolwich', in C Bates & A Rhys-Taylor (eds), *Walking through Social Research*, Routledge, pp. 54–69.
Bawaka Country, Suchet-Pearson, S, Wright, S, Lloyd, K & Burarrwanga, L 2013 'Caring as Country: towards an ontology of co-becoming in natural resource management', *Asia Pacific Viewpoint*, vol. 54, no. 2, pp. 185–197.
Bawaka Country, Wright, S, Suchet-Pearson, S, Lloyd, K, Burarrwanga, L Ganambarr, R, Ganambarr-Stubbs, M, Ganambarr, B & Maymuru, D 2015

'Working with and learning from Country: decentring human author-ity', *Cultural Geographies*, vol. 22, no. 2, pp. 269–283.

Bawaka Country, Wright, S, Suchet-Pearson, S, Lloyd, K, Burarrwanga, L, Ganambarr, R, Ganambarr-Stubbs, M, Ganambarr, B, Maymuru, D & Sweeney, J 2016, 'Co-becoming Bawaka: towards a relational understanding of place/space', *Progress in Human Geography*, vol. 40, no. 4, pp. 455–475.

Bell, SJ, Instone, L & Mee, KJ 2017, 'Engaged witnessing: researching with the more-than-human', *Area*, doi:10.1111/area.12346.

Bennett, J 2007, 'Edible matter', *New Left Review*, vol. 45, pp. 133–145.

Bennett, J 2010, *Vibrant Matter: A Political Ecology of Things*, Duke University Press.

Bennett, J 2011, 'Author response', *Dialogues in Human Geography*, vol. 1, no. 3, pp. 404–406.

Bennett, J 2015, 'Ontology, sensibility and action', *Contemporary Political Theory*, vol. 14, pp. 82–89.

Braun, B & Whatmore, S 2010, 'The stuff of politics: an introduction', in B Braun & S Whatmore (eds), *Political Matter: Technoscience, Democracy, and Public Life*, University of Minnesota Press, pp. ix–xl.

Burghardt, GM 2004, 'Ground rules for dealing with anthropomorphism', *Nature*, vol. 430, no. 6995, p. 15.

Burghardt, GM 2007, 'Critical anthropomorphism, uncritical anthropocentrism, and naive nominalism', *Comparative Cognition and Behavior Reviews*, vol. 2, pp. 136–138.

Castree, N 2003, 'Environmental issues: relational ontologies and hybrid politics', *Progress in Human Geography*, vol. 27, no. 2, pp. 203–211.

Cloke, P & Jones, O 2004, 'Turning in the graveyard: trees and the hybrid geographies of dwelling, monitoring and resistance in a Bristol cemetery', *Cultural Geographies*, vol. 11, no. 3, pp. 313–341.

Coole, D 2013, 'Agentic capacities and capacious historical materialism: thinking with new materialisms in the political sciences', *Millennium – Journal of International Studies*, vol. 41, no. 3, pp. 451–469.

Coole, D & Frost, S 2010a, 'Introducing the new materialisms', in D Coole, S Frost & J Bennett (eds), *New Materialisms: Ontology, Agency, and Politics*, Duke University Press, pp. 1–43.

Coole, D & Frost, S 2010b, *New Materialisms: Ontology, Agency, and Politics*, Duke University Press.

Cronon, W 1996, 'Introduction: in search of nature', in W Cronon (ed.), *Uncommon Ground: Rethinking the Human Place in Nature*, WW Norton, pp. 23–56.

Daar, AS, Singer, PA, Leah Persad, D, Pramming, SK, Matthews, DR, Beaglehole, R, Bernstein, A, Borysiewicz, LK, Colagiuri, S, Ganguly, N, Glass, RI, Finegood, DT, Koplan, J, Nabel, EG, Sarna, G, Sarrafzadegan, N, Smith, R, Yach, D & Bell, J 2007, 'Grand challenges in chronic non-communicable diseases', *Nature*, vol. 450, no. 7169, pp. 494–496.

Daston, L & Mitman, G 2005, *Thinking with Animals: New Perspectives on Anthropomorphism*, Columbia University Press.

DeLanda, M 1997, *A Thousand Years of Nonlinear History*, Zone Books.

DeLanda, M 2006, *A New Philosophy of Society: Assemblage Theory and Social Complexity*, Bloomsbury Academic.

Deleuze, G & Guattari, F 1987, *Thousand Plateaus: Capitalism and Schizophrenia*, (translated by Brian Massumi), University of Minnesota Press.

Despret, V 2004, 'The body we care for: figures of anthropo-zoo-genesis', *Body & Society*, vol. 10, nos 2–3, pp. 111–134.

Ferguson, KE 2015, 'Engaging new and old materialisms', *Contemporary Political Theory*, vol. 14, pp. 79–82.

Fox, NJ 2016, 'Health sociology from post-structuralism to the new materialisms', *Health*, vol. 20, no. 1, pp. 62–74.

Fuentes, A & Baynes-Rock, M 2017, 'Anthropogenic landscapes, human action and the process of co-construction with other species: making anthromes in the Anthropocene', *Land*, vol. 6, no. 1, p. 15.

Ginn, F 2014, 'Sticky lives: slugs, detachment and more-than-human ethics in the garden', *Transactions of the Institute of British Geographers*, vol. 39, no. 4, pp. 532–544.

Gorzelak, MA, Asay, AK, Pickles, BJ & Simard, SW 2015, 'Inter-plant communication through mycorrhizal networks mediates complex adaptive behaviour in plant communities', *AoB PLANTS*, vol. 7, no. 1, doi:10.1093/aobpla/plv050.

Greenhough, B 2010, 'Vitalist geographies: life and the more-than-human', in B Anderson & P Harrison (eds), *Taking-place Non-representational Theories and Geography*, Ashgate, pp. 37–54.

Gregson, N 2011, 'Book review forum: *Vibrant Matter: A Political Ecology of Things*', *Dialogues in Human Geography*, vol. 1, no. 3, pp. 402–404.

Haraway, DJ 2008, *When Species Meet*, University of Minnesota Press.

Haraway, DJ 2016, *Staying with the Trouble: Making Kin in the Chthulucene*, Duke University Press.

Head, L, Atchison, J & Phillips, C 2015, 'The distinctive capacities of plants: re-thinking difference via invasive species', *Transactions of the Institute of British Geographers*, vol. 40, no. 3, pp. 399–413.

Hein, SF 2016, 'The new materialism in qualitative inquiry: how compatible are the philosophies of Barad and Deleuze?', *Cultural Studies ↔ Critical Methodologies*, vol. 16, no. 2, pp. 132–140.

Herring, A 2008, 'Viral panic, vulnerability and the next pandemic', in C Panter-Brick & A Fuentes (eds), *Health, Risk and Adversity*, 2nd edn, Berghahn Books, pp. 78–97.

Hillier, J 2013, 'More than meat: rediscovering the cow beneath the face in urban heritage practice', *Society and Space*, vol. 31, no. 5, pp. 863–878.

Hinchliffe, S 2011, 'Book review forum: *Vibrant Matter: A Political Ecology of Things*', *Dialogues in Human Geography*, vol. 1, no. 3, pp. 396–399.

Hinchliffe, S & Whatmore, S 2006, 'Living cities: towards a politics of conviviality', *Science as Culture*, vol. 15, no. 2, pp. 123–138.

Houston, D, Hillier, J, MacCallum, D, Steele, W & Byrne, J 2017, 'Make kin, not cities! Multispecies entanglements and "becoming-world" in planning theory', *Planning Theory*, doi:10.1177/1473095216688042.

Kaika, M 2005, *City of Flows: Modernity, Nature, and the City*, Routledge.

Kimmerer, RW 2013, *Braiding Sweetgrass: Indigenous Wisdom, Scientific Knowledge and the Teachings of Plants*, Milkweed Editions.

Kirksey, SE & Helmreich, S 2010, 'The emergence of multispecies ethnography', *Cultural Anthropology*, vol. 25, no. 4, pp. 545–576.

Konok, V, Nagy, K & Miklósi, Á 2015, 'How do humans represent the emotions of dogs? The resemblance between the human representation of the canine and the human affective space', *Applied Animal Behaviour Science*, vol. 162, pp. 37–46.

Kuhn, TS 1970, *The Structure of Scientific Revolutions*, University of Chicago Press.

Latham, A & McCormack, DP 2004, 'Moving cities: rethinking the materialities of urban geographies', *Progress in Human Geography*, vol. 28, no. 6, pp. 701–724.

Latour, B 1992, 'Where are the missing masses? The sociology of a few mundane artifacts', in WE Bijker & J Law (eds), *Shaping Technology/Building Society: Studies in Sociotechnical Change*, MIT Press, pp. 225–258.

Latour, B 2000, 'When things strike back: a possible contribution of "science studies" to the social sciences', *British Journal of Sociology*, vol. 51, no. 1, pp. 107–123.

Latour, B 2005, *Reassembling the Social: An Introduction to Actor-Network-Theory*, Oxford University Press.

Lemke, T 2015, 'New materialisms: Foucault and the "Government of Things"', *Theory, Culture & Society*, vol. 32, no. 4, pp. 3–25.

Li, TM 2007, 'Practices of assemblage and community forest management', *Economy and Society*, vol. 36, no. 2, pp. 263–293.

Maller, C 2017, 'Epigenetics, theories of social practice and lifestyle disease', in A Hui, TR Schatzki & E Shove (eds), *The Nexus of Practices: Connections, Constellations, Practitioners*, Routledge, pp. 68–80.

Maller, C, Townsend, M, Pryor, A, Brown, PR & St Leger, L 2006, 'Healthy parks, healthy people: "contact with nature" as an upstream health promotion intervention for populations', *Health Promotion International*, vol. 21, no. 1, pp. 45–54.

Marcus, GE & Saka, E 2006, 'Assemblage', *Theory, Culture & Society*, vol. 23, nos 2–3, pp. 101–106.

Mol, A 1999, 'Ontological politics: a word and some questions', *Sociological Review*, vol. 47, no. S1, pp. 74–89.

Phillips, J 2006, 'Agencement/Assemblage', *Theory, Culture & Society*, vol. 23, nos 2–3, pp. 108–109.

Pickering, A 2008, 'Against human exceptionalism', paper presented at a workshop: *What Does It Mean to Be Human?*, 25 January, https://ore.exeter.ac.uk/repository/bitstream/handle/10036/18873/XTRwrkshp-250108.pdf?sequence=1, accessed 30 May 2016.

Pickering, A 2013, 'Being in an environment: a performative perspective', *Natures Sciences Sociétés*, vol. 21, no. 1, pp. 77–83.

Plumwood, V 2009, 'Nature in the active voice', *Australian Humanities Review*, vol. 46, pp. 113–129.

Rose, DB 1996, *Nourishing Terrains: Australian Aboriginal Views of Landscape and Wilderness*, Australian Heritage Commission.

Simard, SW 2009, 'The foundational role of mycorrhizal networks in self-organization of interior Douglas-fir forests', *Forest Ecology and Management*, vol. 258, Supplement, pp. S95–S107.

Simard, SW, Perry, DA, Jones, MD, Myrold, DD, Durall, DM & Molina, R 1997, 'Net transfer of carbon between ectomycorrhizal tree species in the field', *Nature*, vol. 388, no. 6642, pp. 579–582.

St. Pierre, EA, Jackson, AY & Mazzei, LA 2016, 'New empiricisms and new materialisms: conditions for new inquiry', *Cultural Studies ↔ Critical Methodologies*, vol. 16, no. 2, pp. 99–110.

Stengers, I 2010, 'Including nonhumans in political theory: opening Pandora's Box?', in B Braun & S Whatmore (eds), *Political Matter: Technoscience, Democracy, and Public Life*, University of Minnesota Press, pp. 3–34.

Strengers, Y, Nicholls, L & Maller, C 2016, 'Curious energy consumers: humans and nonhumans in assemblages of household practice', *Journal of Consumer Culture*, vol. 16, no. 3, pp. 761–780.

Thrift, N 2008, *Non-representational Theory: Space, Politics, Affect*, Taylor & Francis.

Van Dooren, T, Kirksey, E & Münster, U 2016, 'Multispecies studies: cultivating arts of attentiveness', *Environmental Humanities*, vol. 8, no. 1, pp. 1–23.

Washick, B & Wingrove, E 2015, 'Politics that matter: thinking about power and justice with the new materialists', *Contemporary Political Theory*, vol. 14, no. 1, pp. 63–79.

Whatmore, S 2006, 'Materialist returns: practising cultural geography in and for a more-than-human world', *Cultural Geographies*, vol. 13, no. 4, pp. 600–609.

Williams, EA 2003, *A Cultural History of Medical Vitalism in Enlightenment Montpellier*, Routledge.

Wilson, EO 1984, *Biophilia*, Harvard University Press.

Wohlleben, P 2016, *The Hidden Life of Trees: What They Feel, How They Communicate – Discoveries from a Secret World*, Black.

Yong, E 2016, *I Contain Multitudes: The Microbes within Us and a Grander View of Life*, Bodley Head.

4 The Practice Turn

Social practices, performance and routine

Introduction

This chapter first provides a brief historical overview of social practice theories, followed by a section covering some criticisms and perceived weaknesses. I then provide a discussion explaining some of the differences between practices and (other) more-than-human theories presented in Part I, concluding with a section that presents practices as a useful organising frame, or leading theory, for how to think about and intervene in health in cities from a more-than-human perspective. Although all the theories reviewed in Part I provide valuable new ways of seeing, understanding and knowing more-than-human worlds, post-humanist theories of practice have several advantages over other approaches when contemplating intervening with a more-than-human healthy urban environment agenda. Practice theories have had a long period of development across the social sciences and humanities, and are well established compared to other more-than-human theories, many of which default to practices as the unit of enquiry; they can accommodate the main features of the more-than-human theories already outlined, and there is a substantial body of empirical work related to policy and applied problems relevant to a healthy cities agenda that draw on theories of practice. For example, there are practice-based studies on domestic energy and water consumption (Browne et al. 2013; Shove et al. 2014; Strengers 2012; Walker et al. 2014), food (Halkier & Jensen 2011; Warde et al. 2007), transport and mobilities (Spurling & McMeekin 2015; Watson 2012) and human health (Blue et al. 2016; Maller et al. 2016; Supski et al. 2016).

Practice and other more-than-human theories share the following five broad features: (1) they collapse common boundaries such as agency and structure, macro and micro (and advocate 'flat' ontologies); (2) they emphasise ongoing process, doing and performance through the enactment of everyday or mundane activities or practices; (3) they privilege embodied or tacit knowledges, affects and emotions over cognition or consciousness; (4) they acknowledge various types of agencies and materials, human, non-human and more-than-human; and (5) they see rhythms, patterns and textures through relations that link past and present, near and far, but subscribe to open-ended futures where practices or performances are not always predetermined, and are always changing. These are the main ideas this book draws on for rethinking healthy cities.

The unique contribution of practice theories lies in understanding everyday activity as recognisable practices, regularly and routinely performed over time-spaces, linking and connecting with other practices – for example, the practices that make up daily routines, such as showering and dressing, commuting, studying, working, socialising, caring for humans and non-humans, preparing and eating meals, and getting ready for bed. Other practices may occur less frequently than daily, but still be repeated regularly or routinely, such as gardening or hobbies. Practice theories therefore differ from the other more-than-human theories in that they concentrate on repeated activities rather than the affective (Chapter 2) or new materialisms approaches (Chapter 3) that are more concerned with events or entanglements that may or may not be ongoing or repeated. Although practice theories are based on the premise of a human practitioner and can be considered human-focused, they are not human-centric as they are interested in practices and their material and spatial compositions, rather than simply what individual humans do, think or say. This is a valuable approach when attempting to rethink complex environments, such as cities that comprise extended and interlinked material arrangements and the activities and doings carried out by humans and non-humans. Despite being focused on routines, practice theories also take the view that activity is not always predictable or pre-determined (Shove 2015). Despite being considered 'potentially subversive and innovative' (Nicolini 2012, p. 23), the notion of practices as essential to understanding social life is 'an increasingly influential supposition' (Hui et al. 2017, p. 1).[1] Although some brief examples are included here, Chapter 5 contains further detail about understanding health using social practices, and Chapter 6 expands on these ideas by looking at practices involving living non-humans, such as animals and plants.

A brief history of theories of social practice

Arriving in two main waves or generations (Postill 2010; Schatzki 2016a; 2016b), practice theories originate from the work of the philosophers Wittgenstein, Heidegger (Rouse 2007; Schatzki 2016a; 2016b), Marx (Nicolini 2012) and Foucault (Rouse 2007; Schatzki 2001). From there, they were adopted by various influential social theorists. The first wave included Giddens (1984), Bourdieu (1990) and Ortner (1984). These thinkers foregrounded the performative aspects of doing and action, arguing that the agency of individuals and the formation of social structures were co constitutive rather than separate domains for inquiry and analysis of social life. Moving away from 'intellectualism, representationalism, individualisms' (Schatzki 2001, p. 2), they were interested in (human) bodies, performance and practical consciousness over rational thought, grounding ideas of social practice in the unfolding of everyday or ordinary life (Maller 2015).[2] This makes practices highly relevant to researching, designing and intervening for healthy cities, where health is said to be created in the ordinary settings where people (and non-humans) live, work and play (World Health Organization 1986), such as homes, educational institutions and workplaces.

In the second wave of the practice tradition,[3] theorists such as Schatzki (2002), Reckwitz (2002b), Warde (2005), Nicolini (2012), Pickering (1995) and Shove and colleagues (Shove & Pantzar 2005; Shove et al. 2012) pursued and refined the parameters of practice generated by first-wave scholars,[4] particularly by drawing out the material or more-than-human aspects of practice. The absence of non-humans in the first wave of practice theories remarked upon by Reckwitz (2002a), Schatzki (2002) and picked up by others (e.g., Schatzki 2010; Shove et al. 2012) was particularly seen as deficient in contrast to developments in science and technology studies and actor–network theory (ANT) (e.g., Latour 1992; Law & Hassard 1999). Found most consistently in the disciplinary streams of sociology, STS and cultural studies, theories under the practice mantle continue to evolve across a wide range of fields, including geography (e.g., Browne 2016; Walker 2015), media studies (e.g., Postill 2010), organisation studies (e.g., Gherardi 2012; Nicolini 2012), public health (e.g., Blue & Spurling 2017; Maller 2015; 2017) and technology and design (e.g., Kuijer et al. 2013; Strengers 2013). However, as discussed in more detail later, in the main, practices are said to only be carried by people, despite their reliance on non-humans.

Like the other theories in this book, there is no consistent definition of practice theory (Gherardi 2017; Rouse 2007; Schatzki 2016b; Warde 2014),[5] but what are common to the diverse body of work grouped under the practice heading are ontologies and epistemologies that unite rather than divide agency and structure, and the premise that practices make up the basic unit of enquiry into social life. Essentially, practices are organised sets of linked actions carried out or performed across time and space (Shove et al. 2012). Practices do not exist in isolation, and are joined by meshes of links and relations to other practices to form a 'nexus' (Hui et al. 2017) or 'plenum' of practices (Schatzki 2015; 2016b). Put simply, the plenum of practices makes up the observable and experienced socio-material worlds of cities and urban environments. Because the later theorists emphasised non-humans and the material components of practices, this work is prioritised in this chapter – being the most relevant for thinking about how to create healthy urban environments as defined by the presence of multiple living non-humans, materials, built structures and technologies.

Despite considerable variability in definitions of practice, two are most commonly cited in the literature. The first is from Reckwitz (2002b), who describes practices as 'routinised' actions, or blocks or patterns of activity, involving interconnected elements of bodies and minds, objects/materials and socially shared competencies, knowledge and skills. This was one of the first clear definitions of a practice, and is widely cited (e.g., Horne et al. 2011; Hui 2017; Spaargaren et al. 2016; Strengers & Maller 2015a; Warde 2005). More recently, this definition was superseded by an alternative from Shove et al. (2012), who pared practices down to be comprised simply of three interlocking elements: materials, meanings and competences. Materials are all the things, or non-humans, required to perform a practice; meanings are the reasons it is performed; and competences are the necessary actions and skill, know-how and technique required to carry it out. For example, the practice of running for exercise in cities requires certain materials (e.g., roads, shoes, clothing), competences (e.g., how to run and how to avoid traffic), and lastly, a reason to run (e.g., enjoyment, and an understanding of running as beneficial to health and well-being) (Maller et al. 2016).[6] Clearly, practices are carried out by people or 'carriers' (Reckwitz 2002b; Shove et al. 2012) who are recruited to practices and perform them at regular moments in time. Evident here is another requirement – that practices are comprised of neither single performances nor performed by a single practitioner; they are recognisable entities routinely or habitually carried out by multiple practitioners or groups of people (Schatzki 2016a; 2016b; Shove 2014).[7] Think of practices such as playing competitive sports or being a member of a garden club. To ensure their continued performance or 'survival', practices must attract or recruit sufficient cohorts of carriers (Shove 2015; Shove & Pantzar 2007). For example, recruitment of new practitioners can happen when practices 'travel' to various places through the movement of existing practitioners (Maller & Strengers 2013), as occurs in migration from one country to another, holiday travel and global sporting competitions.

Another way to think about practices is as easily recognisable 'doings and sayings' (Schatzki 2002, p. 73) that are part of daily routines or other regularly occurring activities – for example, mundane things such as getting to work, exercising or washing clothes.[8] There is now a substantial body of empirical work on many types of practices. These include working in organisations (Gherardi 2012; Nicolini 2012), mobility (Spurling & McMeekin 2015; Watson 2012), doing leisure activities such as physical activity (Maller et al. 2016; Shove & Pantzar 2005; 2007), washing (Browne et al. 2013), cooking (Halkier & Jensen 2011) and keeping homes or offices warm or cool (Gram-Hanssen 2010; Hitchings 2011; Strengers & Maller 2012; Walker et al. 2014), together with other less frequently performed practices, such as renovating or buying houses (Judson et al. 2013; Maller 2016).[9]

In describing practices and their component elements, it is important to recognise that practices are simply considered the basic building blocks – it is their relations and intersections with other practices to form bundles and complexes, a nexus, system or plenum, that is essential to understand and explain social life (Shove et al. 2012).[10] For example, practices are often co-located in similar sites or settings, such as in particular rooms of buildings (e.g., a bathroom or office) or parts of cities (e.g., a park or football stadium) where technical and material infrastructures support or are integral to their performance. Such 'bundles' of practices form 'loose-knit patterns based on co-location and coexistence' and may not be co-dependent (Shove et al. 2012, p. 66). However, they are likely to be connected through shared or common elements whose role may vary in different practices. When practices are 'stickier and [have] more integrated arrangements, including co-dependent forms of sequence and synchronization', they are said to form a complex (Shove et al. 2012, p. 66). Complexes of practice are connected and co-dependent in both space and time. A useful example is to consider the complex of 'getting ready in the morning', comprising sequential and dependent practices starting at one's home, including waking, bathing, dressing, and food preparation and eating (breakfasts and/or lunches). This might be followed by practices taking place outside the home, such as in vehicles and on roads and tracks to transport children to school, and then finally commuting to work. Before turning to a discussion of social practice theories as more-than-human, I outline some of the assumed limitations of theories of social practice, how these have been dealt with in the literature and how practice theories are continuing to develop.

Critiques of social practice theories

As highlighted by Hui et al. (2017), two of the main charges directed at theories of practice are as follows. First, that they have a limited scale and can only account for small and not large phenomena (such as what individual households do compared with infrastructure like roads and highways), and thereby they inadequately deal with hefty things such as power, economies and bureaucracies (among others). Second, sensations and experiences of people are said to be neglected or overlooked, especially regarding affect and emotions – for example, how practices, such as driving to work or taking a bath, might feel. Both criticisms are relevant to a more-than-human healthy cities agenda – the first, because cities and their component non-human parts and contributors are often large in scale, and the second because cities are constantly imbued with and create affects and emotions that are important to understanding if they are to become more-than-human habitat.

Regarding the first criticism, practice theorists are not in agreement about the issue of scale, particularly whether to recognise seemingly 'small' and 'large' phenomena (Nicolini 2017). Nicolini (2017, p. 99) describes the first camp, who follow the 'traditional layered view of the social', where social life functions at various different levels, often referred to as 'micro' and 'macro' (also critiqued by Schatzki 2016b). Some scholars claim some 'macro' social phenomena are the product of 'long-term, complex and far reaching social processes' beyond the realm of practices (Nicolini 2017, p. 100). So-called 'large' things like institutions and social classes are therefore seen as quite different from 'small' everyday occurrences such as the 'mundane social intercourse' used in greeting people; in other words, small and large phenomena 'are made of different ontological stuff'(Nicolini 2017, p. 100). This is a common view shared by many social scientists and theorists, not just those interested in practices.

The issue of scale has most directly been dealt with by Schatzki (2015; 2016b), along with Nicolini (2017) and Watson (2017), through arguments for the 'flatness' of the social world (i.e., social life does not have any levels). Large-scale phenomena include a range of familiar socio-material structures. These include financial markets, educational systems and institutions (Nicolini 2017), disciplines such as those in the arts or sciences, sources of power such as governments (Schatzki 2016b), and energy and water infrastructures, such as roads, cities and other socio-material features of urban environments. Poignantly using the simple example of everyday greetings, Nicolini (2017) shows how labels such as 'large' and 'small' or 'complexity' and 'size' are not as useful as they first appear in trying to understand and explain social life. Phenomena perceived as small or micro-instances of action, but that have widespread recurring performances throughout social worlds, cannot be said to have insignificant or unimportant effects, nor be appropriately labelled as 'small':

> The practice of greeting other people at the beginning of a social encounter . . . [is] in fact ubiquitous, pervasive and critical to sustain the fabric of social relationships and its orderliness. Indeed, one can hardly think of a phenomenon that is more 'macro' and 'large-scale' than greetings.
>
> (Nicolini 2017, p. 100)

This is consistent with thinking in the second camp of practice theorists (and with the more-than-human theories presented in Chapters 2 and 3), who view social phenomena as comprising the same materials, whether they appear large or small, micro or macro (DeLanda 2006; Schatzki 2016b; Thrift 2008; Watson 2017). A corollary of this requirement is that social life therefore exists on a single plane, rather than multiple levels. This view is often confusingly referred to as 'flat' (or a flat ontology)[11] (Nicolini 2017; Schatzki 2015; 2016b). However, a more visual and dynamic way to think about social practices existing on a single plane is through similes of fabric and textiles, such as wefts, weaves and webs, or in other words, viewing links and relations between practices with a 'rhizomic sensitivity' (Nicolini 2017, p. 102). This sensitivity to inter-relations recalls DeLanda (2006) and Thrift (2008, p. 17), who, in assemblage and non-representational theory respectively, argue that 'a multiplicity of "scales" is always present in inter-actions'. Flatness does not imply that all relations between and produced by practices are equal, or that inequalities and inequities do not exist – for example, the distribution of income or access to public transport in cities.

As Nicolini (2017) shows, among flat ontologists there are also differences in the ways that practices are thought to recur through the performances of practitioners or carriers. One view is that people uncritically follow a predetermined block, template or practice pattern that leaves little room for innovation or adjustments. This way of thinking about practices has been criticised as overly deterministic, and Nicolini (2017) considers that it suffers similar deficiencies to rational choice theory. By decentring people, practice theorists following this line of thought may be guilty of 'muting' the agency of the practitioner. Furthermore, this critique shares similarities with the concern that practice theories neglect individual experience (discussed shortly). However, this criticism is countered by others who consider that despite a general continuity between practice performances to form the recognisable entity, each performance is unique in its situation in time and space (Nicolini 2017).[12] In this view, practices are less predetermined, and importantly, each performance presents an opportunity for innovation, change and emergence (Shove et al. 2012). Moreover, taking a relational position on practice performances means that studying one practice in isolation without looking to how it is connected to other practices and their performance across time and space may be futile. For Nicolini (2017, p. 102), this resolves the question of scale, because following the 'living and pulsating connections among practices' means that 'large phenomena appear as textures, nexuses, meshes or assemblages of practices'.[13]

It follows that what might be thought of as large, single entities, such as a company, government or economy, are made up of myriad interwoven practices, bundles and complexes that can collectively appear as more or less coherent wholes. In the context of practices and scale, it is important here to briefly discuss issues relating to power. In the social sciences, power is usually considered an object or property of people, such as the 'capacity to act with effect' or 'to direct or purposively influence the actions of others' (Watson 2017, p. 170). In theories of practice, however, power is instead 'rendered a relational, socially constituted effect' produced by practices, rather than a property of a person or group of people (Watson 2017, p. 173). Foucault has been influential in shifting thinking about power from object to effect through his ideas of governmentality, and related ideas about power as distributed (Watson 2017). In practice ontologies, power as an effect or an outcome of the multiple performances of practices makes more sense than being a force beyond or bearing down on practices. Nevertheless, if power is the product of practice performances, the effects of 'enduringly powerful social agents such as corporations or governments' must be accounted for (Watson 2017, p. 171). Watson (2017) draws on ANT and the notion that through their relations to and connections with other practices, some practices can 'govern' others through processes of alignment, 'correction' or 'discipline'. Hence, although practices are made of the same stuff, some have distinctive characteristics achieved through alliances or alignment with other practices in different sites or contexts that produce and reproduce arrangements or effects over time. This means that some practices 'have a disproportionate capacity for shaping action elsewhere' (Watson 2017, p. 181), which can be observed as the differential spread of power – for example, the practices of urban policymaking or city planning. Thinking of power this way is consistent with practices as being more-than-human, as explained in the next section.

Turning now to the second criticism directed at theories of social practice, concerns have been raised about the backgrounding or absence of sensations and experiences of practice performances (Latham & Conradson 2003; Pink 2012). This relates to the status of bodies and the affective experience of individuals or groups of practitioners in theories of practice. As there is a lot to say concerning bodies and affects as a lacuna in practice theories, and as an important part of understanding healthy urban environments, I spend some time examining each. I also explicate notions of bodies and affects in the next section on theories of practice as more-than-human.

Apart from the acknowledgement of the body/mind complex, and bodies being continually 'shaped by and through practices' (Reckwitz 2002b, p. 251), bodies[14] are not consistently dealt with in practice theory. Bodies tend to either be foregrounded and present as carriers and agents of practices (e.g., Wallenborn and Wilhite 2014) or simply assumed to always be there and relatively backgrounded (e.g., Shove and Pantzar 2005), depending on the scholar and the context or problem-focus. It is also assumed that all bodies are equally capable of performing practices, an oversight picked up on by Fox et al. (2017). In short, bodies appear to have a 'present-absent' status in practice theories, where their 'physical and sensory qualities are unrecognised or dematerialised' (Maller 2017, p. 72).

When thinking about health and the health status of human bodies, I have previously suggested that bodies play a key material role in practices, and in fact can be thought of as either a material part of practices or supplying materials to practices (Maller 2017). For example, bodies provide the energy to perform or carry out practices, and provide cellular and molecular materials or substances necessary for basic functioning (Maller 2017). Taking a different tack, Rouse (2007, pp. 651–652) posits that 'practice theorists . . . understand human bodies as both the locus of agency, affective response and cultural expression, and the target of power and normalization'. Affects and emotions as sensory bodily experiences are typically a 'blind spot' in theories of practice (Reckwitz 2017, p. 116). In disciplines such as cultural geography and anthropology, there are many examples where bodies and their sensations have come to the fore to 'develop the sensuous character of practice' (Simonsen 2007, p. 169) – for instance, Pink (2012) on sensory ethnographies, Simonsen (2007, p. 170) on Merleau-Ponty's ideas of perception as 'a dialectical relationship of the body and its environment', and Ingold's (2010, p. S121) notions of bodies 'walking along' in weather.

Aside from their potential irrelevance to some research, Reckwitz (2017, p. 118) argues that affects, sensations and emotions may have been neglected in practice scholarship because they have either been dismissed as properties of individuals (and therefore non-social), or rationality and modernity have been assumed to override them. Regardless, as two prominent practice theorists, both Reckwitz (2002b; 2017) and Schatzki (1996; 2002) have much to say about the affective dimensions of practices. For example, Reckwitz (2002b, p. 254) claims: 'Every practice contains a certain practice-specific emotionality (even if that means a high control of emotions). Wants and emotions thus do not belong to individuals but – in the form of knowledge – to practices.'

Reckwitz (2017, p. 115) argues that the statuses of affect, emotions and feelings have 'a special question of fundamental importance in current social theory', situating them in relation to The Affective Turn (discussed in Chapter 2). Together with interests in space and time, more-than-human perspectives (as post-humanism), and a 'rediscovery' of the senses, Reckwitz (2017, p. 115) places affects and emotions as aligning 'the cultural and the material, the symbolic and the objective (or the living)' through performance. In other words, affects are 'built into' practices. Schatzki (Schatzki 1997; 2002; 2016b) takes a similar stance through his use of 'teleo-affectivities', which include emotions, goals and ends as part of practices.[15] Reckwitz (2017) then explains practice theory's perspective on affects: (1) affects are relations between practice entities and are therefore social, not individual; (2) affects are not properties, but activities or part of practices that involve motivations, desires and fascinations;[16] and (3) affects are states of physical arousal (e.g., pleasure or displeasure) directed at something of significance, such as people, things or ideas. These types of 'affective objects' or artefacts are intensely charged with positive or negative qualities – for example, the 'glamourous fascination' with a thing (e.g., new technology or a device), or the fear or pleasure of being in a city (e.g., a 'spatial atmosphere') (Reckwitz 2017, p. 122). Although Wetherell (2012, p. 12) has a different take on affect, as highlighted in Chapter 2, she declares: 'the familiar social science concept of practice offers the best, bare bones, synthesising rubric for research on affect. It offers the most effective, accurate and productive account of affect's pattern and logic'.

As noted above, I will return to more detailed discussion of affects and emotions subsequently in the section that examines how theories of practice intersect with more-than-human theories, such as non-representational thinking. Before that, I now address, albeit, briefly, how practice theories can intervene and create social change.

The final criticism sometimes directed at theories of practice that is worth briefly discussing in regard to urban environments is that, as observed by Maller and Strengers (2015) and Watson (2017), they have a limited capacity to intervene in or create social change. Although the field of empirical work using practices demonstrates this is not the case, part of this criticism could be associated with earlier work using practice theories that focused on historical analyses of practice change to describe and document the trajectories of practices in considerable detail (e.g., Shove 2003). Of course, much work in the mid- to late 2000s has sought to rectify this perceived weakness. For example, in a volume I co-edited titled *Social Practices, Intervention and Sustainability: Beyond Behaviour Change* (Strengers & Maller 2015b), contributors provide numerous, diverse examples of attempts at steering and intervening in social life using practice-based approaches. Similarly, work from the DEMAND Centre at Lancaster University in the UK has tackled steering and changing practices in a policy context.[17] With the popularity of practice theories not waning any time soon, no doubt further work will continue to develop the use of practice approaches for interventions and creating change to improve social and environmental outcomes in urban contexts. The next section examines theories of practice regarding their similarities and differences with more-than-human theories. Here I make a case for labelling practice theories 'more-than-human'.

Comparing social practices to affective and new materialist thinking

With their verifiable post-humanist position,[18] practice theories share enough in common with the more-than-human theories in Part I to be considered messmates. In my view, however, theories of social practice have had wider purchase than other theories, in that they have been used and cited more frequently in the literature, evidenced by their recurring reference, directly and indirectly, in affective, assemblage, new materialist and non-representational approaches (e.g., Anderson & Harrison 2010; DeLanda 2006; Thrift 2008; Wetherell 2012). In sum, what unites these theories is that they 'share an emphasis on the ongoing composition of the social from within the "rough ground"' of practices (Anderson & Harrison 2010, p. 17). At their core, theories of practice along with other more-than-human theories owe a considerable debt to ANT and the work of STS in elevating the status of non-humans (Shove et al. 2012). However, there are of course subtle (and not so subtle) similarities and differences between the various more-than-human theories in this book, some of which this section briefly elaborates. There are three areas of differentiation or varying positioning between practice theories and other more-than-human approaches that I clarify here before concluding with a case for using practice theories as the 'lead' theory in trying to rethink healthy cities: (1) the location of agency, (2) the inclusion of affect and emotions (partially addressed above) and (3) the types of action studied in empirical enquiries.

First (and requiring the most discussion) is the question of agency and how it is distributed (or not) between non-humans implicated in practices, and following this, the tantalising and radical prospect of whether humans are needed to perform practices. At the core of this issue is the question of human-centrism. To a degree, the more-than-human theories I have covered shift in subtle ways around this question, and the extent humans are centred depends on the ontology of the theorist. The centring or decentring of people has implications for the locus of agency and whether it is concentrated in human practitioners, distributed across practices or their elements, or (partially or fully) assigned to non-humans, which (as indicated, controversially) perform practices with or without a human counterpart (Maller & Strengers in press). Without assigning definitive labels, I suggest that one way of thinking about the status of human-centrism in more-than-human theories is a sliding scale, with practices on the more human-centric end, new materialisms and assemblages[19] on the opposite more decentred end, and affective and non-representational approaches somewhere in the middle.[20] Where a theory sits regarding human-centrism becomes important when implementing its ideas into practice for a more-than-human healthy cities agenda – for example, regarding practices of decision-making for biodiversity and sustainability.

Theories of practice, in the main, assume that only people carry practices. From their origins to recent more post-humanist formulations, they rely on the premise of a human practitioner, with some theorists more than others overtly declaring this stance (e.g., Shove et al. 2012; Simonsen 2012). Although acknowledging practice theory's alignment with ANT, Shove et al. (2012) do not agree with Latour (2000) that non-humans can construct social orders. They argue 'that human and non-human relations can be better understood when located in terms of a more encompassing, but *suitably materialised*, theory of practice' (Shove et al. 2012, p. 18; emphasis added). In decentred stances like ANT, assemblage thinking and new materialisms, non-humans are attributed equal agencies and capacities to act as humans. For example, in explaining how humans are decentred in assemblage thinking, Li (2007, p. 265) states: 'the situated subjects who do the work of pulling together disparate elements [do so] without attributing to them a master-mind or a totalising plan'.

In a relatively controversial move, some practice theorists have considered whether non-humans can perform practices without humans, or if that is a step to far, at least be considered as co-performers of practice (Maller & Strengers in press). For example, in considering whether companion animals might perform or be implicated in practices involving energy consumption in households, Strengers et al. (2016, p. 762) write: 'While pets and pests cannot talk or "choose" energy products and are not (normally) involved in turning appliances on and off, they can sit suggestively next to heaters, or make a mess on clean laundry hung out to dry.' There is no doubt that more-than-human agency is present in these examples which affect how much energy households consume. In seeking to satisfactorily account for their role in practices which arguably are more than simple materials or even bystanders of practice, Strengers et al. (2016, p. 767) turn to assemblage thinking: '[We] illustrate how various humans, animals, plants and objects can be thought of as "consumers" of energy, not in the traditional sense, but as part of assemblages of practice in which they necessarily participate, perform and co-construct.'

Similarly, Giaccardi et al. (2016, p. 6) also make the case that technologies can be co-performers in practices, as they become increasingly competent, and relied-upon, to achieve certain actions in an increasingly technologically advanced world because: 'By viewing competences as distributed between people and technologies, the idea that technologies have certain unique . . . capabilities that people do not have means that technologies can complement people in areas where they excel.'

Although they do not declare that technologies perform practices in themselves, some theorists point to increasing advances in artificial intelligence; hence, the idea that things and other non-humans could perform practices, or actively participate in practices, has validity (Maller & Strengers in press). However, a hybrid stance, where agency is accepted as shared between humans and non-humans, seems to capture the current position of most more-than-human theories, with varying degrees of residual human-centrism present. In explaining the position of non-representational theories on human-centrism, Thrift (2008, p. 13) argues strongly for a decentred human stance, but suggests that decentring humans completely is going 'too far'; and this is despite non-representational thinking giving equal weight to the agency of things. In short, as discussed respectively in Chapters 3 and 2, assemblage and new materialisms push non-humans forward as the loci of action and performance compared to affective, non-representational and social practice theories. Nevertheless, the bulk of empirical work to date that draws on more-than-human theories is decidedly, but not surprisingly, human-centric, or at least human-focused. Given the recognition that cities are already habitat for human and non-humans and animals and considering the rise and effects of technological agents, more empirical work with human and non-humans is needed if cities are to become sustainable and healthy more-than-human environments.

The second area of difference between practice theory and other more-than-human theories is their treatment of or interest in affect and emotions. The way affect and emotions are germane to practice theories was discussed earlier. From this discussion, it is apparent that emotions and affect are of varying interest to practice theorists, dependent on different conceptualisations of practices. However, in comparison to non-representational and affective approaches, practice theories are significantly less interested in affect and emotions. As discussed in detail in Chapter 2, of all the more-than-human theories, non-representational theory and others under the mantel of The Affective Turn distinctly position themselves around affects and emotions.

Finally, where practice theories and some other more-than-human theories differ slightly relates to the types of action they are typically concerned with. Practices are regular activities performed multiple times, whereas encounters, events and other emergent non-representational phenomena may or may not be repeated or ongoing. Although more-than-human theories share an interest in the indeterminacy and unpredictability of action and performance, theories of practice are, to a degree, more interested in contingent predictability because they focus on repeated or routine activities across time and space. Overall, it is worth noting that more-than-human theories differ about the types of action they pursue in their enquiries. These different approaches mean there is a palette of options to inform the study of cities and how they might be changed; however, empirical applications often involve investigations of practice.[21]

Conclusion

This chapter commenced with an overview of theories of social practice which, as another 'wild' idea, have recently gained prominence in many fields in the social sciences and humanities, and consequently are increasingly influential. Practice theories share much in common with the other more-than-human theories covered in Part I. For example, like other more-than-human theories, they elevate materials and other non-humans in everyday life, recognising and respecting their complex relations and in some cases their capacities to act, such as digital or 'smart' technologies or companion animals and plants. However, in theories of practice, there is a clear emphasis on regularly and routinely performed recognisable practices over time and space that connect with other practices, such as those comprising weekday routines. With their focus on routine, practices are well placed to understand how different more-than-human activities and encounters in cities are connected, shape and reshape each other in productive, but not always beneficial ways – for example, traffic problems caused by work and school commutes. With their minimalist, but still present, humanism, practices are also useful because in thinking about how to change cities, it makes sense to start by 'following' routine and regular performances of more-than-human action.

Considering these advantages, together with their long genealogy, their ability to incorporate the main contributions from a range of more-than-human theories and the substantial body of empirical work drawing on theories of practice, this chapter argued that practice theories are useful to begin rethinking about how to intervene in cities to make them more-than-human habitat. Although theories of practice have been chosen as a 'lead' theory, the more-than-human theories reviewed in Part I are close companions, providing important support and taking precedence at different moments. This hybrid model of drawing on different theories at various times and contexts is recommended because, as illustrated in the following chapters, despite sharing many features in common, ultimately each theoretical standpoint brings a distinctive advantage that can be important or useful when thinking about healthy urban environments.

Now that the fit between more-than-human theories presented in Part I has been established, Part II turns to more practical matters – specifically, how practice theories, supported by the rich perspectives of other approaches, can change the way human health is thought about in urban environments, and how more-than-human theories can be used to intervene for healthier, more-than-human habitat.

Notes

1 I recommend Schatzki (2001), Shove et al. (2012), Warde (2014), Reckwitz (2002b) or Nicolini (2012) for accessible overviews of the history of theories of practice.
2 A variety of reasons are said to motivate the rise of practice theories. According to Warde (2014, p. 284): 'The most common explanation of the emergence of theories of practice is that they were a response to a number of fundamental problems of social theory at the point of the passing of economism and Marxism in the 1970s.'
3 Also known as the 'turn' (Schatzki 2001) or 're-turn' to practice (Gherardi 2017).
4 I have written elsewhere more extensively on the limitations and criticisms of Bourdieu and Giddens's views on practice (Maller 2015).
5 Schatzki (2016b) argues this is a strength of practice theories because pluralist understandings allow for different conceptual directions and of different empirical phenomena.
6 Discussed in more detail in Chapter 5.
7 Hence the 'social' of social practices.
8 Practices generally refer to doings and sayings that practitioners recognise, not just those activities described by theorists.
9 Importantly, Hui et al. (2017, p.2) note that, until now, this broad adoption of ideas of practice is not accompanied by a 'corresponding refinement in the theoretical ideas that are used to inform empirical research'.
10 I recommend Shove et al. (2012) and the edited collection by Hui et al. (2017) to explore detailed relations between practices.
11 Schatzki (2016b) points out that practice theories are not the only ontologies that argue all social life is carried out on one level.
12 Nicolini (2017, p. 101) calls this view of practices and their relations 'connected situationalism'.
13 Although Nicolini (2017, p. 103) uses some of the language of assemblage thinking, he does not directly link his ideas to assemblage theorists, apart from referring to generally in his comment about how the language of webs, mesh and assemblage is used by 'other relational social scientists'.
14 In using the term 'bodies' here, I mean 'body-minds', to avoid the classic Cartesian dualism and remain consistent with a more-than-human take on practices.
15 To elaborate, Schatzki (1997, pp. 302–303) writes: 'The sole universal feature of teleoaffectivity is the omnipresence of affectivity: human activity continuously expresses the emotions, moods, and feelings ignored in Bourdieu and underplayed in Giddens, thereby manifesting its dependence on how things matter to people.'
16 Keeping in mind that these are properties of the practice, and not ascribed to individual people.
17 The DEMAND (Dynamics of Energy, Mobility and Demand) Centre has produced some valuable working papers on steering and changing practices, available at www.demand.ac.uk/publications/ (accessed 22 January 2018).
18 For those interested in the detail of theoretical arguments made for post humanism in theories of social practice, see Part III in Schatzki et al. (2001).

19 Discussed in Chapter 3.
20 Discussed in Chapter 2.
21 How different more-than-human approaches can be used in research and policymaking is discussed in Chapter 7.

References

Anderson, B & Harrison, P 2010, 'The promise of non-representational theories', in B Anderson & P Harrison (eds), *Taking-place: Non-representational Theories and Geography*, Ashgate, pp. 1–34.

Blue, S, Shove, E, Carmona, C & Kelly, MP 2016, 'Theories of practice and public health: understanding (un)healthy practices', *Critical Public Health*, vol. 26, no. 1, pp. 36–50.

Blue, S & Spurling, N 2017, 'Qualities of connective tissue in hospital life: how complexes of practice change', in A Hui, TR Schatzki & E Shove (eds), *The Nexus of Practices: Connections, Constellations, Practitioners*, Routledge, pp. 24–37.

Bourdieu, P 1990, *The Logic of Practice*, Polity Press.

Browne, AL 2016, 'Can people talk together about their practices? Focus groups, humour and the sensitive dynamics of everyday life', *Area*, vol. 48, no. 2, pp. 198–205.

Browne, AL, Medd, W & Anderson, B 2013, 'Developing novel approaches to tracking domestic water demand under uncertainty – a reflection on the "up scaling" of social science approaches in the United Kingdom', *Water Resources Management*, vol. 27, no. 4, pp. 1013–1035.

DeLanda, M 2006, *A New Philosophy of Society: Assemblage Theory and Social Complexity*, Bloomsbury Academic.

Fox, E, Hitchings, R, Day, R & Venn, S 2017, 'Demanding distances in later life leisure travel', *Geoforum*, vol. 82, Supplement C, pp. 102–111.

Gherardi, S 2012, *How to Conduct a Practice-based Study: Problems and Methods*, Edward Elgar.

Gherardi, S 2017, 'Sociomateriality in posthuman practice theory', in A Hui, TR Schatzki & E Shove (eds), *The Nexus of Practices: Connections, Constellations, Practitioners*, Routledge, pp. 38–67.

Giaccardi, E, Kuijer, L & Neven, L 2016, 'Design for resourceful ageing: intervening in the ethics of gerontechnology', paper presented to *Design+Research+Society (DRS): Future Focused Thinking*, Brighton, United Kingdom, 27–30 June.

Giddens, A 1984, *The Constitution of Society: Outline of the Theory of Structuration*, Polity Press.

Gram-Hanssen, K 2010, 'Residential heat comfort practices: understanding users', *Building Research & Information*, vol. 38, no. 2, pp. 175–186.

Halkier, B & Jensen, I 2011, 'Methodological challenges in using practice theory in consumption research: examples from a study on handling nutritional contestations of food consumption', *Journal of Consumer Culture*, vol. 11, no. 1, pp. 101–123.

Hitchings, R 2011, 'Researching air-conditioning addiction and ways of puncturing practice: professional office workers and the decision to go outside', *Environment and Planning A*, vol. 43, no. 12, pp. 2838–2856.

Horne, R, Maller, C & Lane, R 2011, 'Remaking home: the reuse of goods and materials in Australian households', in R Lane & A Gorman-Murray (eds), *Material Geographies of Household Sustainability*, Ashgate, pp. 89–111.

Hui, A 2017, 'Variation and the intersection of practices', in A Hui, TR Schatzki & E Shove (eds), *The Nexus of Practices: Connections, Constellations, Practitioners*, Routledge, pp. 52–67.

Hui, A, Schatzki, TR & Shove, E 2017, *The Nexus of Practices: Connections, Constellations, Practitioners*, Routledge.

Ingold, T 2010, 'Footprints through the weather-world: walking, breathing, knowing', *Journal of the Royal Anthropological Institute*, vol. 16, pp. S121–S139.

Judson, E, Iyer-Raniga, U & Horne, R 2013, 'Greening heritage housing: understanding homeowners' renovation practices in Australia', *Journal of Housing and the Built Environment*, pp. 1–18.

Kuijer, L, De Jong, A & Van Eijk, D 2013, 'Practices as a unit of design: an exploration of theoretical guidelines in a study on bathing', *ACM Transactions on Computer–Human Interaction*, vol. 20, no. 4, pp. 21:1–21:22.

Latham, A & Conradson, D 2003, 'The possibilities of performance', *Environment and Planning A*, vol. 35, no. 11, pp. 1901–1906.

Latour, B 1992, 'Where are the missing masses? The sociology of a few mundane artifacts', in WE Bijker & J Law (eds), *Shaping Technology/Building Society: Studies in Sociotechnical Change*, MIT Press, pp. 225–258.

Latour, B 2000, 'When things strike back: a possible contribution of "science studies" to the social sciences', *British Journal of Sociology*, vol. 51, no. 1, pp. 107–123.

Law, J & Hassard, J 1999, *Actor Network Theory and After*, Wiley.

Li, TM 2007, 'Practices of assemblage and community forest management', *Economy and Society*, vol. 36, no. 2, pp. 263–293.

Maller, C 2015, 'Understanding health through social practices: performance and materiality in everyday life', *Sociology of Health & Illness*, vol. 37, no. 1, pp. 52–66.

Maller, C 2016, *Homemaking Practices of Provision and Maintenance: Implications for Environmental Action*, Oxford University Press.

Maller, C 2017, 'Epigenetics, theories of social practice and lifestyle disease', in A Hui, TR Schatzki & E Shove (eds), *The Nexus of Practices: Connections, Constellations, Practitioners*, Routledge, pp. 68–80.

Maller, C & Strengers, Y 2013, 'The global migration of everyday life: investigating the practice memories of Australian migrants', *Geoforum*, vol. 44, pp. 243–252.

Maller, C & Strengers, Y 2015, 'Conclusion: transforming practice interventions', in Y Strengers & C Maller (eds), *Social Practices, Intervention and Sustainability: Beyond Behaviour Change*, Routledge, pp. 196–200.

Maller, C & Strengers, Y (eds) in press, *Social Practices and Dynamic Non-humans: Nature, Materials and Technologies*, Palgrave Macmillan.

Maller, C, Nicholls, L & Strengers, Y 2016, 'Understanding the materiality of neighbourhoods in 'healthy practices': outdoor exercise practices in a new master-planned estate', *Urban Policy and Research: Special Issue on Health*, vol. 34, pp. 55–72.

Nicolini, D 2012, *Practice Theory, Work, and Organization: An Introduction*, Oxford University Press.

Nicolini, D 2017, 'Is small the only beautiful? Making sense of "large phenomena" from a practice-based perspective', in A Hui, TR Schatzki & E Shove (eds), *The Nexus of Practices: Connections, Constellations, Practitioners*, Routledge, pp. 98–113.

Ortner, SB 1984, 'Theory in anthropology since the sixties', *Comparative Studies in Society and History*, vol. 26, no. 1, pp. 126–166.

Pickering, A 1995, *The Mangle of Practice: Time, Agency and Science*, University of Chicago Press.

Pink, S 2012, *Situating Everyday Life: Practices and Places*, SAGE Publications.

Postill, J 2010, 'Introduction: theorising media and practice', in B Bräuchler & J Postill (eds), *Theorising Media and Practice*, Berghahn Books, pp. 1–32.

Reckwitz, A 2002a, 'The Status of the "Material" in Theories of Culture: From "Social Structure" to "Artefacts"', *Journal for the Theory of Social Behaviour*, vol. 32, no. 2, pp. 195–217.

Reckwitz, A 2002b, 'Toward a theory of social practices: a development in culturalist theorizing', *European Journal of Social Theory*, vol. 5, no. 2, pp. 243–263.

Reckwitz, A 2017, 'Practices and their affects', in A Hui, TR Schatzki & E Shove (eds), *The Nexus of Practices: Connections, Constellations, Practitioners*, Routledge, pp. 114–125.

Rouse, J 2007, 'Practice theory', in MW Risjord (ed.), *Philosophy of Anthropology and Sociology*, North-Holland, pp. 639–681.

Schatzki, TR 1996, *Social Practices: A Wittgensteinian Approach to Human Activity and the Social*, Cambridge University Press.

Schatzki, TR 1997, 'Practices and actions: a Wittgensteinian critique of Bourdieu and Giddens', *Philosophy of the Social Sciences*, vol. 27, no. 3, pp. 283–308.

Schatzki, TR 2001, 'Introduction: practice theory', in TR Schatzki, K Knorr Cetina & E Von Savigny (eds), *The Practice Turn in Contemporary Theory*, Routledge, pp. 1–14.

Schatzki, TR 2002, *The Site of the Social: A Philosophical Account of the Constitution of Social Life and Change*, Pennsylvania State University Press.

Schatzki, TR 2010, 'Materiality and social life', *Nature and Culture*, vol. 5, no. 2, pp. 123–149.

Schatzki, TR 2015, 'Practices, governance and sustainability', in Y Strengers & C Maller (eds), *Social Practices, Intervention and Sustainability: Beyond Behaviour Change*, Routledge, pp. 15–30.

Schatzki, TR 2016a, 'Multiplicity in social theory and practice ontology', in M Jonas & B Littig (eds), *Praxeological Political Analysis*, Taylor & Francis.

Schatzki, TR 2016b, 'Practice theory as flat ontology', in G Spaargaren, D Weenink & M Lamers (eds), *Practice Theory and Research: Exploring the Dynamics of Social Life*, Routledge, pp. 28–42.

Schatzki, TR, Knorr Cetina, K & Von Savigny, E 2001, *The Practice Turn in Contemporary Theory*, Routledge.

Shove, E 2003, *Comfort, Cleanliness and Convenience: The Social Organization of Normality*, Berg.

Shove, E 2014, 'Putting practice into policy: reconfiguring questions of consumption and climate change', *Contemporary Social Science*, vol. 9, no. 4, pp. 415–429.

Shove, E 2015, 'Linking low carbon policy and social practice', in Y Strengers & C Maller (eds), *Social Practices, Intervention and Sustainability: Beyond Behaviour Change*, Routledge, pp. 31–44.

Shove, E & Pantzar, M 2005, 'Consumers, producers and practices: understanding the invention and reinvention of Nordic walking', *Journal of Consumer Culture*, vol. 5, no. 1, pp. 43–64.

Shove, E & Pantzar, M 2007, 'Recruitment and reproduction: the careers of and carriers of digital photography and floorball', *Human Affairs*, vol. 17, pp. 154–167.

Shove, E, Pantzar, M & Watson, M 2012, *The Dynamics of Social Practice: Everyday Life and How It Changes*, SAGE Publications.

Shove, E, Walker, G & Brown, S 2014, 'Transnational transitions: the diffusion and integration of mechanical cooling', *Urban Studies*, vol. 51, no. 7, pp. 1506–1519.

Simonsen, K 2007, 'Practice, spatiality and embodied emotions: an outline of a geography of practice', *Human Affairs*, vol. 17, no. 2, pp. 168–181.

Simonsen, K 2012, 'In quest of a new humanism: embodiment, experience and phenomenology as critical geography', *Progress in Human Geography*, vol. 37, no. 1, pp. 10–26.

Spaargaren, G, Lamers, M & Weenink, D 2016, 'Introduction: using practice theory to research social life', in G Spaargaren, D Weenink & M Lamers (eds), *Practice Theory and Research: Exploring the Dynamics of Social Life*, Routledge, pp. 3–27.

Spurling, N & McMeekin, A 2015, 'Sustainable mobility policies in England', in Y Strengers & C Maller (eds), *Social Practices, Intervention and Sustainability: Beyond Behaviour Change*, Routledge, pp. 78–94.

Strengers, Y 2012, 'Peak electricity demand and social practice theories: reframing the role of change agents in the energy sector', *Energy Policy*, vol. 44, pp. 226–234.

Strengers, Y 2013, *Smart Energy Technologies in Everyday Life: Smart Utopia?*, Palgrave Macmillan.

Strengers, Y & Maller, C 2012, 'Materialising energy and water resources in everyday practices: insights for securing supply systems', *Global Environmental Change*, vol. 22, no. 3, pp. 754–763.

Strengers, Y & Maller, C 2015a, 'Introduction: social practices, intervention and sustainability, beyond behaviour change', in Y Strengers & C Maller (eds), *Social Practices, Intervention and Sustainability: Beyond Behaviour Change*, Routledge, pp. 1–12.

Strengers, Y & Maller, C (eds) 2015b, *Social Practices, Intervention and Sustainability: Beyond Behaviour Change*, Routledge.

Strengers, Y, Nicholls, L & Maller, C 2016, 'Curious energy consumers: humans and nonhumans in assemblages of household practice', *Journal of Consumer Culture*, vol. 16, no. 3, pp. 761–780.

Supski, S, Lindsay, J & Tanner, C 2016, 'University students' drinking as a social practice and the challenge for public health', *Critical Public Health*, pp. 1–10.

Thrift, N 2008, *Non-representational Theory: Space, Politics, Affect*, Taylor & Francis.

Walker, G 2015, 'Beyond individual responsibility: social practice, capabilities and the right to environmentally sustainable ways of living', in Y Strengers & C Maller (eds), *Social Practices, Intervention and Sustainability: Beyond Behaviour Change*, Routledge, pp. 45–60.

Walker, G, Shove, E & Brown, S 2014, 'How does air conditioning become "needed"? A case study of routes, rationales and dynamics', *Energy Research & Social Science*, vol. 4, pp. 1–9.

Wallenborn, G & Wilhite, H 2014, 'Rethinking embodied knowledge and household consumption', *Energy Research & Social Science*, vol. 1, pp. 56–64.

Warde, A 2005, 'Consumption and theories of practice', *Journal of Consumer Culture*, vol. 5, no. 2, pp. 131–153.

Warde, A 2014, 'After taste: culture, consumption and theories of practice', *Journal of Consumer Culture*, vol. 14, no. 3, pp. 279–303.

Warde, A, Cheng, S-L, Olsen, W & Southerton, D 2007, 'Changes in the practice of eating: a comparative analysis of time-use', *Acta Sociologica*, vol. 50, no. 4, pp. 363–385.

Watson, M 2012, 'How theories of practice can inform transition to a decarbonised transport system', *Journal of Transport Geography*, vol. 24, pp. 488–496.

Watson, M 2017, 'Placing power in practice theory', in A Hui, TR Schatzki & E Shove (eds), *The Nexus of Practices: Connections, Constellations, Practitioners*, Routledge, pp. 169–182.

Wetherell, M 2012, *Affect and Emotion: A New Social Science Understanding*, SAGE Publications.

World Health Organization 1986, 'Ottawa Charter for Health Promotion', paper presented to *International Conference on Health Promotion: The Move Towards a New Public Health*, Ottawa, 17–21 November.

Part II

Making more-than-human healthy urban environments

Turning to the practical implications of this book, Part II uses the ideas and theories of the three turns presented in Part I to reconceptualise health and well-being in cities as more-than-human. It also shows how more-than-human theories can help rethink how to make cities more-than-human habitat. The former is the subject of Chapter 5, while cities as more-than-human habitat is covered in Chapter 6. Chapters 5 and 6 address the book's second aim: to open ways of thinking, knowing and understanding cities and urban environments as more-than-human habitat. Building on the more-than-human framings of health and cities, as argued in Chapters 5 and 6, Chapter 7 takes innovative more-than-human methods and ideas for changing research and policymaking practices to transform the way we think about, know, live and change cities. This chapter addresses the third aim of the book, which is to encourage experimentation with new concepts and ideas from a more-than-human perspective and to think about intervening for change differently, accepting there will be unpredictable or unforeseen outcomes.

5   Understanding health as more-than-human

Introduction

This chapter turns its attention to human health and well-being in urban environments to reconceptualise health using the more-than-human theories of Part I. Despite its initial appearances of being overly humanist, my interest in human health is an entry point for the book's overtly more-than-human agenda to see, know and understand the non-humans who make and remake cities in general, and more particularly, healthy urban environments. Specifically, thinking about human health as more-than-human is a useful way to contemplate the book's second aim: to open ways of thinking, knowing and understanding cities and urban environments as more-than-human habitat. There are several reasons for this. First, starting with humans and their health is pragmatic because of the way healthy urban environments have been conceptualised in the past, and continue to be positioned in global initiatives like the Sustainable Development Goals (United Nations 2016). It is also consistent with, and therefore able to connect to, the dominance of human-centric and essentialist thought in urban planning, public health and policymaking, as well as many other domains of modernist thought (Latour 2012). Second, focusing on human health is a self-interested approach to understanding more-than-human ideas because it may not only lead to new ways think about and improve human health and well-being, but also the conditions and quality of urban environments, their sustainability and impacts on non-humans. Despite decades of environmental activism, campaigns and other strategies, humans are still causing vast amounts of pollution and are destroying ecosystems at unprecedented levels (Ripple et al. 2017). Bennett (2010, pp. 110–111) makes a similar point when she wonders 'whether environmentalism remains the best way to frame the problems' like over-consumption and sustainability, and 'would a discursive shift from environmentalism to vital materialism enhance the prospects for a more sustainability-oriented public?' Third, thinking about health leads to the question of 'healthy for whom?' In unpacking this question, the default definition of 'whom' would usually refer to various groups of people and variations in socio-economic or other variables. Consistent with my aim in this book, I argue that living non-humans should also be considered as both recipients and creators of healthy urban environments. In other words, the point of reframing health as more-than-human is to critique the notion of healthy urban environments being only about people. Rather, to be considered healthy, urban environments must be eco-centric urban places.

As highlighted in Chapter 1, despite calling for paradigm shifts, current ideas for creating more liveable cities and healthier urban environments suffer from limited or reductionist understandings of everyday interactions and encounters in urban places. Significantly, these ingrained ways of thinking about the world ask the same questions and rely on the same methods (Kaika 2017) that have been unsuccessful in delivering the sustainable development sought by global initiatives. These include the Brundtland Report (Brundtland 1987), and the health for all visualised in the Ottawa Charter (World Health Organization 1986b) and the Healthy Cities Programme.[1] Looking more closely at how human health is understood in the context of urban environments, the first section of this chapter reviews current ways of thinking, including the social determinants of health, health promotion and ecological health perspectives. In discussing these mainstream ideas, I draw on work that intersects with policymaking, planning and urban design. The concluding section discusses some of the limitations of how human health in urban environments is currently conceived, and more particularly, how current understandings of health could transcend healthy/ unhealthy and agency/structure binaries and be conceived of as more-than-human.

The second half of the chapter reframes human health in urban settings using more-than-human thinking. Familiar activities such as walking and running, usually framed as behaviours, are used to illustrate how health could be recast as arising from practices dependent on the many non-humans that comprise everyday life. Four types of human–non-human interaction that affect health are considered:

- the materials and materialities that make up urban infrastructure, such as roads and paths;
- the co-presence and habitation of living non-humans in cities such as trees;
- the close interactions and practices carried out between humans and plants or animals;
- close interactions and practices carried out between humans and technologies, 'apps' and robots.

Although I focus on the positive outcomes of a more-than-human approach to health, it is equally important to acknowledge the potential negative outcomes, as not all human–non-human relations are beneficial or wanted. For both humans and living non-humans, there is the potential for ill-health and harm via disease transmission, conflict and violence, and other environmental and ecosystem impacts.

A final note, by way of introduction: while the chapter explicates theories of practice as the 'lead' theory, other contributions from the more-than-human theories presented in Chapters 2 and 3 augment the argument.

Current ideas of urban health

Although it has long been recognised that the planning and design of cities affects health and well-being, the fact that most people now live in cities has intensified interest in urban health issues. This section briefly reviews two ways of understanding urban health, starting with the social determinants of health, followed by socio-ecological or ecological models of health.

The social determinants of health and health promotion

Moving beyond biomedical understandings and an illness-focus, urban health is often conceptualised as the relations between people and the environments in which they live, understood through ideas such as the social or environmental determinants of health (Baum 2008; Bentley 2014; Wilkinson & Marmot 1998). The social determinants approach recognises that people's social and economic circumstances and histories are often beyond individual control, but have a profound effect on health status, well-being and longevity (Wilkinson & Marmot 1998). Although lists vary, there are usually ten recognised determinants of health: the social gradient, stress, early life, social exclusion, work, unemployment, social support, addiction, food and transportation. Spread across a range of policy domains, the determinants approach seeks to spread responsibility outwards from the health and medical sector to address the conditions in which health is created (Wilkinson & Marmot 1998).[2]

A closely related approach that tackles urban health is health promotion. In this modality, health is understood to be more than simply the absence of disease. Instead, it is 'a state of complete physical, mental, and social wellbeing' (World Health Organization 1946, p. 1). Health promotion is enabling people to have greater control over their health, and like the social determinants approach, it also seeks to put health on the agenda of policy makers in all sectors, not just health (World Health Organization 1986b). As explained in Chapter 1 (Box 1.1), in 1986, the first conference on health promotion was held in Ottawa, Canada. As a call to arms, the Ottawa Charter was an agreement created and endorsed by delegates, and included, among other aims, the goal of creating 'health for all' by the year 2000. A series of actions were listed, as well as recognition of various health prerequisites. These included: peace, shelter, education, food, income, a stable ecosystem, sustainable resources, social justice and equity (World Health Organization 1986b). In other words, like the social determinants, there was a formal recognition of the social and environmental conditions in which health is created and sustained.

There are two main approaches in health promotion. The first targets policies and programmes to create health through improving social, economic and environmental conditions, and the second is to strengthen the skills of individuals, usually through behaviour change or related approaches. Typically, when faced with complex, multisector and increasingly politicised problems such as obesity, lack of physical activity, pollution and over-consumption of fat and sugar, much attention and effort has been directed towards individuals and their behaviour (Baum 2008; Lindsay 2010). As Frohlich et al. (2001, pp. 783–784) observe, in most traditional health research, 'behaviours are studied independently of the social context, in isolation from other individuals, and as practices devoid of social meaning'. One reason for this is that any attempt to construct an all-encompassing model of health and well-being means that complexity can become an excuse for inaction (Rayner 2009). Instead there is a resort to 'lifestyle drift', the 'tendency for policy to start off recognising the need for action on upstream social determinants of health inequalities only to drift downstream to focus largely on individual lifestyle factors' (Popay et al. 2010, p. 148). It is unfortunate that such behavioural explanations for health and well-being dominate much public health policy in a healthy cities context (Delormier et al. 2009). These explanations harmfully isolate humans from the social determinants while simultaneously blaming them for their health status due to 'poor' attitudes, behaviour or choices (Coutts et al. 2014; Petersen et al. 2010). They also ignore the many more-than-human dimensions that underpin human health and well-being, as this chapter will explain.

Ecological models of health and well-being

Other typical attempts to better understand the social and environmental dimensions of health originate from socio-ecological or ecological models, also developed in the 1980s and 1990s (Bentley 2014). These models see individual people embedded within larger social and natural systems, and describe interactive and reinforcing characteristics that underlie health outcomes (Hancock 1985; 1993).[3] Ecological models seek to prioritise or elevate nature more than the social determinants of health and health promotion approaches, thereby redressing a neglected aspect of the Ottawa Charter, as Hancock (2011, p. ii168) argues: 'the health of our ecosystems is in fact – and always has been – THE most important determinant of the health and wellbeing of the Earth's [human] population'. Broader than the simple inclusion of nature, ecological models draw on principles of social justice and environmental values, such as those from the Earth Charter. These include conviviality, described as respect and care for the entire 'community of life'; equity or social and economic justice; sustainability, which implies the ecological integrity of urban systems; and global responsibility based on principles of democracy, non-violence and peace (Bentley 2014, p. 531; Kickbusch 1989).

I briefly review a few typical ecological models here, as most share common characteristics. The first and most common model is the Mandala of Health, initially developed by Hancock and Perkins (Hancock 1985; Hancock & Perkins 1985) and later expanded by Hancock (1993) (Figure 5.1). It depicts nested circles or spheres of humans, community, the built environment, culture and the biosphere to represent the determinants of health. As Hancock (1993, p. 42 after Dansereau 1966) explains: 'human ecology is the interaction of culture with environment'. A key feature of the Mandala was that it aimed to address all dimensions of health and well-being through multiple strategies and multi-disciplinary approaches. Anticipating that the model might be interpreted as fixed or unresponsive, Hancock (1993, p. 42) claims the model is 'a dynamic three-dimensional model in which the various elements "change" in shape and size according to their relative importance over time and in different communities'.

To assist in capturing this dynamism, Hancock (1993) also designed two complementary models to accompany the Mandala of Health, each with three intersecting circles. The second model was designed to foreground or prioritise human development that is socially and environmentally equitable for present and future generations. It has three intersecting circles: health,

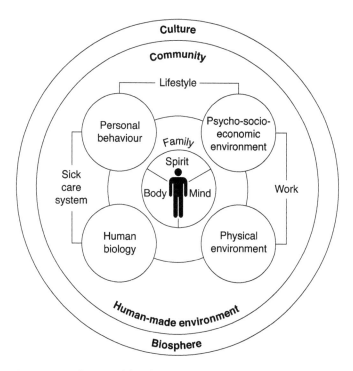

Figure 5.1 The Mandala of Health

Source: Reprinted from Hancock (1993, p. 42) with permission from Oxford University Press.

environment, economy (Hancock 1993). The third model aimed to integrate health, social and community well-being, and environmental sustainability with economic vitality, recognising the need for a holistic, multisectoral approach. Its three interlocking circles are community, environment and economy (Hancock 1993). All three models were designed to be integrated, although exactly how and when each would be most useful is unclear.

Socio-ecological or ecological approaches and models for urban health still hold currency because nature, or the health of ecosystems, has received little attention in health promotion and public health more broadly (Coutts et al. 2014; Hartig et al. 2014). However, some recent health scholarship has started to converge or connect with ideas found in more-than-human thinking – recognised as the 'evolving ecological public health paradigm' (Coutts et al. 2014, p. 1006). For example, acknowledging the dependency of humans on nature, Coutts et al. (2014, p. 1006) comment: 'until somewhat recently, our ecological models have not fully reflected the complex ecological nature of humans as inseparable from the natural environment'. Similarly in advocating the decentring of humans in urban environments, Bentley argues: 'the challenge for the twenty-first century is crafting an ecological public health' that 'acknowledges *humans as part of the ecosystem*, not separate from it and not central to it' (2014, p. 529; emphasis added). Regardless of their orientation towards nature and recognition of the need to decentre humans, people remain central in current ecological models, and this inadvertently maintains the human/nature binary, among other problems.

Limitations of current approaches to understanding urban health

Although ecological paradigms and conceptualisations are a useful starting point for understanding how cities affect human health and well-being, they are limited in their capacity to bring about change or radically challenge the status quo, to enable cities to truly be thought of as more-than-human habitat. This is evident from the fact that despite being in existence for more than 30 years – together with the recognition of the importance of 'the environment' in calls to arms such as the Ottawa Charter and, more recently, in the New Urban Agenda – very little has changed in the way cities are conceived and how public health and urban planning understand the health and well-being of urban human inhabitants and their dependence on, and embeddedness, in nature.

There are three principal critiques of current thinking about urban health that apply to the social determinant and ecological models. First, the centrality of humans is not thoroughly questioned or interrogated. This is not surprising considering the humanist mandate of public health, also common to disciplines such as urban planning. Maintaining a (westernised) humanist focus, however, precludes other ways of understanding and knowing the world and inhibits innovative thinking required to tackle urban problems

(Connell 2007). Particularly, as discussed in Part I, the assumed superiority of text and language together with adherence to universalised representational methodologies are maintained at the expense of affects (Chapter 2), materiality and material relations (Chapter 3) and practices (Chapter 4), which are largely ignored.

Second, concepts and tools, such as the social determinants and ecological models of health, cannot escape criticisms of dualism and segmentation that, despite intentions, separate nature from culture, among other divisions. For example, the artificial divisions between various levels or layers of 'environment', 'behaviour' and 'community' (Figure 5.1) are often poorly explained, and result in opaque interactions between the given layers and, as acknowledged by Hancock (1993), are misleadingly thought of as fixed or static. In fact, despite good intentions, macro models and concepts reveal little about how health and well-being are created and experienced on an everyday basis. As described in Chapter 2, the categories represented in these models can also be selectively applied to positivist and representational agendas, leading to idealised measurement approaches, such as social or environmental indicators, rather than looking at processes and networks (Kaika 2017). The centring of individuals in these models also supports neoliberal agendas (Coutts et al. 2014; Petersen & Lupton 1996) and tendencies to resort to lifestyle drift (Popay et al. 2010), where poor health outcomes are blamed on people rather than the social and environmental conditions in which they live.

Third, aside from ecological health paradigms, in current thinking about urban health, 'nature' or 'the environment' is described in universal and homogenous terms and also problematised as passive, or lacking in agency (Cronon 1996) (see also Chapter 3 on new materialisms). Regarding urban contexts, Kaika (2017, p. 91) captures this idea by stating: 'we keep treating nature as if it were something that could be injected into cities in the form of parks or green roofs, [or] an aesthetic artefact'.

Conflating all animal and plant species, landscapes and ecosystems into the macro category of 'nature' cannot capture the myriad ways human health and well-being are affected by various parts and types of ecosystems (Coutts & Hahn 2015). For example, despite a large body of evidence on a range of health benefits derived from contact with nature (broadly defined), it is unclear how various levels of biodiversity in cities might be beneficial, or harmful, to human residents because 'we know little about which aspects of biodiversity trigger the positive human wellbeing benefits reported in studies to date' (Pett et al. 2016, p. 578).

These problems show that trying to come up with a model sophisticated enough to encapsulate the many complex aspects of human health and well-being in cities is a challenging task, and why extant models, notwithstanding their good intentions (and popularity), continue to appear reductionist and suffer from the limitations mentioned. To their credit, it is important to recognise that no model can be a complete or true representation – it will always be spatially and temporally constrained. This conundrum indicates that it is timely to move away from models and representations as they are currently understood towards the ideas found in more-than-human theories. As discussed in Part I, these can lead to alternative ways of understanding human health and well-being, and connect to a richer understanding of healthy urban environments.

A more-than-human approach to health

As introduced in Chapter 4, theories of social practice, as the lead more-than-human approach motivating this book, have enormous potential to 'reinvent' health promotion (Baum 2008, p. 457). Aside from addressing some of the limitations of current ways of thinking about health in urban settings described above, practice theories help reconceptualise health because they collapse structure and agency, see health as the product of the practices of everyday life rather than individual behaviours (or the sole responsibility of individuals) and connect with ideas of 'working upstream' to create the conditions for health instead of focusing 'downstream' on illness (World Health Organization 1986a). From a practice theory perspective, health is therefore understood as the result of participation in a set of social practices rather than 'healthy' or 'unhealthy' behaviours (i.e., individual agency), or because of external factors or context (e.g., structures bearing down on agents or people) (Blue et al. 2016; Frohlich et al. 2001; Maller 2015).

Using dichotomous labels such as 'healthy' and 'unhealthy' perpetuates binaries of 'good' and 'bad', simplifies much of the complexity and diversity created by the routines of everyday life (Maller 2015), and ignores the notion that practices are materially interwoven with one another to create complexes, bundles and nexuses (Hui et al. 2017; Shove et al. 2012). Of course, there may be some obvious practices that have more direct and clear implications for human health, such as practices related to food consumption and physical activity. However, there are impacts of other practices that may not be as obvious, for example driving to work, socialising or working seated at a desk all day. Overall, using theories of social practice, health is the product of participation in entire sets of practices, complexes and bundles (Maller 2015). This more-than-human, relational take on health contrasts starkly with one that is solely focused on the actions of individual people and their 'healthy' or 'unhealthy' attitudes, behaviours and choices – or what might be termed the 'ABC' of health (after Shove 2010b). Such ABC approaches ignore the environmental context, materiality and the myriad non-humans that comprise cities. Even when environments and non-humans are acknowledged, they are framed insufficiently – but perhaps conveniently – as external or contextual factors (Maller 2015; Shove 2010a).

Every practice can potentially have both positive and negative impacts on human health (especially over the long term), and practices compete for limited resources like time, with each day only having so many hours available for activity (Pantzar & Shove 2010). For instance, the practice 'complex' of working long hours and commuting over large distances between home and work means that little time is left in the day for other practices such as physical activity or cooking (Maller et al. 2016). As Pantzar and Shove (2010, p. 19) explain, 'the integration, sequence and synchronicity between social practices define, constitute and reproduce the rhythmic ordering of daily life'. A more-than-human understanding of health also considers the actions, presence and roles of non-humans in everyday lives – things like animals, plants, the weather, roads, lights and technologies, and the ways in which they are experienced spatially, temporally and sensorily as elements of practices (Maller et al. 2016), or even as co-performers of practices (Maller & Strengers in press).

Figure 5.2 illustrates the practice of neighbourhood walking using the elements described by Shove et al. (2012) introduced in Chapter 4. Here, certain materials are required or experienced (e.g., roads, clothing, grass, trees), as well as skills or competences (e.g., how to cross roads, knowing where to go) and lastly, a reason to walk (e.g., running an errand, getting 'out and about' or being able to observe animal and plants). The combination and integration of elements comprising different varieties practices of walking vary according to the various non-humans involved, people, times and places.

Meanings: someone to walk with (dogs, people), having 'me-time', to be healthy, get some exercise, get 'out and about', going to a destination, going on an errand, appreciating and observing plants, birds, animals, experiencing weather

Materials/materiality: tracks, paths, roads, pedestrian lights, clothing, dog leads and gear, a destination (e.g., shops/parks/waterways), wind, rain, sun, grass, trees, allergens

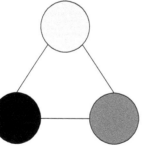

Competences: knowing where to walk, how to get there, choosing among routes, time management, how to cross roads and overcome obstacles, wearing appropriate clothing, dog handling competences

Figure 5.2 The practice of neighbourhood walking, with examples of meanings, materials and competences

Source: Adapted from Shove et al. (2012, p. 29) with permission from SAGE Publications.
Note: This example was developed from some research funded by the Victorian Health Promotion Foundation (VicHealth), supported by Stockland, the City of Casey, the Metropolitan Planning Authority (Victorian Government) and RMIT University. For further details, see Maller and Nicholls (2016) and Maller et al. (2016).

At any given moment, if one or more elements of the practice are changed, missing, unavailable and unable to be substituted, it is less likely that the practice of walking will be performed (Maller & Strengers 2013). For example, if it begins to rain or the season changes, the practice may be postponed or cancelled (Maller et al. 2016), or it may be substituted with another practice (Maller & Strengers 2013). Elements have properties of connectivity whereby they connect practices, bundles and complexes through various material arrangements (Schatzki 2002). Many materials are physically connected in time and space and are used in multiple, related practices (e.g., bike-paths may be shared or conjoined with paths that support practices of dog-walking and running).

Considering materials and materiality in more detail, it is easy to think of clothing and equipment as material elements of practices, but it is less common to conceive the features of urban environments as elements. However, roads and paths are vital materials or surfaces without which physical activity, such as running or walking, would not take place or would take place differently. These non-humans in urban environments also shape and mould bodies, with various materials and surfaces impacting bodies in a variety of ways. For example, running or walking on grass compared to asphalt, concrete, gravel or a running track changes how muscles, sinews, tissues and bones respond to maintain balance and momentum, prevent injury and build strength.[4] As practice performances are repeated, bones can become denser, muscles and sinews strengthen, and there are metabolic and other system changes so that over time the body is transformed (Wainwright & Turner 2006). Such materialities also have implications when accidents or injuries are sustained, such as falling off a bike on the road compared to a grassy surface.

In addition to the specific qualities of materials, there are other health and well-being benefits arising from practices involving living non-humans, such as animals and plants. Despite nuances still being worked through (Coutts & Hahn 2015; Pett et al. 2016), it is now widely accepted that there are numerous human health and well-being benefits associated with the presence of various types of living non-humans in urban environments. For example, tree cover in urban areas is associated with lower rates of obesity, improved social cohesion, and fewer incidences of type 2 diabetes, high blood pressure and asthma (Ulmer et al. 2016). Views of parks are also associated with reduced stress and higher life satisfaction (Honold et al. 2016). Interacting with other species is known to bring even more benefits, including to physical, psychological and mental health (Fawcett & Gullone 2001; Maller et al. 2006; Soulsbury & White 2016; Wood et al. 2007). Through practices of care and co-habitation, companion animals have various positive impacts on human health, including reduced blood pressure, increased physical activity levels and better self-esteem (Amiot et al. 2016). As evidence for the profound effects animals can have on humans, some dogs, with their human carers, are engaged as 'animal therapists' (Amiot et al. 2016, p. 556).

co-performing therapy in visits to nursing homes to provide stress relief and companionship; this results in improved emotional states and quality of life for human residents (Sollami et al. 2017). Caring for plants through gardening has been shown to have similar positive impacts, including improving mood (Wood et al. 2016) and providing physical, nutritional and social benefits (Sanchez & Liamputtong 2017). Practices of caring that involve animals and plants are, in fact, a good beginning to comprehend the many relations and entanglements humans have with non-humans in everyday life (see Chapter 6). However, through its more comprehensive aims related to healthy urban environments, this book presents a set of deeper arguments for caring for living non-humans in cities.

Besides practices involving living animals and plants, there are other practices with non-living non-humans that similarly open and shift thinking towards a more-than-human position. Although some non-humans that people regularly encounter are not alive, they can respond and interact with humans in numerous life-like ways. These include the artificial intelligence of digital assistants and health 'apps' on mobile phones or tablets (e.g., McMillan et al. 2016; Powell et al. 2017), and the various and increasingly smart appliances commonly found in homes. These include 'smart' fridges that inform you when food stocks are low (Hachani et al. 2016) or even entire 'smart' homes filled with devices that intend to make human lives more convenient, pleasant and energy-saving and less labour-intensive (Hargreaves et al. 2018; Strengers & Nicholls 2017). Among other recent developments, socially assistive robots have begun to be used in nursing homes and other therapeutic settings where living animals which may normally co-perform these practices may be at risk. Instead, 'pet' robots co-perform caring practices, interacting with elderly patients to reduce stress levels and reliance on pain medication (Petersen et al. 2017).

Although there are many reported benefits from urban non-human–human interactions, there are also risks to human health, harms, unintended consequences and negative health impacts for non-humans – which may also be ethically questionable (Amiot et al. 2016; Soulsbury & White 2016; Strengers & Nicholls 2017; Strengers et al. 2016; Taylor et al. 2016). For example, in animal-assisted therapy scenarios, the needs of animals may be overlooked in pursuit of human therapeutic outcomes, resulting in animal stress and decreased health and welfare (Taylor et al. 2016). Domestic pets have been associated with the transmission of infectious diseases and parasites between humans and animals, as well as injury from bites (Amiot et al. 2016), and pets can be subject to domestic violence (Newberry 2016), inadequate care and human-centric rules and regulations. Moreover, regarding other non-human agents, instead of saving energy and time, smart homes have been found to create new forms of household labour and are overall more likely to increase energy consumption (Hargreaves et al. 2018; Strengers & Nicholls 2017). In sum, these examples provide further evidence that humans need to be more cognisant of the myriad non-humans in everyday life, understand their practices and relations, both beneficial and harmful, and consider what these practices mean for making healthy urban environments from a more-than-human stance. Hence, more-than-human theories can offer new ways of thinking about human health and can help us understand how urban environments and their health impacts are negotiated, experienced, made and remade by relations between humans and non-humans.

As the first step to thinking about healthy cities as more-than-human, this chapter reframed the concept of health in more-than-human terms. Initially, non-humans may be considered important only regarding their capacity to impact humans and their health and well-being. However, using human health to take the initial move towards more-than-human framings of healthy urban environments leads to the second step – to consider living non-humans as actors with capacities for sensing, feeling, responding and acting autonomously in the world. At the most basic level, this shift in perspective views non-humans as having agencies and co-producing or co-performing practices that affect human and non-human 'health', rather than merely being a passive backdrop or resource. This agency is most apparent when a practice involves living non-humans, such as animals and plants. As explained further in Chapter 6, in gardening and pet-keeping, plants, animals and humans are shaped by, and shape, these practices and relations with each other through lively, regularly carried out performances.

Conclusion

This chapter showed how more-than-human thinking can reconceptualise health in urban settings to move beyond the failings of the social determinants and other current understandings. It has shown new ways of understanding how human health might be created in urban places through a more detailed and emergent understanding of how places and environments are conceptualised, experienced and formed through multiple relations between people, things, living creatures, infrastructures and technologies. In particular, more-than-human thinking could help resolve some of the problems with current understandings of human health by collapsing structure/agency, healthy/unhealthy and other binaries, moving beyond an individual focus or 'lifestyle drift' to incorporate the roles of materials, materialities, living and non-living non-humans and their relations across space and time, and account for the complexity of everyday life that ecological and similar models have struggled to capture. Using social practices and more-than-human thinking enriches, and could dramatically shift, current perspectives on urban health and provide fruitful new avenues for planners, policymakers and others seeking to improve health outcomes, equity and the liveability of cities (see Chapter 7).

Ultimately, conceiving health as more-than-human could help achieve the aims of earlier declarations, such as the Ottawa Charter, the Brundtland

Report, the Healthy Cities Programme and their reincarnation respectively in the United Nations' New Urban Agenda and Sustainable Development Goals. However, there is an urgent need to rethink cities and who they are for beyond humans. Chapter 6 explores cities as more-than-human habitat.

Notes

1 See Chapter 1.
2 See Wilkinson and Marmot (1998) for full descriptions, and Wilkinson and Marmot (2003) for evidence.
3 See Coutts et al. (2014) for an overview of various ecological models of health.
4 See Wainwright and Turner's (2006) work on how dancers' bodies change over time in response to the materiality of surfaces.

References

Amiot, C, Bastian, B & Martens, P 2016, 'People and companion animals: it takes two to tango', *BioScience*, vol. 66, no. 7, pp. 552–560.

Baum, F 2008, 'The Commission on the Social Determinants of Health: reinventing health promotion for the twenty-first century?', *Critical Public Health*, vol. 18, no. 4, pp. 457–466.

Bennett, J 2010, *Vibrant Matter: A Political Ecology of Things*, Duke University Press.

Bentley, M 2014, 'An ecological public health approach to understanding the relationships between sustainable urban environments, public health and social equity', *Health Promotion International*, vol. 29, no. 3, pp. 528–537.

Blue, S, Shove, E, Carmona, C & Kelly, MP 2016, 'Theories of practice and public health: understanding (un)healthy practices', *Critical Public Health*, vol. 26, no. 1, pp. 36–50.

Brundtland, GH 1987, *Our Common Future: Report of the United Nations World Commission on Environment and Development*, Oxford University Press.

Connell, R 2007, *Southern Theory: The Global Dynamics of Knowledge in Social Science*, Allen & Unwin.

Coutts, C, Forkink, A & Weiner, J 2014, 'The portrayal of natural environment in the evolution of the ecological public health paradigm', *International Journal of Environmental Research and Public Health*, vol. 11, no. 1, p. 1005.

Coutts, C & Hahn, M 2015, 'Green infrastructure, ecosystem services, and human health', *International Journal of Environmental Research and Public Health*, vol. 12, no. 8, p. 9768.

Cronon, W 1996, 'Introduction: in search of nature', in W Cronon (ed.), *Uncommon Ground: Rethinking the Human Place in Nature*, WW Norton, pp. 23–56.

Delormier, T, Frohlich, KL & Potvin, L 2009, 'Food and eating as social practice – understanding eating patterns as social phenomena and implications for public health', *Sociology of Health & Illness*, vol. 31, no. 2, pp. 215–228.

Fawcett, NR & Gullone, E 2001, 'Cute and cuddly and a whole lot more? A call for empirical investigation into the therapeutic benefits of human–animal interaction for children', *Behaviour Change*, vol. 18, no. 2, pp. 124–133.

Frohlich, KL, Corin, E & Potvin, L 2001, 'A theoretical proposal for the relationship between context and disease', *Sociology of Health & Illness*, vol. 23, no. 6, pp. 776–797.

Hachani, A, Barouni, I, Said, ZB & Amamou, L 2016, 'RFID based smart fridge', paper presented to *8th IFIP International Conference on New Technologies, Mobility and Security*, 21–23 November.

Hancock, T 1985, 'The Mandala of Health: a model of the human ecosystem', *Family & Community Health*, vol. 8, no. 3, pp. 1–10.

Hancock, T 1993, 'Health, human development and the community ecosystem: three ecological models', *Health Promotion International*, vol. 8, no. 1, pp. 41–47.

Hancock, T 2011, 'It's the environment, stupid! Declining ecosystem health is THE threat to health in the 21st century', *Health Promotion International*, vol. 26, Supplement 2, pp. ii168–ii172.

Hancock, T & Perkins, F 1985, 'The Mandala of Health: a conceptual model and teaching tool', *Health Education*, vol. 24, no. 1, pp. 8–10.

Hargreaves, T, Wilson, C & Hauxwell-Baldwin, R 2018, 'Learning to live in a smart home', *Building Research & Information*, vol. 46, no. 1, pp. 127–139.

Hartig, T, Mitchell, R, Vries, S & Frumkin, H 2014, 'Nature and health', *Annual Review of Public Health*, vol. 35, no. 1, pp. 207–228.

Honold, J, Lakes, T, Beyer, R & Van der Meer, E 2016, 'Restoration in urban spaces', *Environment and Behavior*, vol. 48, no. 6, pp. 796–825.

Hui, A, Schatzki, TR & Shove, E 2017, *The Nexus of Practices: Connections, Constellations, Practitioners*, Routledge.

Kaika, M 2017, '"Don't call me resilient again!": the New Urban Agenda as immunology . . . or . . . what happens when communities refuse to be vaccinated with "smart cities" and indicators', *Environment and Urbanization*, vol. 29, no. 1, pp. 89–102.

Kickbusch, I 1989, 'Approaches to an ecological base for public health', *Health Promotion*, vol. 4, no. 4, pp. 265–268.

Latour, B 2012, *We Have Never Been Modern*, Harvard University Press.

Lindsay, J 2010, 'Healthy living guidelines and the disconnect with everyday life', *Critical Public Health*, vol. 20, no. 4, pp. 475–487.

Maller, C 2015, 'Understanding health through social practices: performance and materiality in everyday life', *Sociology of Health & Illness*, vol. 37, no. 1, pp. 52–66.

Maller, C & Nicholls, L 2016, *Planning and Designing Healthy New Communities: Selandra Rise – Research Summary*, Victorian Health Promotion Foundation, Melbourne, Australia, https://www.vichealth.vic.gov.au/-/media/ResourceCentre/PublicationsandResources/General/Selandra_Rise_Final_Summary_Report.pdf, accessed 9 February 2018.

Maller, C & Strengers, Y 2013, 'The global migration of everyday life: Investigating the practice memories of Australian migrants', *Geoforum*, vol. 44, pp. 243–252.

Maller, C & Strengers, Y (eds) in press, *Social Practices and Dynamic Non-humans: Nature, Materials and Technologies*, Palgrave Macmillan.

Maller, C, Nicholls, L & Strengers, Y 2016, 'Understanding the materiality of neighbourhoods in "healthy practices": outdoor exercise practices in a new master-planned estate', *Urban Policy and Research: Special Issue on Health*, vol. 34, pp. 55–72.

Maller, C, Townsend, M, Pryor, A, Brown, PR & St Leger, L 2006, 'Healthy parks, healthy people: "contact with nature" as an upstream health promotion intervention for populations', *Health Promotion International*, vol. 21, no. 1, pp. 45–54.

McMillan, KA, Kirk, A, Hewitt, A & MacRury, S 2016, 'A systematic and integrated review of mobile-based technology to promote active lifestyles in people with type 2 diabetes', *Journal of Diabetes Science and Technology*, vol. 11, no. 2, pp. 299–307.

Newberry, M 2016, 'Pets in danger: exploring the link between domestic violence and animal abuse', *Aggression and Violent Behavior*, vol. 34, pp. 273–281.

Pantzar, M & Shove, E 2010, 'Temporal rhythms as outcomes of social practices', *Enthnologia Europaea*, vol. 40, no. 1, pp. 19–29.

Petersen, A & Lupton, D 1996, *The New Public Health: Health and Self in the Age of Risk*, SAGE Publications.

Petersen, A, Davis, M, Fraser, S & Lindsay, J 2010, 'Healthy living and citizenship: an overview', *Critical Public Health*, vol. 20, no. 4, pp. 391–400.

Petersen, S, Houston, S, Qin, H, Tague, C & Studley, J 2017, 'The utilization of robotic pets in dementia care', *Journal of Alzheimer's Disease*, vol. 55, pp. 569–574.

Pett, TJ, Shwartz, A, Irvine, KN, Dallimer, M & Davies, ZG 2016, 'Unpacking the people–biodiversity paradox: a conceptual framework', *BioScience*, vol. 66, no. 7, pp. 576–583.

Popay, J, Whitehead, M & Hunter, DJ 2010, 'Injustice is killing people on a large scale – but what is to be done about it?', *Journal of Public Health*, vol. 32, no. 2, pp. 148–149.

Powell, AC, Chen, M & Thammachart, C 2017, 'The economic benefits of mobile apps for mental health and telepsychiatry services when used by adolescents', *Child and Adolescent Psychiatric Clinics of North America*, vol. 26, no. 1, pp. 125–133.

Rayner, G 2009, 'Conventional and ecological public health', *Public Health*, vol. 123, no. 9, pp. 587–591.

Ripple, WJ, Wolf, C, Newsome, TM, Galetti, M, Alamgir, M, Crist, E, Mahmoud, MI & Laurance, WF 2017, 'World scientists' warning to humanity: a second notice', *BioScience*, vol. 67, no. 12, pp. 1026–1028.

Sanchez, EL & Liamputtong, P 2017, 'Community gardening and health-related benefits for a rural Victorian town', *Leisure Studies*, vol. 36, no. 2, pp. 269–281.

Schatzki, TR 2002, *The Site of the Social: A Philosophical Account of the Constitution of Social Life and Change*, Pennsylvania State University Press.

Shove, E 2010a, 'Beyond the ABC: climate change policy and theories of social change', *Environment and Planning A*, vol. 42, pp. 1273–1285.

Shove, E 2010b, 'Social theory and climate change: questions often, sometimes and not yet asked', *Theory, Culture & Society*, vol. 27, nos 2–3, pp. 277–288.

Shove, E, Pantzar, M & Watson, M 2012, *The Dynamics of Social Practice: Everyday Life and How It Changes*, SAGE Publications.

Sollami, A, Gianferrari, E, Alfieri, M, Artioli, G & Taffurelli, C 2017, 'Pet therapy: an effective strategy to care for the elderly? An experimental study in a nursing home', *Acta Bio Medica*, vol. 88, no. 1, pp. 25–31.

Soulsbury, CD & White, PCL 2016, 'Human–wildlife interactions in urban areas: a review of conflicts, benefits and opportunities', *Wildlife Research*, vol. 42, no. 7, pp. 541–553.

Strengers, Y & Nicholls, L 2017, 'Convenience and energy consumption in the smart home of the future: industry visions from Australia and beyond', *Energy Research & Social Science*, vol. 32, Supplement C, pp. 86–93.

Strengers, Y, Nicholls, L & Maller, C 2016, 'Curious energy consumers: humans and nonhumans in assemblages of household practice', *Journal of Consumer Culture*, vol. 16, no. 3, pp. 761–780.

Taylor, N, Fraser, H, Signal, T & Prentice, K 2016, 'Social work, animal-assisted therapies and ethical considerations: a programme example from Central Queensland, Australia', *British Journal of Social Work*, vol. 46, no. 1, pp. 135–152.

Ulmer, JM, Wolf, KL, Backman, DR, Tretheway, RL, Blain, CJA, O'Neil-Dunne, JPM & Frank, LD 2016, 'Multiple health benefits of urban tree canopy: the mounting evidence for a green prescription', *Health & Place*, vol. 42, pp. 54–62.

United Nations 2016, *Sustainable Development Goals*, www.un.org/sustainable development/sustainable-development-goals/, accessed 23 June 2017.

Wainwright, SP & Turner, BS 2006, '"Just crumbling to bits"? An exploration of the body, ageing, injury and career in classical ballet dancers', *Sociology*, vol. 40, no. 2, pp. 237–255.

Wilkinson, R & Marmot, M (eds) 1998, *Social Determinants of Health: The Solid Facts*, World Health Organization.

Wilkinson, R & Marmot, M (eds) 2003, *Social Determinants of Health: The Solid Facts*, World Health Organization.

Wood, CJ, Pretty, J & Griffin, M 2016, 'A case-control study of the health and well-being benefits of allotment gardening', *Journal of Public Health*, vol. 38, no. 3, pp. e336–e344.

Wood, LJ, Giles-Corti, B, Bulsara, MK & Bosch, D 2007, 'More than a furry companion: the ripple effect of companion animals on neighborhood interactions and sense of community', *Society and Animals*, vol. 15, pp. 43–56.

World Health Organization 1946, *Constitution of the World Health Organization*, World Health Organization.

World Health Organization 1986a, 'Ottawa Charter for Health Promotion', paper presented to *International Conference on Health Promotion: The Move Towards a New Public Health*, Ottawa, 17–21 November.

World Health Organization 1986b, *The Ottawa Charter for Health Promotion*, World Health Organization, Health and Welfare Canada, and Canadian Public Health Association, www.who.int/healthpromotion/conferences/previous/ottawa/en/, accessed 11 May 2016.

6 Cities as more-than-human habitat

Introduction

In this book, I make the case that we need to rethink cities and who they are for. In Chapter 1, I defined 'healthy urban environments' as places – or habitats – that benefit, and are healthy for, humans and (some) living non-humans. Chapter 5 explained how human health could be conceptualised as more-than-human; this chapter focuses on urban animals[1] and plants, exploring the various ways cities provision, are utilised by and benefit a range of species, including humans. With the human population continuing to grow, the subsequent increase in urbanisation places further pressure on ecosystems and ensuing health affects, and there is an urgent need to question human exceptionalism (Franklin 2007; Houston et al. 2017; Wolch 1996) and reframe cities as habitat for more than just humans. Humans can no longer – and must not be – the only urban 'beings that count' (Whatmore 2002, p. 155). In highlighting the inherent more-than-humanness of cities and the paucity of standard binary categories, Swyngedouw (1996, p. 66) argues: 'there is nothing "purely" social or natural about the city'.

In support of this idea, there is mounting evidence from conservation biology and urban ecology that cities provide crucial habitat for many species, including some under threat (Garrard & Bekessy 2014; Ives et al. 2016; Kowarik 2011; Low 2003). This evidence calls into question conservation management, planning and other policies that focus on preserving habitat *outside* of urban areas (Garrard & Bekessy 2014; Houston et al. 2017). The idea of 'nature'[2] being not only present, but active in urban places remains controversial because it contests beliefs that cities are separate from nature and primarily for humans, and raises questions about the implications of shifting this stance towards a more-than-human position. However, cities are not necessarily 'against nature' (Head et al. 2014). For example, due to its enormous efforts to create urban habitat for both humans and other species, Singapore is now an excellent example of a 'biophilic city' (Newman 2014).

Drawing on this context that challenges the city/nature divide, this chapter brings more-than-human thinking together with insights about 'human–nature' relations in cities from conservation, urban ecology and human geography. Some of the work in human geography is already steeped in more-than-human ideas, but taking a more systematic view and including broader literature (and evidence) from other disciplines helps to highlight the presence, importance and health outcomes of human–nature relations in urban environments. A more-than-human perspective and (re)interpretation of this literature bring to the fore the many multispecies relations that already characterise urban environments, but are often not seen – or are taken for granted – because, since they are an ordinary part of everyday urban life, they often go unnoticed. This means that non-human species are marginalised, ignored and exploited in urban environments (Hinchliffe et al. 2005; Narayanan 2017; Wolch 1996), a scenario which I argue is detrimental and counter-productive to the achievement of healthy cities.

The first section of the chapter focuses on the ways cities provide habitat for non-human species. Rather than simply being on the receiving end of habitat provision, however, a more-than-human perspective also considers agencies and the variety of ways non-human animals and plants shape and remake cities – how they take advantage of a range of 'habitats', whether intentionally made or provided by humans or not. This section argues that cities are not made, nor made healthy, by humans alone, thereby representing a key step in working towards a more-than-human conceptualisation of cities. Drawing on the more-than-human thinking from Part I (Chapters 2, 3 and 4), the following section explores gardening and wildlife feeding practices as activities that benefit, and are healthy for, humans as well as other living non-humans. It presents evidence from an established body of literature documenting the health benefits of contact with nature and the contributions of urban non-human species to human health and well-being. A more-than-human understanding of gardening and wildlife feeding practices means that the enactment of the 'distinctive agencies' (Head 2016, p. 75) of living non-humans, and their varied relations with humans and other non-humans in everyday life, is a key part of understanding their health outcomes. More-than-human thinking helps to show that seeing, knowing and continuing to live with the animals and plants already extant in cities is a key part of making cities biodiverse, more eco-centric and healthier places for both humans and other species. The final section and conclusion strengthen the case that cities already are more-than-human habitat continually made and remade through entanglements and processes of 'becoming with' (Haraway 2008, p. 4)[3] between humans and innumerable non-humans. Using a more-than-human lens repositions existing knowledge about the benefits of 'nature' in cities which, importantly, can be used to further decentre humans and change the way we think about cities.

Reasons for recentring humans and their health were provided in Chapter 5; however, two further points justify this move. First, humans are an animal species, which, like many others, depend on and make habitats of various kinds. Second, humans are simply one species among many in urban environments, and it is our various relations and entanglements with other species (and other non-humans) in cities that not only make them liveable, but healthy more-than-human habitat.

Cities as habitat for non-human species

Despite their human-centrism and privilege, cities accommodate, provide for and are made by many other forms of life[4]. Although in general cities have been considered degraded and impoverished forms of habitat, this idea is now being questioned as new research shows how some species directly benefit from cities and that others can adapt more readily than previously assumed (Ives et al. 2016; Jones 2002). As Low (2003, pp. 1 and 2) declares: 'we hear so much these days about wildlife dying out as if nature *en masse* were sliding down the drain' whereas in fact 'many native things . . . have never known better times'.

All cities, regardless of their size, geography, degree of urbanisation and density (among other characteristics), provide a range of habitats that can support a surprising array of non-human species. Most obviously, habitat is provided through the creation of greenspaces, parklands, gardens, lawns and other vegetation. Moreover, it is also delivered through built structures, water sources and other substrates or forms of nourishment and protection not necessarily intended for use by, or to benefit, species other than humans. These include homes, offices and buildings (Power 2009; Sumasgutner et al. 2014), landfill and transfer stations, tips, general rubbish or litter (Jones 2002) and waste treatment plants (Low 2003). Some species can thrive in polluted parts of cities avoided by humans, which inadvertently can result in their protection. A good example of this is the endangered green and golden bell frog, discovered in a polluted site during the extensive works undertaken for the 2000 Sydney Olympics (Darcovich & O'Meara 2008).

Other ways cities support non-human species are through indirect means such as road-kill as a source of food for scavengers and, more directly, through human residents supplying nest boxes and feeding birds and mammals in their backyards (Jones 2002; 2018). Once ideas about the purity and idealism of habitat are put aside, cities are unexpectedly rich in the types and forms of habitat they can provide. This is not to diminish or ignore the environmental impact of cities, nor to override the significance of 'intact' or fully functioning ecosystems, remnants, conservation zones or national parks. These forms of habitat are vital and of incredible importance. The point is that binaries of wilderness versus urban or other simplistic conceptualisations of what is and what is not habitat are no longer useful in worlds that have always shaped, and have been shaped by, many diverse lifeforms, including, but not limited to, humans. This is particularly true of the current era acknowledged as 'the Anthropocene', a post-Holocene era denoting the influence (and in many cases, significant alteration) of every ecosystem on the planet by *Homo sapiens* (Steffen et al. 2007; Waters et al. 2016).[5] There is no doubt that these scenarios bring forth a range of largely negative affects (Chapter 2), including dystopian concerns, but also a genuine concern, and even acceptance (Head 2016). Rather than being overlooked or dismissed, the ecological value of urban habitats has been recognised as 'novel ecosystems' (Kowarik 2011; Morse et al. 2014). A novel ecosystem is defined by Morse et al. (2014, p. 12) as created by 'the direct result of intentional or unintentional alteration by humans . . . sufficient to cross an ecological threshold'. Once this threshold has been crossed, it leads to 'a new ecosystem trajectory' that permanently deviates from the previous system (Morse et al. 2014, p. 12).

This shift from purity towards hybridity reflects ideas in a range of disciplines that there is no longer, or in fact ever was, any 'pure' form of nature (Cronon 1996; Head 2016; Low 2003; Marris et al. 2013; Swyngedouw 2006), which also means that humans cannot be distinguished from it. Given the validation of urban environments as habitats, this section reviews some examples of where non-human species have adapted to, and shaped, urban environments in ways that are not always congruent with human-centric ideas about cities. In many geographically dispersed cities where dwellings comprise detached forms of housing in suburban settings, humans are 'remarkably similar to other highly territorial species . . . [and] live in uniform patches of land, with very definite boundaries, within which we construct a local landscape' (Jones 2002, p. 3). With defining characteristics of suburban gardens including lawn, trees and shrubs, these local landscapes are the first place to look for evidence of urban habitat construction and provision, some of which are surprisingly disruptive from a purely human perspective.

Australian brush turkeys are a large mound-building bird from the megapode family. Typically found in moist mountain forests and coasts of Eastern Australia, they occur as far south as the Illawarra region of Sydney (Jones & Goth 2008). Rather than constructing nests in trees, male brush turkeys build large mounds of decomposing leaves and other organic matter for incubating eggs. In more recent times, they have become increasingly common in suburban areas of Brisbane and Sydney; this follows a period of decline when they were hunted by humans, especially during the Great Depression (Jones & Goth 2008). Brush turkeys were first reported in Brisbane in the early 1970s in an area adjacent to a bushland reserve where they seemed to make the transition from their traditional habitat into suburban backyards (Jones & Everding 1991). During this time, there was an increase in the number of Brisbane households engaging in gardening practices, planting and encouraging subtropical rainforest plants in their gardens (see below for a more detailed discussion of human–plant entanglements). The increased access to native plants may have encouraged the birds to urbanise (Jones & Everding 1991).

Undeterred by the expansion of houses accompanied by hungry cats and speeding cars, since the 1980s, the number of brush turkeys in Brisbane has increased dramatically, and a similar pattern is observed in Sydney (Jones et al. 2004; Skatssoon 2009). Once they have decided on a location, these adaptable birds will make use of any suitable organic matter to make their mounds, often scraping up the entire plant communities of suburban gardens into one steaming mound that can weigh 4 tonnes – or the size of a small car (Collerton 2009; Jones & Everding 1991). Such dramatic interventions in garden practices are hard to ignore. Brush turkeys are incredibly difficult to deter and are known to efficiently and doggedly reconstruct a mound, despite repeated attempts by humans to re-rake the mound contents back into something resembling the garden from which it came (Collerton 2009). As well as humans providing suitable mound-building materials from encouraging 'natural' bush gardens to the establishment of rotting compost heaps, outdoor feeding practices of domestic dogs and cats may also inadvertently be providing a supplementary food source as brush turkeys adapt their diet to whatever it is local cats and dogs consume.

Not surprisingly, the presence and activities of brush turkeys in suburbia have not been uniformly welcomed by humans. Local council workers, naturalists and scientists are required to respond to complaints (Skatssoon 2009) where avian and human residents have been caught up in episodes of what is termed 'human–wildlife conflict' (Soulsbury & White 2016). Given their tenacity and ubiquity, the response by councils is to generally encourage acceptance and neighbourly tolerance between humans and birds. This example is one of many that illustrate how species can actively make and remake habitat in an urban setting through demonstrating agencies in multiple more-than-human entanglements, and, overall, benefiting from these interactions.

Other stories of adaptation are found the world over. In the eastern parts of the USA, the white-tailed deer, a native species once hunted by humans to the extent that populations were reduced, has returned with vigour. This is due to the proliferation of suburban gardens that provide food and shelter from predators and hunters because 'their adaptability, acute senses, and other physical attributes allow them to flourish in metropolitan suburbs as well as in the wilderness' (DeNicola et al. 2010, p. 3). The deer have actively made use of the processes of American urbanisation and are now part of several complex more-than-human entanglements where the impacts include both positive and negative affects. Positive affects are associated with the reestablishment of a native animal species considered by human residents as a 'welcome sight' in the suburbs; while negative affects are associated with the 'destruction' of gardens; injuries and costs arising from collisions with vehicles; and the potential transmission of pathogens; for example, the deer host black-legged ticks, the primary vector for the bacteria that causes Lyme disease (DeNicola et al. 2010, pp. 3–4).

Some populations of non-human species, like brush turkeys in Australia and the white-tailed deer in the USA, have flourished from a diminished basis due to their ability to adapt to and profit from urbanisation, particularly the proliferation of suburban backyards and gardens. However, as well as common species, cities all around the world have also been found to house many species at risk of extinction (Ives et al. 2016). The reasons for this include the fact that cities are often founded in areas of high biodiversity (Jones 2018; Luck 2007), and due to the processes of urbanisation homogenising habitats (McKinney 2006), extinction rates can be exacerbated. In the UK, for example, three species of song thrush of conservation concern are now largely restricted to urban or built environments in eastern England due to the rise of industrialised farming practices and the subsequent reduction of their usual habitat (Mason 2000). Instead, the thrushes are making use of housing and gardens, factories, schools and other urbanised areas that include greenspace. These areas are found to have significantly more bird territories than rural areas (Mason 2000).

An Australian plant example is the endangered Nielsen Park she-oak which now occurs exclusively within the metropolitan area of greater Sydney (Ives et al. 2016). Although examples such as this may appear to present evidence for the adaptability and agency of these species, of concern is that their presence in cities 'may represent an "extinction debt"' – a problem associated with newly established cities (Ives et al. 2016). An extinction debt means the threatened species currently found in urban environments, like those mentioned above, may not survive. Consequently, although some cities are 'biodiversity hotspots' (Garrard & Bekessy 2014, p. 63), and suburbs have been found to be more diverse than other forms of habitat, species able to survive and reproduce in urban environments are those that can adapt to 'the rather special conditions and challenges of this new landscape' (Jones 2002, p. 4).

Low (2003) refers to the 'winners' and 'losers' of urbanisation to describe how some non-human species readily adapt to and take advantage of the urbanised city habitats, while others do not. Some adaptations are unexpected, such as species of birds and bats preferring to roost in scraggly trees at busy suburban intersections full of noise and light pollution, rather than relatively intact, 'quiet' forest not too far away (Low 2003). Traffic-centred intersections do not seem ideal forms of habitat according to human understandings of quality, but rethinking this scenario from and with the perspective of a bat or bird – as advocated by more-than-human scholars such as Wolch (1996) and Puig de la Bellacasa (2017) – such places can offer superior protection from predators and more readily available food sources compared to their usual forms of habitat (Low 2003). In other cases, cities can provide stable food and water supplies through gardens and supplementary food provision that are taken advantage of throughout the year changing the overwintering habits of some species, particularly birds (Jones 2002; 2018; Low 2003).

Animals are not the only living non-humans that make and remake cities as habitat. Plants are also active agents, and are increasingly valued as key actors for liveability, sustainability and biodiversity in urban environments. However as Pellegrini and Baudry (2014, p. 876) comment, 'vegetation has always grown in cities, not only in a domestic form as a tool for town planning but also unbidden'. In their study of street vegetation in Paris and Montpellier, the authors studied the persistent plants that occupy tree pits (shallow indented gardens in footpaths where street trees are planted) and other unexpected places. Despite the challenges of competing against traffic and apparently impermeable surfaces, the authors record the 'uncontrolled vegetation which grows in the cracks of the asphalt, between the cobblestones of sidewalks, in street tree pits and flower boxes, [and] on walls' (Pellegrini & Baudry 2014, p. 876). Indicative of how far thinking has come in some disciplines, the capacity of urban plants determined to grow where they should not is known as 'spontaneous flora', and consequently 'hard surfaces are considered as real ecosystems' (Pellegrini & Baudry 2014, p. 877). The authors' notion of 'previously unbidden flora' challenges the assumed static or passive character of cities (Pellegrini & Baudry 2014, p. 873).

These examples provide evidence of the various agencies of non-human species, some of which are quick to adapt to the often rapidly changing circumstances of urban environments, more so than humans usually give them credit. Overall, despite there being 'more of some species and fewer of others' (Jones 2002, p. 2), any adaptations that result in persistence are evidence of the capacities of non-human species to adapt to and materially and affectively shape cities. This refutes the idea they are universally passive recipients or automatic victims of urbanisation.

Urban environments are therefore repositioned as dynamic places constantly being made and remade by humans and other species. Despite being considered 'a strange and diverse environment when viewed as habitat for both wildlife and people' (Jones 2002, p. 3), cities are intense sites and products of more-than-human entanglements. Moreover, these phenomena debunk the idea of human exceptionalism that implies that, as a product of human effort, cities have somehow conquered 'raw nature' (Wolch 1996). In fact, cities have not 'somehow risen above the physical constraints of "nature"– as places of enlightened human value and technological mastery' (Houston et al. 2017, p. 3). Elucidating some of the ideas introduced in Chapter 5, the next section explores how 'nature' in cities is beneficial to humans, and how the active presence, materiality and agencies of plants and animals make cities more-than-human.

More-than-human encounters and human health and well-being

The previous section illustrated how cities can provide habitat to non-human species, and how some species are actively making and remaking the materiality of cities, usually to their benefit. This section turns to animals and plants entangled in relations with humans as vibrant non-humans, and how this can be beneficial for human health. It also has a few caveats regarding its human view. First, despite its flaws, for brevity, I use the term 'nature' temporarily to distinguish (i.e., artificially bifurcate) non-domesticated living animals and plant species, vegetated areas and, in general, the ecosystems of cities, from humans.[6] I do not give specific attention to non-living substrates and materials, the built environment and other 'infrastructural dimensions' of cities because these were introduced in Chapter 5. Furthermore, I do not include animals and plants consumed as food. Second, although innumerable assemblages and multispecies relations with and without humans make cities what they are, this section is mostly limited to multispecies encounters that include humans, for reasons explained shortly. Third, the health outcomes from multispecies entanglements are mostly limited to humans rather than non-human species – the reason being that there is more readily available evidence for human outcomes from these encounters, and to sufficiently cover all the reciprocal benefits and potential harms for non-human species is beyond the scope of the book. I also do not give much attention to the potential harms to humans from human–non-human animal relations – for example, from potential predators, although they are touched on briefly. In drawing on the health benefits of multispecies relations for people, what I want to demonstrate is that humans are part of 'nature', and vice versa, and furthermore, that our everyday lives in cities are characterised by multispecies encounters that can have powerful health impacts on both humans and other species, some more obvious than others.

As noted in Chapter 5, a range of benefits for humans have been attributed to the presence and contact with trees, plants and animals in cities.[7] Psychosocial benefits from having access to nature include stress reduction and increased capacity for attention (Kaplan 1995; Maller et al. 2006; Ulrich et al. 1991), opportunities for social connection and improved emotional health (Coley et al. 1997; Maller 2009; Soulsbury & White 2016) and higher life satisfaction (Honold et al. 2016). However, there are also a range of physical health benefits, including improved immune function, increased physical activity, reduced cardiovascular morbidity and improved pregnancy outcomes (Egorov et al. 2016). Originating with the parks movement in the US and Europe in the nineteenth century, and now backed by global evidence from diverse disciplines including environmental psychology, epidemiology and health promotion (Egorov et al. 2016; Maller et al. 2008), access to and contact with nature is increasingly regarded as a key determinant of liveable and healthy cities for humans (Frumkin 2003; Hinchliffe & Whatmore 2006; Lowe et al. 2015; Maller et al. 2010; Pellegrini & Baudry 2014). Together with built infrastructures and technologies, the agencies and presence of nature in cities also make them more-than-human.

Most of the ways nature forms part of urban environments is via greenspaces and bluespaces (i.e., parks and public gardens, sports grounds, remnant vegetation or conservation zones, rivers, ponds, reservoirs, wetlands, coastal areas), including cemeteries, roadside verges, street trees, roof-top gardens, green walls, community gardens and residential front and backyards, and 'indeed any place where there is a natural surface or where trees are growing' (Egorov et al. 2016, p. 3). These areas include a mix of private and public land tenures. There are also 'informal' greenspaces (Rupprecht et al. 2015) – that is, vegetated parts of cities not necessarily delineated as formal parks or open spaces (Akkerman & Cornfeld 2010). Informal greenspaces include drainage channels, vacant lots and railway verges. Of course, animal and plant species can be incredibly mobile and are not confined to these areas, frequently inhabiting buildings, infrastructure and other substrates not typically considered habitat (see, e.g., Hinchliffe & Whatmore 2006; Low 2003; Pellegrini & Baudry 2014). Due to the increasing knowledge about how nature can benefit health, there are calls for urbanised humans to have regular 'doses of nature' and for health professionals to prescribe nature-based immersion treatments for patients suffering a range of health conditions (Townsend 2006; Ulmer et al. 2016). Humans having access to nature in cities is also reflected in global charters such as the UN's Sustainable Development Goals (United Nations 2016) (see Chapter 1). There is little doubt that, in general, humans like, enjoy, seek out and benefit from interactions and encounters with nature or non-human species.[8]

While these calls for improving access to nature in cities are encouraging, and are a good beginning, more-than-human thinking can be used to see how nature is already intimately entangled in everyday human lives such that, as argued in Part I, they are always more-than-human, and the human/nature divide is problematic. More-than-human thinking offers a new way to understand some of the evidence for the beneficial (and harmful) effects for humans from co-habiting with animals, trees and plants in cities, as noted in human and cultural geography (e.g., Head et al. 2014; Power 2005). Hence, rather than review the literature and the apparent mechanisms or pathways towards beneficial outcomes for humans,[9] in this section I focus on specific examples of human–non-human entanglements and opportunities for 'becoming with' that arise from everyday practices involving encounters between species. Although my interest is in human–non-human species encounters, I acknowledge the many multispecies entanglements that occur without humans that also make cities more-than-human habitat.

As argued in Chapter 4, theories of social practice are a useful lead approach for exploring more-than-human entanglements in urban settings because they are readily identifiable, comprise multiple performances in space and time, connect with other practices, and are carried out by humans and multiple non-humans. They can also help frame possible interventions to make cities healthier, despite acknowledging the possibility of contingent outcomes (discussed in Chapter 7). The following discussion explicates two related practices that involve multispecies encounters and care in more detail – gardening and wildlife feeding. As discussed in Chapter 5, practices of caring are a useful way to begin to understand how human lives are comprised of more-than-human relations. As well as being beneficial for human health, practices of caring are also a key pathway towards making cities more-than-human habitat.

Gardening

Gardens are ubiquitous in cities around the world (Kendal et al. 2012), and gardening is a typical way humans have contact with nature (Kaplan & Kaplan 1989; Lewis 1996). It is also recognised that gardens can play a significant role in the liveability, biodiversity and sustainability of healthy cities (Gosh & Head 2009; Head & Muir 2007; Mumaw & Bekessy 2017). Although gardening can be classified into different types – for example, productive gardening (Head et al. 2004), wildlife gardening (Mumaw et al. 2017), and community (Glover 2004; Wood et al. 2016), school (Maller 2009; Waliczek et al. 2001) and therapeutic gardening (Johnson et al. 2002) – all forms of gardening involve similar ingredients and are often, but not always, based on reciprocal relations between various humans and non-humans, including plants, insects and other pollinators, solar energy, water, microorganisms, soil and nutrients. Various types of gardening are known to provide different benefits for people. For example, volunteering or working in community vegetable gardens, such as allotments (Wood et al. 2016), has been shown to improve self-esteem, while gardening at home to encourage wildlife creates feelings of contributing to 'the common good' (Mumaw 2017). School-age children participating in gardening programmes can benefit from problem-solving skills and other learning outcomes (Maller 2009).

To clarify the multiplicity of affects attributed to gardening, it is important to note that there is not a single gardening practice, but instead a complex of connected and co-dependent practices (Chapter 4) that take place in common settings or locations, carried out with a certain logic and order (Shove et al. 2012). Practices that comprise the complex of gardening include sowing and cultivation of seeds and cuttings, bed preparation and soil management, pruning, watering, harvesting, pest management and killing. Many of these practices would share elements, such as competences in how to use tools and handle plants, meanings about when and why specific practices should be carried out and the sequence, and various materials and equipment, such as gloves, clippers, fertilisers, buckets, rakes and wheel-barrows. Although plants have material characteristics that manifest in a characteristic 'planty-ness' (Head et al. 2014), they also have planty-capacities and agencies (Head et al. 2015) that vary among species and individuals.

Compared to animals, the capacities and agencies of plants may not be as readily detected by human eyes (Hitchings & Jones 2004). To conceptualise the capacities of plants, Head et al. (2015, p. 410) describe them as 'including a particular materiality; mobility (without human intervention); sensing and communicating; and taking shape as flexible bodies'. Furthermore, they argue that, in fact, plants 'enact distinctive agencies – sun eating, mobile, communicative and flexibly collective' (Head et al. 2015, p. 410). Therefore, as vibrant non-humans with distinct capacities, plants cannot be classified simply as 'materials' in gardening practices and complexes. As pointed out in Chapter 4, plants, pets, birds, technologies, robots and other dynamic or vibrant non-humans can be co-performers of, and participants in, practices (Amiot et al. 2016; Maller & Strengers in press; Petersen et al. 2017; Strengers et al. 2016).

From the outset, gardening practices are premised on, and produced by, relations and multiple entanglements between humans and non-humans. To succeed, gardening practices require compliance and cooperation on the part of the plants and other non-humans implicated in the action. Head et al. (2014, p. 864) highlight the importance of paying attention to the specific capacities of plants and humans in an ongoing sense: this is because 'categories and configurations of human entanglement with the nonhuman world are not pre-existing givens, but become and are worked out in a process of relation'. As demonstrated in Part I, this emphasis on processes and dynamics of 'becoming with' is a key feature of taking a more-than-human approach.

Although gardeners may often start with certain outcomes, goals or meanings in mind, through their entanglements and relations with plants and other non-humans in the garden they relinquish control; like the garden itself and its planty inhabitants, gardeners also find themselves being shaped and changed by gardening practices (Power 2005). They often benefit from these encounters as they 'tune-in' to nature's seasons and experience the rewards of having healthy plants and trees (Mumaw 2017). This outcome is illustrative of the capacities and agencies of plants in gardening practices where 'different plant characters' draw humans 'down into their world, and make for an understanding of their concerns and a commitment to their care' (Hitchings 2003, p. 107). In his study of the gardens of North London, Hitchings (2003, p. 107) explains that: 'the status of the garden and the gardener were not fixed. They were constantly shifting between the enroller and the enrolled, the performer and the stagehand.'

Capturing these shifting dynamics, Power (2005, p. 40) writes it is 'moments of collaboration, negotiation, challenge and competition that make gardening a dynamic and lively relation'. In this way, plants exercise agencies in the co-performance of practices, recommending themselves to gardeners and enlisting humans in their care (Hitchings 2003; Power 2005). Rather than being 'forced' into the garden and gardening practices by 'calculating gardeners', plants 'may be amenable to the role and have as much to gain as the gardeners' (Power 2005, p. 50).

Nevertheless, not all plants are congenial or cooperative all the time. Plants can be non-compliant or even downright subversive. For example, in North London, Hitchings (2003, p. 105) found that 'whilst the humans of the garden wanted . . . to have things ordered and organised into attractive docile landscapes, the plants . . . had some other concerns'. He explains that different plants had different strategies enabling them to survive in the garden. Similarly, in her study of gardens in Sydney, Power (2005, p. 48) reports that plants considered weeds by gardeners were those that 'attempted to ensure their own garden performance. . . [by entering] ongoing, competitive relations with the gardeners by refusing their enrolment into the gardeners' plans'.

Gardeners and plants do not have exclusive relationships. In addition to other materials and co-performers enrolled in specific gardening practices, there are numerous other non-humans that can, inadvertently or otherwise, intervene in and disrupt practices in beneficial or detrimental ways. These include animals and birds such as white-tailed deer and brush turkeys that might unexpectedly eat, trample or uproot plants; damaging winds that break branches; weeds that compete for space and nutrients; or sun and frost that burn delicate leaves. As Hitchings (2003, p. 102) observes, for these and other reasons, gardens can 'be seen as an ephemeral and precarious outcome, whose achievement – both symbolically and materially – is constructed and negotiated through the interaction of different actors'.

These contestations in the performance of gardening practices carried out across urban gardens in cities globally are part of larger practice complexes that comprise the liveability and biodiversity of urban environments. Based on a wide range of evidence from horticulture, public health, environmental education and geography, gardeners benefit health-wise, and are changed through, the ongoing performance of gardening practices (e.g., see Bhatti & Church 2004; Glover 2004; Graham & Connell 2006; Lewis 1996; Maller et al. 2008; Mumaw et al. 2017; Power 2005; Waliczek et al. 2001; Wood et al. 2016). In an urban liveability context, gardening practices can result in increased physical activity levels, have positive impacts in drug rehabilitation centres, prisons and hospitals, improve mental and emotional health, and enhance community cohesion (Maller et al. 2008). Gardeners' selection, care and nurturing of native or introduced plants can, in turn, attract certain bird and animal species over others, impacting urban biodiversity and the health of ecosystems, as highlighted earlier in this chapter. Through gardening, 'people, plants and many others are entangled in ways that both enhance and constrain each other's lives' (Head et al. 2014, p. 863) and collectively make and remake urban habitat. There is now growing interest in 'wildlife gardening' and enhancing the 'wild spaces' of cities as a key strategy to make cities both more liveable and biodiverse (Mumaw et al. 2017; Soulsbury & White 2016; Threlfall & Kendal 2017). Higher biodiversity levels in cities have been associated with better psychological health for humans (Fuller et al. 2007), and there is increasing interest in the connection between human microbiomes and urban biodiversity levels, particularly of microbes – what is now referred to as the 'environmental microbiome' (Flies et al. 2017; Mills et al. 2017). Higher biodiversity levels may be associated with higher diversity in the microorganisms living in human digestive systems, known to be beneficial to health (Yong 2016) and potentially regulate immune function (Flies et al. 2017).

Wildlife gardening (or gardening for wildlife) involves removing weeds, planting and keeping native vegetation, and other means of providing habitat for native animal and plant species in domestic gardens (Mumaw

2017). As a result of wildlife gardening practices, wildlife gardeners can develop a form of land stewardship through their relations of care with the plants and animals inhabiting their gardens (Mumaw 2017; Mumaw et al. 2017). As argued by Haraway (2008, p. 4), the entanglements between gardeners, plants and animals in wildlife gardening – in fact, in all gardening – is a process of 'becoming with'. However, in practices that involve intense relations of care via multispecies entanglements, rather than becoming 'with', which retains a sense of separation without moral obligation or ethics, Cloke and Jones (2003, p. 210) argue 'being-for-the-other' is more appropriate.[10] Similarly, Puig de la Bellacasa (2017, p. 83) advocates 'living-with', highlighting the quotidian context of human–non-human relations of care. Both Cloke and Jones (2003) and Puig de la Bellacasa (2017) argue that such thinking is a form of 'ethical mindfulness' that decentres and deprivileges humans in multispecies relations, and engenders respect for non-human species. Regarding domestic gardening, Power (2005, p. 48) explains further: '"being-for-the-other" unsettles nature–culture frameworks by drawing people and plants into a relation of care'.

More-than-human notions like being-for-the-other recognise and elevate non-human agencies and assign both humans and living non-humans a sense of mutual responsibility. These ideas illustrate the vibrancy and agencies of living non-humans in cities, further dispelling their assumed passivity and liberating them of the dubious status of 'context'. Beyond urban gardens and gardening practices, plants exert incredible agencies in numerous other ways beneficial for urban environments. For example, trees can perform 'ecosystem services', including carbon sequestration, air quality improvement, reduction of storm water flows and assist with energy conservation (Roy et al. 2012). Humans would therefore do well to pay plants more attention through humble gardening practices, and more broadly as non-human agents and makers of healthy urban environments. This is because 'as both individuals and different kinds of collectives, [plants] play a key role in the emerging environmental political issues of the twenty-first century' (Head et al. 2014, p. 867).

In addition to relations of caring with, and for, plants in domestic gardens, some urban gardeners and residents extend these practices to animals. Although these entanglements most commonly involve pets, there is a growing global phenomenon of humans providing significant amounts of food for urbanised non-human species, particularly birds (Galbraith et al. 2014; Jones 2018; Reynolds et al. 2017).

Feeding birds

Garden bird feeding[11] is the intentional supply of food materials to wild birds in domestic gardens. Beginning centuries ago, mostly in the northern parts of Europe during winter to provide food during times of scarcity, bird feeding now also occurs in the southern hemisphere and is no longer restricted to winter; instead, it occurs all year round (Jones 2018; Reynolds et al. 2017). The types of food provided include seeds, sugar mixtures, human food scraps and meats (Jones & Reynolds 2008).

The scale of this phenomenon is enormous, comprising a billion-dollar global industry, concentrated in the US and UK (Reynolds et al. 2017). The food supplied through bird feeding dramatically exceeds bird populations for which it is intended. For example, in the UK, residents provide five times the amount of seed needed for the entire blue tit population (Reynolds et al. 2017), and in the US, the equivalent of 22,000 railway carriages full of seed is provided to birds every year (Jones 2018). Despite the volume of food provided, there is little evidence that birds become dependent or rely on food provisioning by humans; it is always only a supplementary part of their diet, despite the firmly held beliefs of feeders (Jones 2018). Like gardening practices, bird feeding requires certain competences, meanings and materials that are necessary for its performance. It is also associated with, and dependent on, other practices such as shopping for avian food supplies and feeders, gardening, feeder hygiene and maintenance, and bird watching. It might therefore more accurately be described as a complex of practices. It is also connected to extensive professional and commercialised practices and complexes of producing, packaging, distributing and selling food, supplements and feeding apparatuses.

The popularity and widespread distribution of bird feeding as a practice indicates that urban humans and birds are easily recruited to and enjoy these opportunities for multispecies entanglements. However, surprisingly very little is known about bird feeding and its impacts on humans, birds and ecosystems. Recent studies have explored why people feed birds, and the main reasons reported are care and pleasure (Jones 2018), happiness, joy (Galbraith et al. 2014) and responsibility (Reynolds et al. 2017). The commitment to care for the birds they feed runs so deep that some humans worry that if they stop feeding, 'their' birds will starve, and hence never break 'the feeder's Golden Rule: Once you start, don't stop' (Jones 2018, p. 263). This practice and its intense relations of care is a clear example of 'being-for-the-other' and how it produces affective outcomes. Although both humans and birds can profit from the relations of care expressed through feeding, there are concerns about the spread of disease, avian epidemics, benefiting the 'wrong' (introduced or aggressive) species, the overall lack of evidence of food shortages, and far-reaching ecosystem impacts (Jones 2018; Reynolds et al. 2017). Considering these potential harms to birds and other non-human species, there are well-grounded suspicions that people benefit much more from this practice than birds (Jones 2018). Puig de la Bellacasa (2017, p. 83) argues that 'living-with' non-human animals requires humans to be 'aware of [such] troubling relations'.

It follows that not all multispecies entanglements between humans and non-human species in urban environments are positive or beneficial, and there can be unintended or unpredictable outcomes at various scales (Field et al.

1999; Soulsbury & White 2016). Viewed from an ecosystem or urban metabolism perspective, potential harms are considered by Swyngedouw (2006, p. 118), who argues that 'processes of metabolic change are never socially or ecologically neutral' because 'particular trajectories of socioenvironmental change undermine the stability or coherence of some social groups, places or ecologies, while their sustainability elsewhere might be enhanced'.

Other harmful outcomes include human–wildlife conflicts and other experiences that have detrimental impacts on humans or non-human species: 'nature in the city can and is indeed often a matter of life or death' (Swyngedouw 2004). This is most apparent when considering places where humans and apex predators, or large and powerful animals, co-exist, such as elephants in India, crocodiles in Australia and mountain lions in North America. Human–wildlife conflicts are classified into four main categories: aggression, injury and death; nuisance and damage; disease; and economic costs (Soulsbury & White 2016). However, as with the benefits literature on contact with nature, these impacts are all human-centric rather than accounting for wildlife or non-human species affects. This recalls Cloke and Jones's (2003) argument for ethical mindfulness, where humans have a responsibility to the numerous other species that call cities home. More specifically, Swyngedouw (2006, p. 115) calls for a 'just urban socio-environmental perspective' that 'always needs to consider the question of who gains and who pays and to ask serious questions about the multiple power relations'.

To summarise this section, describing practices of gardening and wildlife feeding using social practices and more-than-human thinking has shown how the vibrancy, agencies and capacities of non-human species are articulated through the ongoing negotiation and collaboration of practice performances with humans. Although the benefits (and harms) arising from these entanglements and relations have focused on humans, there are many circumstances where these relations are reciprocal, and non-human species can also benefit or suffer harm.

Conclusion

In further dispelling the myth of passivity by using more-than-human thinking, this chapter has illustrated the agencies and vibrancy of non-human species, and how they actively make and remake cities through various entanglements with humans and other non-humans. Urban environments are now known to provide special forms of habitat for threatened and endangered species as well as unconventional, unintentional habitat for unbidden species. Interpreting research from urban ecology and human geography through an overt more-than-human framing, the chapter revealed new insights about 'human–nature' relations in cities and how multispecies entanglements are a key way to make them healthy places to live. Cities are forged in myriad more-than-human relations – a dance of interactions that can be beneficial to both humans and non-humans or potentially cause conflict and harm. For these reasons, among others, cities should be conceptualised as more-than-human habitat. Patterns of rising global urbanisation and increasing extinctions and threats to non-human species mean there is an urgent need to see and know cities in this way.

Aside from changing practices that contribute to negative human impacts on the Earth, particularly the destruction of traditional habitats, practices of gardening and wildlife feeding are examples of caring and ethical mindfulness that show how humans and other urban species are constantly entangled in processes of becoming-and being-for-the-other. Such practices bring non-human agencies to our attention and show how cities are home to, and made by, many other species. There are other practices involving multispecies entanglements, both caring and deleterious, that could also be examined in this light and tested for their potential to change the way we think about cities and who they are for – as well as redress some of the harms of urbanisation. There is still a lot to learn about how humans can know urban nature better and continue to transcend human–nature boundaries, and much needs to be done to reconceptualise and make cities healthy places for both humans and other species. Chapter 7 tackles this topic.

Notes

1 Including insects.
2 Binaries and homogenous or problematic terms like 'nature' are difficult to avoid and are used here as heuristic devices. The clumsiness of some terminology used in this and other chapters in the book reflects the inherent difficulties encountered, and contradictions performed, in attempting to shift ideas, language and practice beyond humans (Head 2016). As Castree (2003, p. 208) observes: 'it remains difficult to operationalize a nonanthropo-/ecocentric politics . . . [and the] deployment of neologisms and metaphors that challenge existing mind-sets can be difficult to digest'.
3 See also Chapter 3.
4 In this chapter, there is an emphasis on animal and plant species rather than microorganisms due to limitations of space and scope.
5 Without absolving (predominantly western) human responsibility and accountability (Head 2016), the Anthropocene can be argued as maintaining human-centrism and exceptionalism, contradicting the goals of more-than-human theories (Loftus 2016). However, the rapid, unpredictable and nonlinear changes now becoming evident in cities and globally are acknowledged as the result of more-than-human, rather than solely human, activity (Head 2016).
6 See Cronon (1996), Instone (1998) and Castree (2014) for a comprehensive discussion of the social construction of nature.
7 There is a large body of work on the health impacts and benefits of domesticated companion animals, such as cats, dogs and birds (e.g., Anderson et al. 1992; Bauman et al. 2001; Beck & Katcher 1989; 1996; Friedmann et al. 1983; Headey et al. 2002; Schaefer 2002; Serpell 1991; Siegel 1990). However, the focus in this chapter is on 'wild' living non-humans, such as native species.
8 In fact, as introduced in Chapter 3, evolutionary reasoning for this is supported by the biophilia hypothesis that argues humans are genetically predisposed to be

attracted to, or fascinated by, other species as this contributed to survival (Kellert & Wilson 1995; Wilson 1984).
 9 I suggest Egorov et al. (2016) or Maller et al. (2008) for reviews, acknowledging that this is a rapidly growing field.
10 Haraway (2016) has also experimented with other more expansive terms such as 'make-with' and 'compose-with'.
11 Although ritualistic provisioning of food is common in the Indian subcontinent, most bird feeding is associated with the developed/western parts of the world (Reynolds et al. 2017).

References

Akkerman, A & Cornfeld, AF 2010, 'Greening as an urban design metaphor: looking for the city's soul in leftover spaces', *The Structurist*, vol. 49, no. 50, pp. 30–35.
Amiot, C, Bastian, B & Martens, P 2016, 'People and companion animals: it takes two to tango', *BioScience*, vol. 66, no. 7, pp. 552–560.
Anderson, WP, Reid, CM & Jennings, GL 1992, 'Pet ownership and risk factors for cardiovascular disease', *Medical Journal of Australia*, vol. 157, pp. 298–301.
Bauman, AE, Russell, SJ, Furber, SE & Dobson, AJ 2001, 'The epidemiology of dog walking: an unmet need for human and canine health', *Medical Journal of Australia*, vol. 175, pp. 632–634.
Beck, A & Katcher, A 1989, 'Bird-human interaction', *Journal of the Association of Avian Veterinarians*, vol. 3, no. 3, pp. 152–153.
Beck, A & Katcher, A 1996, *Between Pets and People: The Importance of Animal Companionship*, Purdue University Press.
Bhatti, M & Church, A 2004, 'Home, the culture of nature and meanings of gardens in late modernity', *Housing Studies*, vol. 19, no. 1, pp. 37–51.
Castree, N 2003, 'Environmental issues: relational ontologies and hybrid politics', *Progress in Human Geography*, vol. 27, no. 2, pp. 203–211.
Castree, N 2014, *Making Sense of Nature*, Routledge.
Cloke, P & Jones, O 2003, 'Grounding ethical mindfulness for/in nature: trees in their places', *Ethics, Place & Environment*, vol. 6, no. 3, pp. 195–213.
Coley, RL, Kuo, FE & Sullivan, WC 1997, 'Where does community grow? The social context created by nature in urban public housing', *Environment & Behavior*, vol. 29, no. 4, pp. 468–495.
Collerton, S 2009, 'Man v bird: the brush turkey battle', ABC News, www.abc.net.au/news/2009-08-17/man-v-bird-the-brush-turkey-battle/1394040, accessed 19 June 2017.
Cronon, W 1996, 'Introduction: in search of nature', in W Cronon (ed.), *Uncommon Ground: Rethinking the Human Place in Nature*, WW Norton, pp. 23–56.
Darcovich, K & O'Meara, J 2008, 'An Olympic legacy: green and golden bell frog conservation at Sydney Olympic Park 1993–2006', *Australian Zoologist*, vol. 34, no. 3, pp. 236–248.
DeNicola, AJ, VerCauteren, KC, Curtis, PD & Hyngstrom, SE 2010, *Managing White-tailed Deer in Suburban Environments: A Technical Guide*, Cornell University Press.
Egorov, AI, Mudu, P, Braubach, M & Martuzzi, M 2016, *Urban Green Spaces and Health*, WHO Regional Office for Europe, Copenhagen.

Field, R, Csanyi, S & Slate, D 1999, 'Wildlife and people in suburbs: a comparison of history, ecology, and management of two continents', paper presented to *International Wildlife Management Congress*, Hungary.

Flies, EJ, Skelly, C, Negi, SS, Prabhakaran, P, Liu, Q, Liu, K, Goldizen, FC, Lease, C & Weinstein, P 2017, 'Biodiverse green spaces: a prescription for global urban health', *Frontiers in Ecology and the Environment*, vol. 15, no. 9, pp. 510–516.

Franklin, A 2007, 'Human–nonhuman animal relationships in Australia: an overview of results from the first national survey and follow-up case studies 2000–2004', *Society and Animals*, vol. 15, pp. 7–27.

Friedmann, E, Katcher, A & Meislich, D 1983, 'When pet owners are hospitalized: significance of companion animals during hospitalization', in A Katcher & A Beck (eds), *New Perspectives on Our Lives with Companion Animals*, University of Pennsylvania Press, pp. 346–350.

Frumkin, H 2003, 'Healthy places: exploring the evidence', *American Journal of Public Health*, vol. 93, no. 9, pp. 1451–1456.

Fuller, RA, Irvine, KN, Devine-Wright, P, Warren, PH & Gaston, KJ 2007, 'Psychological benefits of greenspace increase with biodiversity', *Biology Letters*, vol. 3, no. 4, pp. 390–394.

Galbraith, JA, Beggs, JR, Jones, DN, McNaughton, EJ, Krull, CR & Stanley, MC 2014, 'Risks and drivers of wild bird feeding in urban areas of New Zealand', *Biological Conservation*, vol. 180, pp. 64–74.

Garrard, GE & Bekessy, SA 2014, 'Land use and land management', in Byrne J, Sipe N & J Dodson (eds), *Australian Environmental Planning: Challenges and Future Prospects*, Routledge, pp. 61–72.

Glover, TD 2004, 'Social capital in the lived experiences of community gardeners', *Leisure Sciences*, vol. 26, no. 2, pp. 143–162.

Gosh, S & Head, L 2009, 'Retrofitting the suburban garden: morphologies and some elements of sustainability potential of two Australian residential suburbs compared', *Australian Geographer*, vol. 40, no. 3, pp. 319–346.

Graham, S & Connell, J 2006, 'Nurturing relationships: the gardens of Greek and Vietnamese migrants in Marrickville, Sydney', *Australian Geographer*, vol. 37, no. 3, pp. 375–393.

Haraway, DJ 2008, *When Species Meet*, University of Minnesota Press.

Haraway, DJ 2016, *Staying with the Trouble: Making Kin in the Chthulucene*, Duke University Press.

Head, L 2016, *Hope and Grief in the Anthropocene: Re-conceptualising Human–nature Relations*, Routledge.

Head, L & Muir, P 2007, 'Changing cultures of water in eastern Australian backyard gardens', *Social & Cultural Geography*, vol. 8, no. 6, pp. 889–905.

Head, L, Atchison, J & Phillips, C 2015, 'The distinctive capacities of plants re-thinking difference via invasive species', *Transactions of the Institute of British Geographers*, vol. 40, no. 3, pp. 399–413.

Head, L, Atchison, J, Phillips, C & Buckingham, K 2014, 'Vegetal politics: belonging practices and places', *Social & Cultural Geography*, vol. 15, no. 8, pp. 861–870.

Head, L, Muir, P & Hampel, E 2004, 'Australian backyard gardens and the journey of migration', *Geographical Review*, vol. 94, no. 3, pp. 326–347.

Headey, B, Grabka, M, Kelley, J, Reddy, P & Tseng, Y-P 2002, 'Pet ownership i good for your health and saves public expenditure too: Australian and German longitudinal evidence', *Australian Social Monitor*, vol. 5, no. 4, pp. 93–99.

Hinchliffe, S & Whatmore, S 2006, 'Living cities: towards a politics of conviviality', *Science as Culture*, vol. 15, no. 2, pp. 123–138.

Hinchliffe, S, Kearnes, MB, Degen, M & Whatmore, S 2005, 'Urban wild things: a cosmopolitical experiment', *Environment and Planning D: Society and Space*, vol. 23, no. 5, pp. 643–658.

Hitchings, R 2003, 'People, plants and performance: on actor network theory and the material pleasures of the private garden', *Social & Cultural Geography*, vol. 4, no. 1, pp. 99–114.

Hitchings, R & Jones, V 2004, 'Living with plants and the exploration of botanical encounter within human geographic research practice', *Ethics, Place & Environment*, vol. 7, nos 1–2, pp. 3–18.

Honold, J, Lakes, T, Beyer, R & van der Meer, E 2016, 'Restoration in urban spaces', *Environment and Behavior*, vol. 48, no. 6, pp. 796–825.

Houston, D, Hillier, J, MacCallum, D, Steele, W & Byrne, J 2017, 'Make kin, not cities! Multispecies entanglements and "becoming-world" in planning theory', *Planning Theory*, doi:10.1177/1473095216688042.

Instone, L 1998, 'The coyote's at the door: revisioning human–environment relations in the Australian context', *Ecumene*, vol. 5, no. 4, pp. 452–467.

Ives, CD, Lentini, PE, Threlfall, CG, Ikin, K, Shanahan, DF, Garrard, GE, Bekessy, SA, Fuller, RA, Mumaw, L, Rayner, L, Rowe, R, Valentine, LE & Kendal, D 2016, 'Cities are hotspots for threatened species', *Global Ecology and Biogeography*, vol. 25, no. 1, pp. 117–126.

Johnson, K, Bland, M, K. & Rathsam, SM 2002, 'Taking root: the development of a hospital garden', *Parks and Recreation*, vol. 37, no. 1, pp. 60–65.

Jones, DN 2002, *Magpie Alert: Learning to Live with a Wild Neighbour*, University of New South Wales Press.

Jones, DN 2018, *The Birds at My Table: Why We Feed Wild Birds and Why It Matters*, Cornell University Press.

Jones, DN & Everding, SE 1991, 'Australian brush-turkeys in a suburban environment: implications for conflict and conservation', *Wildlife Research*, vol. 18, no. 3, pp. 285–297.

Jones, DN & Goth, A 2008, *Mound-builders*, CSIRO Publishing.

Jones, DN & Reynolds, SJ 2008, 'Feeding birds in our towns and cities: a global research opportunity', *Journal of Avian Biology*, vol. 39, no. 3, pp. 265–271.

Jones, DN, Sonnenburg, R & Sinden, KE 2004, 'Presence and distribution of Australian Brushturkeys in the greater Brisbane region', *Sunbird: Journal of the Queensland Ornithological Society*, vol. 34, no. 1, pp. 1–9.

Kaplan, S 1995, 'The restorative benefits of nature: toward an integrative framework', *Journal of environmental psychology*, vol. 15, pp. 169–182.

Kaplan, R & Kaplan, S 1989, *The Experience of Nature: A Psychological Perspective*, Cambridge University Press.

Kellert, SR & Wilson, EO 1995, *The Biophilia Hypothesis*, Island Press.

Kendal, D, Williams, KJH & Williams, NSG 2012, 'Plant traits link people's plant preferences to the composition of their gardens', *Landscape and Urban Planning*, vol. 105, no. 1, pp. 34–42.

Kowarik, I 2011, 'Novel urban ecosystems, biodiversity, and conservation', *Environmental Pollution*, vol. 159, nos 8–9, pp. 1974–1983.

Lewis, CA 1996, *Green Nature/Human Nature: The Meaning of Plants in our Lives*, University of Illinois Press.

Loftus, A 2016, 'On valuing wild encounters', *Dialogues in Human Geography*, vol. 6, no. 1, pp. 106–108.

Low, T 2003, *The New Nature*, Penguin Books.

Lowe, M, Whitzman, C, Badland, H, Davern, M, Aye, L, Hes, D, Butterworth, I & Giles-Corti, B 2015, 'Planning healthy, liveable and sustainable cities: how can indicators inform policy?', *Urban Policy and Research*, vol. 33, no. 2, pp. 131–144.

Luck, GW 2007, 'A review of the relationships between human population density and biodiversity', *Biological Reviews*, vol. 82, no. 4, pp. 607–645.

Maller, C 2009, 'Promoting children's mental, emotional and social health through contact with nature: a model', *Health Education*, vol. 109, no. 6, pp. 522–543.

Maller, C & Strengers, Y (eds) in press, *Social Practices and Dynamic Non-humans: Nature, Materials and Technologies*, Palgrave Macmillan.

Maller, C, Henderson-Wilson, C & Townsend, M 2010, 'Re-discovering nature in everyday settings: or how to create healthy environments and healthy people', *EcoHealth*, vol. 6, no. 4, pp. 553–556.

Maller, C, Townsend, M, Pryor, A, Brown, PR & St Leger, L 2006, 'Healthy parks, healthy people: "contact with nature" as an upstream health promotion intervention for populations', *Health Promotion International*, vol. 21, no. 1, pp. 45–54.

Maller, C, Townsend, M, St Leger, L, Henderson-Wilson, C, Pryor, A, Prosser, L & Moore, M 2008, *Healthy Parks, Healthy People: The Health Benefits of Contact with Nature in a Park Context: A Review of Relevant Literature*, School of Health and Social Development, Faculty of Health, Medicine, Nursing and Behavioural Sciences, Deakin University and Parks Victoria.

Marris, E, Mascaro, J & Ellis, EC 2013, *Perspective: Is Everything a Novel Ecosystem? If So, Do We Need the Concept?*, John Wiley & Sons.

Mason, CF 2000, 'Thrushes now largely restricted to the built environment in eastern England', *Diversity and Distributions*, vol. 6, no. 4, pp. 189–194.

McKinney, ML 2006, 'Urbanization as a major cause of biotic homogenization', *Biological Conservation*, vol. 127, no. 3, pp. 247–260.

Mills, JG, Weinstein, P, Gellie, NJC, Weyrich, LS, Lowe, AJ & Breed, MF 2017, 'Urban habitat restoration provides a human health benefit through microbiome rewilding: the Microbiome Rewilding Hypothesis', *Restoration Ecology*, vol. 25, no. 6, pp. 847–1034.

Morse, NB, Pellissier, PA, Cianciola, EN, Brereton, RL, Sullivan, MM, Shonka, NK, Wheeler, TB & McDowell, WH 2014, 'Novel ecosystems in the Anthropocene: a revision of the novel ecosystem concept for pragmatic applications', *Ecology and Society*, vol. 19, no. 2, pp. 12–22.

Mumaw, L 2017, 'Transforming urban gardeners into land stewards', *Journal of environmental psychology*, vol. 52, pp. 92–103.

Mumaw, L & Bekessy, S 2017, 'Wildlife gardening for collaborative public–private biodiversity conservation', *Australasian Journal of Environmental Management*, pp. 1–19.

Mumaw, L, Maller, C & Bekessy, S 2017, 'Strengthening wellbeing in urban communities through wildlife gardening', *Cities and the Environment (CATE)*, vol. 10, no. 1, pp. 1–18.

Narayanan, Y 2017, 'Street dogs at the intersection of colonialism and informality: "subaltern animism" as a posthuman critique of Indian cities', *Environment and Planning D: Society and Space*, vol. 35, no. 3, pp. 475–494.

Newman, P 2014, 'Biophilic urbanism: a case study on Singapore', *Australian Planner*, vol. 51, no. 1, pp. 47–65.

Pellegrini, P & Baudry, S 2014, 'Streets as new places to bring together both humans and plants: examples from Paris and Montpellier (France)', *Social & Cultural Geography*, vol. 15, no. 8, pp. 871–900.

Petersen, S, Houston, S, Qin, H, Tague, C & Studley, J 2017, 'The Utilization of robotic pets in dementia care', *Journal of Alzheimer's Disease*, vol. 55, pp. 569–574.

Power, ER 2005, 'Human–nature relations in suburban gardens', *Australian Geographer*, vol. 36, no. 1, pp. 39–53.

Power, ER 2009, 'Border-processes and homemaking: encounters with possums in suburban Australian homes', *Cultural Geographies*, vol. 16, no. 1, pp. 29–54.

Puig de la Bellacasa, M 2017, *Matters of Care: Speculative Ethics in More than Human Worlds*, University of Minnesota Press.

Reynolds, SJ, Galbraith, JA, Smith, JA & Jones, DN 2017, 'Garden bird feeding: insights and prospects from a north–south comparison of this global urban phenomenon', *Frontiers in Ecology and Evolution*, vol. 5, no. 24, doi:10.3389/fevo.2017.00024.

Roy, S, Byrne, J & Pickering, C 2012, 'A systematic quantitative review of urban tree benefits, costs, and assessment methods across cities in different climatic zones', *Urban Forestry & Urban Greening*, vol. 11, no. 4, pp. 351–363.

Rupprecht, CD, Byrne, JA, Ueda, H & Lo, AY 2015, '"It's real, not fake like a park": Residents' perception and use of informal urban green-space in Brisbane, Australia and Sapporo, Japan', *Landscape and Urban Planning*, vol. 143, pp. 205–218.

Schaefer, K 2002, 'Human-animal interactions as a therapeutic intervention', *Counselling and Human Development*, vol. 34, no. 5, pp. 1–18.

Serpell, J 1991, 'Beneficial effects of pet ownership on some aspects of human health and behaviour', *Journal of the Royal Society of Medicine*, vol. 84, pp. 717–720.

Shove, E, Pantzar, M & Watson, M 2012, *The Dynamics of Social Practice: Everyday Life and How It Changes*, SAGE Publications.

Siegel, JM 1990, 'Stressful life events and use of physician services among the elderly: the moderating role of pet ownership', *Journal of Personality and Social Psychology*, vol. 58, no. 6, pp. 1081–1086.

Skatssoon, J 2009, 'Brush turkeys find place to roost in the suburbs', *news.com.au*, www.news.com.au/news/brush-turkeys-home-to-roost/news-story/d6e8015f816e683d23457e812180f027, accessed 19 June 2017.

Soulsbury, CD & White, PCL 2016, 'Human–wildlife interactions in urban areas: a review of conflicts, benefits and opportunities', *Wildlife Research*, vol. 42, no. 7, pp. 541–553.

Steffen, W, Crutzen, PJ & McNeill, JR 2007, 'The Anthropocene: are humans now overwhelming the great forces of nature', *AMBIO: A Journal of the Human Environment*, vol. 36, no. 8, pp. 614–621.

Strengers, Y, Nicholls, L & Maller, C 2016, 'Curious energy consumers: humans and nonhumans in assemblages of household practice', *Journal of Consumer Culture*, vol. 16, no. 3, pp. 761–780.

Sumasgutner, P, Schulze, CH, Krenn, HW & Gamauf, A 2014, 'Conservation related conflicts in nest-site selection of the Eurasian kestrel (Falco tinnunculus) and the distribution of its avian prey', *Landscape and Urban Planning*, vol. 127, Supplement C, pp. 94–103.

Swyngedouw, E 1996, 'The city as a hybrid: on nature, society and cyborg urbanization', *Capitalism Nature Socialism*, vol. 7, no. 2, pp. 65–80.

Swyngedouw, E 2004, *Social Power and the Urbanization of Water: Flows of Power*, Oxford University Press.

Swyngedouw, E 2006, 'Circulations and metabolisms: (hybrid) natures and (cyborg) cities', *Science as Culture*, vol. 15, no. 2, pp. 105–121.

Threlfall, CG & Kendal, D 2017, 'The distinct ecological and social roles that wild spaces play in urban ecosystems', *Urban Forestry & Urban Greening*, doi:10.1016/j.ufug.2017.05.012.

Townsend, MA 2006, 'Feel blue? Touch green! Participation in forest/woodland management as a treatment for depression', *Urban Forestry & Urban Greening*, vol. 5, pp. 111–120.

Ulmer, JM, Wolf, KL, Backman, DR, Tretheway, RL, Blain, CJA, O'Neil-Dunne, JPM & Frank, LD 2016, 'Multiple health benefits of urban tree canopy: the mounting evidence for a green prescription', *Health & Place*, vol. 42, pp. 54–62.

Ulrich, RS, Simons, RF, Losito, BD, Fiorito, E, Miles, MA & Zelson, M 1991, 'Stress recovery during exposure to natural and urban environments', *Journal of Environmental Psychology*, vol. 11, pp. 231–248.

United Nations 2016, *Sustainable Development Goals*, United Nations, www. un.org/sustainabledevelopment/sustainable-development-goals/, accessed 23 June 2017.

Waliczek, TM, Bradley, JC & Zajicek, JM 2001, 'The effect of school gardens on children's interpersonal relationships and attitudes towards school', *HortTechnology*, vol. 11, no. 3, pp. 466–468.

Waters, CN, Zalasiewicz, J, Summerhayes, C, Barnosky, AD, Poirier, C, Gałuszka, A, Cearreta, A, Edgeworth, M, Ellis, EC, Ellis, M, Jeandel, C, Leinfelder, R, McNeill, JR, Richter, D, Steffen, W, Syvitski, J, Vidas, D, Wagreich, M, Williams, M, Zhisheng, A, Grinevald, J, Odada, E, Oreskes, N & Wolfe, AP 2016, 'The Anthropocene is functionally and stratigraphically distinct from the Holocene', *Science*, vol. 351, no. 6269, doi:10.1126/science.aad2622.

Whatmore, S 2002, *Hybrid Geographies: Natures Cultures Spaces*, SAGE Publications.

Wilson, EO 1984, *Biophilia*, Harvard University Press.

Wolch, J 1996, 'Zoöpolis', *Capitalism Nature Socialism*, vol. 7, no. 2, pp. 21–47.

Wood, CJ, Pretty, J & Griffin, M 2016, 'A case-control study of the health and well-being benefits of allotment gardening', *Journal of Public Health*, vol. 38, no. 3, pp. e336–e344.

Yong, E 2016, *I Contain Multitudes: The Microbes within Us and a Grander View of Life*, Bodley Head.

7 Changing practices for understanding and making healthy urban environments

Introduction

This chapter tackles the third aim of this book: to encourage experimentation with new concepts and ideas from a more-than-human perspective and to think about intervening for change differently, accepting that, due to the dynamic complexity of cities, any attempt at change will have unpredictable or unforeseen outcomes. Using the innovative ideas from more-than-human thinking developed in previous chapters, it presents exciting ways forward when thinking about applying these ideas to make healthy urban environments.

A more-than-human approach to change

There are several things to consider when drawing together the ideas outlined in previous parts of the book for experimentation and potential application. First, as argued in Chapter 4, theories of social practice are useful as a lead theory or approach from which we can start to think about how to intervene in cities to make them more-than-human habitat. This is not to discredit the other more-than-human theories described in Part I. As explained in the sections below, each theory makes an important contribution when thinking about change from a more-than-human stance.

Second, arguing that things need to change overlooks the fact that practices are *already always changing*, even without deliberate or intended intervention, steering or toolkits (Maller & Strengers 2015a; Shove 2015; Shove et al. 2012). As Chapters 2 and 4 discussed in detail, the very nature of practices is dynamic, a key premise of seeing the world as more-than-human. This dynamism is one explanation for why the usual efforts to intervene have unpredictable or contingent outcomes (Mol 1999; Shove 2014). Furthermore, attempts at steering or intervention do not occur in a vacuum. Existing policy, programmes and related activities already maintain or support extant practices and ways of life, despite the general ignorance of, or an unwillingness to accept, this fact (Shove 2014; 2015). Moreover, global economies and systems of provision circulate elements and structure practices beyond national borders and the control of national policymakers (Shove 2014). Regardless of these conditions and the outcomes of any deliberate intervention being indeterminate, there is an urgent need to respond and attempt to alter the trajectories of some significant global problems affecting all species and current ways of living – particularly increasing urbanisation and climate change (Haraway 2016; Stengers 2015). Although success might be contingent, as advocated by new materialisms, there is merit in establishing optimistic pathways towards better futures.[1]

Third, regarding theories of social practice, it could be argued that to rethink cities as more-than-human habitat, almost *every* practice, bundle and complex should be changed, tweaked or recrafted. This is because, as argued in Chapter 2, each practice performance holds the seeds of future change and, using ideas from new materialisms in Chapter 3, each practice is an opportunity to engage more deeply with non-humans and their vibrancy through ideas such as 'becoming-with' (Haraway 2008, p. 4). Although some practices more directly or straightforwardly involve engaging with non-human actors, like the examples of gardening and garden bird feeding discussed in Chapter 6, 'becoming with' non-humans through practices has relevance in other contexts – for example, eating, where practices involving consumption of food and drink become 'a series of mutual transformations in which the border between inside and outside becomes blurred . . . [where] human and nonhuman bodies re-corporealise in response to each other' (Bennett 2007, p. 134). In becoming-with, 'binary codings of human/ nonhuman dissolve into a coding of more-than-human' (Houston et al. 2017, p. 10). From a human health perspective, paying more attention to such transformations through techniques such as mindfulness have been effective in reducing emotional and binge eating (Katterman et al. 2014), improving eating regulation, dietary patterns and the reduction of anxiety and depression (Miller et al. 2014). More broadly, Bennett (2007, p. 142) argues relatedly that practices of 'artful consumption' of food – for instance, those encouraged by the Slow Food Movement – could change patterns of wasteful consumption and ecological destruction currently characterising the food industry. The idea of a 'movement' like Slow Food fits with the argument of Chapter 4, where rather than single practices, various practices linked through complexes and bundles (Shove et al. 2012) require recrafting to shed their human-centrism and essentialism, and thereby reconsider non-human agencies and environmental impacts in cities. In addition to being an insurmountable task, any attempt to change every practice, complex and bundle is not a practical way forward. Instead, this chapter focuses on two loosely defined domains of intervention, and associated interveners, where more-than-human thinking and experimentation for change could be readily attempted: research and policymaking.

These practice areas are prioritised because changes in these domains could have far-reaching consequences. For example, policies that seek to change what human residents or businesses do would reach into domains of everyday life and industry, which could also be steered towards and benefit from more-than-human thinking. Policymaking also speaks to professional practices because it concerns a range of decision-makers, professions and artefacts that affect what occurs in cities through legislation, project funding, and design and planning from a governance, institutional and infrastructural perspective.

As argued throughout Part I, to rethink healthy cities, more-than-human approaches encourage *both* research and policy to shed typically siloed thinking and practices that separate disciplines and sectors, and instead link with and work across various spheres, including health, land use and conservation, sustainability, housing, employment and transport. In other words, practices, bundles and complexes in these domains need to be steered towards the trans-disciplinary and trans-sectoral. Although already a tenet of the Healthy Cities Programme and the Ottawa Charter, as discussed in Chapters 1 and 5, more-than-human thinking provides new ways to try and achieve this goal where other approaches and methods have had limited success.

This chapter discusses how research and policy problems could be changed using more-than-human thinking, including reframing problems, doing research and using methods differently, and redesigning interventions for healthy cities.

Changing practices of research and policymaking

More-than-human theories have many new and valuable things to say about how to conduct urban-focused research and policymaking differently. Cities are complex places that are best served by approaches that can cope with their multifaceted nature. With the increasing digitisation of homes and workplaces, the rise of artificial intelligence and 'smart' technologies, plus efforts to increase biodiversity, urban living is rapidly changing. Modernist research enterprises that tend to rely on reductive, generalising represent-ationalist theories and methods can only provide a limited understanding of the increasing dynamism and vibrancy of urban environments and what it means for making healthy cities. Rather than avoiding this complexity, more-than-human thinking embraces it. As discussed in Chapters 2 and 3, there are already many dimensions of cities that challenge representational approaches, including affects, vibrant non-human materialities and agencies, and nonlinear concepts of time and temporality. Research and policymak-ing based in, or relying on, representationalist paradigms and methods per se have limited value in rethinking healthy cities regarding current global challenges. To resolve these issues, research and policymaking practices must change.

With more-than-human approaches advocating alternative ways of see-ing, knowing and understanding urban environments, there are implications for changing the practices, bundles and complexes that characterise most research and policymaking endeavours directed at cities and how to improve them. However, rather than rejecting all current research and policymaking outright, whether representationalist or otherwise, more-than-human thinking is of most value in changing the way problems are conceptualised and interpreted, and therefore has implications for how subsequent research practices and programme designs are implemented. The following two subsections on reframing problems and methods are oriented at research, but also apply to policymaking, as this often relies on research for decision-making. The third subsection about conducting interventions for healthy urban environments speaks to both policymaking and research, where research itself is also considered a form of intervention (Browne et al. 2015; Law 2009; Strengers et al. 2015).

Reframing urban problems

The way urban problems are framed and embodied is dependent on particular understandings of the world (epistemology), theories about how it works and changes (ontologies), and how it can be changed (Shove 2011). Briefly discussed in Chapter 1 and elaborated in Chapter 2, discussions of representation and universalising knowledge showed that theories are powerful determinants of what counts as knowledge, what topics or issues are worthy of research and how they should be framed and understood. Once problems are framed in a certain way, they assume a certain character and have a life beyond what was originally intended as they are taken up and replicated by subsequent research. This activity can limit new or alternate framings and marginalise other perspectives (Shove 2010; 2014; Strengers & Maller 2015).

Without revisiting issues with mainstream research and policymaking discussed in Chapter 2, it is important to emphasise that there is a general over-reliance on rational, individualised and universalised human thought and text that is human-centric and ignores the myriad of other ways urban environments are understood, experienced and problematised. The dominant ways urban issues and research problems are framed draw on behavioural, economic and technical theories (Shove 2010; 2015; Strengers & Maller 2015; Strengers et al. 2015), which lead to the proliferation of studies based on representational approaches together with a fascination and preoccupation with quantification, big data and urban analytics (Kaika 2017).

I argue there are three key steps needed to change practices of framing urban problems towards a more-than-human stance. The first is to decentre western and human-centric and essentialist ideas about knowledge and privilege to embrace other ways of knowing and recognising other beings that count and act in cities. Drawing on principles of ethics, empathy and care argued for by non-representational and new materialist approaches (Chapters 2, 3, 6), such as 'being for the other' and ethical mindfulness (Cloke & Jones 2003), would change the way problems are perceived and conceptualised. Instead of seeing situations or 'problems' only from a human perspective, critical anthropomorphism and the work of Despret (2004), Wolch (1996; 2002) and Puig de la Bellacasa (2017) encourage us to 'think' like non-humans, acknowledging the inherent limits of this approach. In this way, encounters with and practices involving non-humans or urban wildlife, which may be perceived detrimental to human health and well-being, would be reconsidered. For example, in scenarios where the activities of wildlife are perceived to be misaligned to human interests, such as large flying fox colonies roosting in cities (Rose 2015), or brush turkeys 'taking over' suburban gardens (Jones & Everding 1991), the 'problem' is often framed as getting rid of these species through relocation. In this scenario, these animals are problematised as being out of place, unwanted or as representing a threat in 'humanist citadels' (Franklin 2017, p. 202). More-than-human thinking would reframe this problem based on the notion that non-human species have a right to call cities home (Wolch 1996). Instead of the problem being framed as one of removal, it would be then be repositioned as 'how to get along' in a multispecies urban habitat, or 'make kin', as argued by Haraway (2016). In fact, this approach has been applied in Queensland, Australia, where the Department of Environment and Heritage Protection believes that some non-human animals have a right to, and are part of, the city ecosystem. Hence, instead of deploying strategies and policies to move flying fox colonies away from urban areas, it provides human residents with tips for living with their flying fox neighbours (Department of Environment and Heritage Protection 2017). Unfortunately, it is a different story in Sydney, where, as Rose (2015) has so richly documented, there is a persistent plan by the Royal Botanic Gardens to remove a maternal colony of grey-headed flying foxes because of the damage done to trees of heritage significance.

The second step in reframing problems is to traverse disciplinary and paradigm boundaries and break down silos that often hold back or thwart innovative thinking. Inspired by new materialisms and other more-than-human theories, there is a need to support disciplinary boundary crossings with the aim of achieving paradigm shifts towards more-than-human ways of knowing and understanding the world. This means resolving divisions between the social and natural sciences, and moving past other divides, such as humans versus non-humans, and considering relational ontologies (Castree 2003) such as those advocated by Bawaka Country et al. (2013; 2015; 2016)[2]. These initiatives are becoming increasingly relevant to urban living due to cities becoming legitimate homes for non-human species, and new 'smart' technologies and artificial intelligence making their way into homes – for example, digital assistants such as Apple's Siri and Amazon's Echo (Alexa) that require new forms, or types of, relations with increasingly animate things and may also change existing relations and practices. More-than-human thinking is useful to understand these emergent more-than-human relations that increasingly characterise and change urban living because it takes a processual and dynamic view of relations to include multiple, ongoing connections in assemblages over space and time.

Scholarship in new materialisms overtly attempts to see beyond disciplinary boundaries and work across disciplines to create *new* knowledge and ways of understanding more-than-human worlds (Lemke 2015). Traversing disciplines is different to multidisciplinarity, where the problem itself is not questioned, but is attempted to be addressed or 'solved' by drawing in multiple perspectives to create a holistic view (Shove 2011). As Lemke (2015, p. 4) surmises regarding new materialisms, they aim to generate 'a new understanding of ontology, epistemology, ethics and politics'. Successful disciplinary crossings are evident in some inspiring scholarship across a range of applied projects and scholarly endeavours (see, e.g., Barad 2007; Bawaka Country et al. 2015; Bennett 2010; Coole & Frost 2010b; Haraway 1991; 2008; Pickering 1993; Whatmore 2002; but there are many others). This work has provided new concepts that embrace the decentring of humans and look to complexity, emergence and process. Examples include Haraway's (2008) 'naturecultures', Barad's (2003) intra-action, Coole's (2013) 'agential capacity' and Bennett's (2010) vibrant matter. Of course, there are some concerns about cross-disciplinary and paradigmatic explorations in the extant literature. For example, noting the importance of the common boundaries at stake, Abrahamsson (2011, p. 399) argues that ecology, biology and politics do not always become intertwined in ways that foster 'a progressive politics'. Shove (2011, p. 262) observes that 'contrasting paradigms ... generate different methods of enquiry, different meanings of evidence, and different sorts of research agendas'. However, these boundaries are becoming increasingly fluid and 'safer' to cross, as discoveries in biotechnology, bio medicine, molecular biology (Coole & Frost 2010a) and physics (Barad 2007) emerge that can be aligned under the 'coherent epistemology' (Shove 2011, p. 263) offered by more-than-human thinking. Work in new materialisms and other more-than-human theories is leading the charge towards a paradigm shift (Pickering 2013) and the meeting, and potential merging, of traditionally separate disciplinary worlds.

The third way problems are reframed in more-than-human approaches is that social practices become the unit of enquiry or analysis, instead of individuals and their behaviours (Shove 2015; Spurling & McMeekin 2015; Strengers & Maller 2015). This strategy has been developed through theories of practice literature and is fundamental to any practice-based approach. Taking social practices, rather than individual people, as the unit of analysis and target for intervention reconceptualises action, and consequently changes how problems are framed and the solutions proposed. For example, working with industry and programme partners on projects attempting to reduce energy consumption in households and businesses, Strengers et al. (2015) explain that, instead of framing problems using epistemologies of behaviour change and rational economic theories to understand what individuals were doing and thinking, the focus was on practices; these included air travel for professional collaboration, washing, cooking, cleaning and heating and cooling homes. This meant that meanings of these practices, the materialities and agencies of appliances, the technologies involved and the competences required to use them came to the fore. Consequently, this approach changed the problem from one of trying to get individuals to consume less energy to being about changing everyday routine work and home practices, some of which were interconnected or co-dependent (Strengers et al. 2015).

Spurling and McMeekin (2015) provide another example through their work on transport and mobility in England. To improve energy efficiency and transition to low-carbon modes of transport and a sustainable future, the 'problem' was framed as one of inefficiency. Inefficient, carbon-fuelled cars were thus the problem, while innovative technologies such as electric vehicles became the solution. However, framing the problem and solution in this way would do nothing to change mobility patterns and their trajectories, and thereby maintained or even exacerbated traffic congestion and reliance on road infrastructure. This would consequently degrade habitats and deprioritise other more sustainable mobility modes such as trains and bicycles (Spurling & McMeekin 2015). Using a practice framing, the problem was instead described as one of mobility practices reliant on private car use. Consequently, adopting a method explained more fully in the subsection on intervention below, the solution was framed as substituting driving practices and their elements with other modes of mobility and changing the ways driving practices interlock and are spatially arranged according to other practices associated with working, home life and leisure (Spurling & McMeekin 2015).

In sum, problems, sites of intervention and routes for change are shifted from individuals and their behaviours to socially shared, and materially enacted, practices. Instead of conceptualising urban problems as what individual people do, problems are framed regarding what practices are being performed, what materials and other non-humans are involved, how they persist across time and space, and how they might be encouraged to change or cease (Shove et al. 2012). Significantly, there is no single 'correct' way to reframe urban problems related to healthy urban environments. However, regarding the dominance of technological, behavioural and individualised framings that currently characterise urban issues, there is a need to generate a greater diversity of approaches (Shove 2011, p. 264). Once problems have been reframed as in the examples described above, research and interventions would be designed, carried out and disseminated using notions of seeing, knowing and doing things differently according to more-than-human thinking; these practices include curiosity, care and empathy. The following subsection discusses how practices could change regarding research methodologies.

Different practices of doing research and using methods

Since understanding and changing the complex nature of cities requires cooperation and collaboration among disciplines, researchers, non-humans and other publics, it requires innovative ways of doing research and using methods. As explained in Chapter 2, non-representational theories, together with other approaches in The Affective Turn, do not oppose representation itself, but the assumed reliability and repeatability of the knowledge generated by those methods. That is, research methods per se are not necessarily at issue,[3] but, as discussed in the previous subsection, the way research problems are framed. In general, more-than-human thinking emphasises nuance, subtlety and the situatedness of encounters rather than definitive, representative, universalised or quantified answers.

Once research problems are reframed, the ways certain methods practices are engaged and applied in a more-than-human framing also change. To decentre humans, a variety of research to understand more-than-human worlds is required. This approach does not mean new or innovative methods are necessarily essential, but instead relates to *how* methods are performed, *who* participates in and conducts the research and *what* combinations are drawn together over relevant timescales. These ways of thinking encourage research design that considers in detail, and more inclusively, human–non-human interactions expressed through practices, encounters, affects and emotions, as well as notions of nonlinearity and emergence in urban environments. It also means that more attention must be applied to research practices and the many materials, meanings and competences that keep certain methods in circulation over others. As Law (2009, p. 239) writes, methods are 'practices that do not simply describe realities but also tend to enact these into being'. Barad (2003, p. 804) is also critical of the processes of making representations and their accuracy regarding 'that which they purport to represent'. In other words, she problematises the lack of reflection, awareness or investigation of the specific *practices* of representing upon which representational research is based. For example, as Law (2009) has shown, and as discussed in Chapter 2, large national surveys produce one way of understanding an issue, but there are often unexpected or unexplainable outcomes because survey questions with a limited set of multiple-choice answers cannot capture the complexity of people's everyday lives. However the limitations of this way of making knowledge are often ignored in a rush to intervene or make policy.

Despite the many methods relevant to more-than-human research, there are some that connect better with the agenda of this book. Instead of representational methods that prioritise the collection or documentation of human languages and texts (explained in Chapter 2) – the sorts of methods advocated by new materialisms, for example – a focus on dynamic more-than-human relations, processes and changes over time is relevant (e.g. Bell et al. 2017). These methods look to the agencies of non-humans and materials; they embrace openness, unpredictability and pre-cognitive affects and emotions (e.g., how cities might be experienced and felt); draw on more democratic methods of empathetic and caring data-making; and, by aiming to be less human- and expertise-centred, they seek to consider phenomena through ideas of nonlinearity and emergence.

However, due to its emergent status, the 'how' of doing more-than-human research is not yet clear or straightforward (Bell et al. 2017). Yet there is much to be learnt from first nations or indigenous practices to inform research and data-making and create change[4] – for example, the engaged witnessing and deep listening practice of Dadirri described by Bell et al. (2017), or the methodologies of attending advocated by Bawaka Country et al. (2013; 2015; 2016) that acknowledge non-humans as participants and authors in the research.[5] This extension of who counts as a researcher (and expert) is important because it is indicative of the decentring of humans and the recentring of more-than-human practices and relations, including those between places, humans and non-humans.

One example of a method used to study non-human animals that decentres researchers as experts is citizen science. Citizen science is increasingly employed in conservation ecology (Dickinson et al. 2012; Silvertown 2009), and involves urban human residents using 'apps', computers and mobile devices to record observations and sightings of non-human species in local habitats in real time. The data is delivered to central databases where conservationists can gain a better understanding of the distribution, abundance and species composition of urban ecosystems. For example, the Aussie Backyard Bird Count is conducted each October and encourages people throughout Australia to engage in practices of identifying and recording the birds they see in their local area (https://aussiebirdcount.org.au/). To participate in this practice, potential citizen scientists download the app to their mobile phone or use an online Web form. Instead of expertise being restricted to scientists, these methods create shared and distributed expertise among householders, devices and scientists whose practices collectively contribute knowledge about the behaviour and ecological characteristics of non-human animals in cities and throughout Australia.

Further expanding notions of who is and is not part of a research project, the depersonalising text and language used to refer to non-humans as 'it' could be repersonalised to recognise their capacities, agencies and roles in the research process (Kimmerer 2013). These ideas of agency connect with work in anthropology using the practice of multispecies ethnography as one example, leveraging off the scholarship of Haraway (2008; 2016), Wolch (1996; 2002) and Puig de la Bellacasa (2017), among others. Kirksey and Helmreich (2010, p. 545) explain: 'multispecies ethnography centres on how a multitude of organisms' livelihoods shape and are shaped by political, economic, and cultural forces'. Rather than one species being studied at a time, multispecies approaches, as the name suggests, explore multispecies entanglements and assemblages, including humans in the mix (Haraway

2016; Houston et al. 2017). Encouragingly, multispecies ethnographies are increasingly covering broader areas of concerns and are a growing phenomenon (Van Dooren et al. 2016). These approaches call for researchers and policymakers to desist in their assumed role of 'impartial observers' (Connell 2007) and involve themselves – past, present and future – in *caring* research and programme endeavours (Bell et al. 2017; Despret 2004).

As discussed in Chapter 3, multispecies ethnographies are also aligned with ideas from the biological sciences that are beginning to repersonalise and enliven research with non-human animals, using techniques such as critical anthropomorphism (Burghardt 2007) (discussed in Chapter 3). Critical anthropomorphism (Burghardt 2007) is used to understand complex animal emotional states and ways of being in the world once thought unique to humans, such as the use of tools and other materials in foraging for and consuming food, and attracting mates. These approaches can help rethink cities as habitat for more-than-just humans, foster understandings of multi-species relationships, who may benefit or be harmed, and help to develop more-than-human understandings of cities and processes of urbanisation.

More-than-human approaches to research also change how research with humans is conducted, where instead of simply following people and their attitudes, behaviours and choices, practices are studied over time and space and at various scales. For example, in studying global practice change and how everyday practices in the home can 'travel' with people as they migrate to different cities around the world, Maller and Strengers (2017) developed the use of a practice memory scrapbook. In studying practices per se, the aim was to understand how practices could migrate and continue to be repli-cated in different cities and contexts through the bodies and memories of their human carriers. In practice literature, the movement and globalisation of practices and how they persist and disappear is relevant to sustainabil-ity and health and well-being. In particular, energy- and water-intensive practices contributing to climate change, like heating and cooling homes with air conditioners, taking multiple daily showers and driving private cars, have been the subject of various studies (e.g., Hitchings & Lee 2008; Maller & Strengers 2015b; Walker et al. 2014). In our study of international students' practices in Melbourne, Australia (Maller & Strengers 2017), we used a scrapbook of images of the various ways students heated and cooled homes, did laundry and kept clean. The images were comprised of current and historical practices, such as swimming in the ocean or having an open wood fire, to technologies such as fans and air conditioners. The idea was that the scrapbook would help researchers and participants look for 'fragmentary clues' (Gaver et al. 2004, p. 53) of past and present practices – not just their own, but the practices they were familiar with in their countries of origin (Maller & Strengers 2017). In focusing on practice memories, the images were designed to reveal how practices had changed over time, in a range of countries and in Australia, and the modification or diffusion of past practices in different climates and contexts. Reframing research projects and methods using more-than-human thinking also leads to thinking differently about interventions to make healthy cities, as the next subsection explains.

Intervening for change

The usual approach for intervening for social and environmental change is to determine which human behaviours or technologies have the most impact or do the most harm, and then target these via strategies to reduce their impacts. The three most common strategies are changing individual attitudes, behaviours and choices; the use of markets and rational economic approaches, such as pricing signals and incentives; and the employment of technologies and devices to prompt, script, disrupt or automate what people do (Strengers & Maller 2015). Such policy interventions are framed 'in terms of simple relations between cause (an intervention) and effect (an outcome)' (Spurling & McMeekin 2015, p. 79). In contrast, more-than-human thinking, and more particularly theories of practice, differ in how they conceptualise interventions through policies and programmes to make healthy urban environments. Overall, interventions to make cities more-than-human habitat aim to shift practices, or the relations, materials and performances between humans and non-humans, over space and time. This would require detailed knowledge of practices and the linkages between them, such as those achieved through methods discussed in the previous subsection.

To change practices requires long-term and systematised efforts across a range of what are currently divided sectors and policy domains, including health, the environment, water, energy, housing, employment and transport (Shove 2015), a stance already advocated by the social determinants and health promotion approaches. However, a more-than-human approach provides further clues as to how to move this agenda forward. At the outset, there would be a need for understanding and 'mapping' intersecting practices across these domains, which together form bundles or complexes of practice (Shove et al. 2012). In this way, multiple sites might be identified for intervention, instead of the usual method of single or one-off interventions (Maller 2017; Maller & Horne 2011). As Spurling and McMeekin (2015, p. 79) explain: 'intervention should [be] viewed . . . as continuous and reflexive, historical and cumulative'.

This means that, rather than interventions directed at single practices identified as being problematic or in need of change, efforts would seek to intervene in multiple intersecting practice bundles, complexes or elements (meanings, materials and competences) at the same time, and support the making and breaking of links between elements that sustain them (Blue et al. 2016; Shove et al. 2012; Spurling & McMeekin 2015). The links between practices refer to how the elements that comprise a practice interconnect and shape each other over time in mutually supporting ways (Shove et al.

2012). For example, in the practice of domestic gardening, *meanings* about the purpose and style of the garden inform, and are informed by, what plant varieties to grow, the materiality and affordances of the local climate, soil, rainfall patterns and availability of light (*materials*), and the sorts of competences required to grow certain plant species in conditions specific to a site. Different combinations of these elements in various places and climates produce different gardens, and are generated by different varieties of gardening practices – for instance, a vegetable and herb garden grown on a balcony in New Delhi, compared to a rooftop garden in Copenhagen or an Australian native garden in subtropical Sydney. In Australia, the long history of migration since British colonisation means that there is a wide variety of gardening practices and types of gardens in cities because various cultural groups have continued the gardening practices of their origin (Graham & Connell 2006; Head et al. 2004). The sorts of gardens found in Australia include predominantly introduced flowering or woodland plants, productive gardens with fruit trees, vegetables and herbs, and native gardens and lawn gardens (Kirkpatrick et al. 2007). The practices that sustain and are replicated as necessary elements of these gardens have remained intact, or are available and interlock, mutually supporting each other and the continued performance of the practice with or without modification (Maller & Strengers 2013).

As indicated above, Spurling and McMeekin (2015) describe how changing practices can occur through three types of inter-related policy intervention: recrafting elements; substituting elements; and changing how practices are bundled together or interlock. Using the example of gardens, to better foster and encourage native and endemic species in cities, the elements comprising domestic gardening could be changed through recrafting. This might mean the introduction of policies to discourage planting of non-native or invasive plants in new or unestablished gardens, training households to identify and remove common 'weeds',[6] and social marketing campaigns to highlight the impact of non-native plants on ecosystems. Furthermore, gardening practices with non-indigenous plants could be substituted with alternative practices that better support urban ecosystems, such as the practice of wildlife gardening (Mumaw et al. 2017). This would mean intervening in two practices at the same time (Spurling & McMeekin 2015) – non-native gardening practices would be phased out through recrafting elements as just described, while interventions to encourage the performance of the substitute practice of wildlife gardening would also be implemented. This might include re-skilling urban gardeners to grow native plants endemic to their neighbourhood; the provision of free native seedlings to households wanting wildlife gardens; advice provided through garden assessments; and campaigns to shift the meanings of gardens from being merely about people to providing habitat for, and being made by, animals and plants (e.g., see Mumaw 2017). Although these ideas may resemble extant methods like those used in behaviour change, the difference is that they would be coordinated and systematised to target practices instead of being one-off interventions aimed at individuals and their behaviour at single points in time (Maller 2017, p. 78).

Finally, to increase urban habitat for non-human species more comprehensively, there could be intervention in the way wider systems of practices interlock and are organised in cities. This means thinking more broadly about habitat protection and provision in urban places and negotiating how land is used and for whom – for example, practices related to where and how new housing and industry sites are provided and their impacts on local ecosystems; the density, style and form of housing developments; and the design of domestic and public gardens and incorporation, encouragement and acceptance of animals and plants in planning processes and legislation. All supporting practices related to these aspects of cities are interlinked across space and time, resulting in specific urban forms (Houston et al. 2017), which may or may not support or protect ecosystems. What this means is that, in addition to intervening in practices of households and industry, it is equally if not more important to intervene in the practices of urban policymakers, planners and other governing professionals (Strengers & Maller 2015), starting with changes to extant practices of problem-framing practices.

By reframing problems, policymakers and practitioners can assist in undoing or 'fossilising' (Shove & Pantzar 2005) practices detrimental to more-than-human habitat that harm human and non-human health. Some examples of practices that could be undone or redirected include car driving, land clearing and industrial pollution. To make cities more-than-human habitat involves the renegotiation of urban spaces as being only for, or 'needed' by, humans to recognising them as important habitat for (native) non-human animals and plants. In other words, there is a need to tackle 'current "needs" [that] are historically contingent, and intimately embedded in *multiple* domains of life, including work, leisure and the home' (Spurling & McMeekin 2015, p. 88; emphasis added). However, the way the non-human animals and plants are considered, conceptualised and responded to through policy and planning in urban environments is 'hyperseparated' (Plumwood 2009, p. 116), and therefore impoverished (Houston et al. 2017; Porter 2010; Wolch 1996). To move beyond and resolve the 'exceptionalism of humanism' in urban planning, humans need to integrate non-humans into our worlds, and 'become enmeshed and interconnected into theirs' (Houston et al. 2017, pp. 2, 10).

One way to do this is to consider and learn from Indigenous Australians' notion of Country. Country is more than just land: 'Country is multidimensional – it consists of people, animals, plants, Dreamings; underground, earth, soils, minerals and waters, surface water, and air. Country . . . exists both in and through time' (Rose 1996, p. 8). Starting from the idea that Country is everywhere, including in urban environments, changes how the governance of cities is conceptualised and enacted. There are various examples of where concepts similar to Country have made their way into policies and legislation.

In 2010, the Bolivian Plurinational Legislative Assembly introduced the Law of the Rights of Mother Earth (Pachamama) to recognise all non-humans on which human life depends and is comprised (Callahuanca 2017). The Law has six 'binding principles', the first of which is 'harmony', where 'human activities, within the framework of plurality and diversity, should achieve a dynamic balance with the cycles and processes inherent in Mother Earth' (Callahuanca 2017). This intervention is a positive step in recognising non-humans, decentring humans and thinking differently even though the policy has not completely eradicated destructive activities such as mining (Plumwood 2009).

Other examples come from New Zealand and India respectively, where the Whanganui, Ganga and Yamuna rivers and the Gangotri and Yamunotri glaciers have been given personhood and are consequently recognised as legal 'persons' with rights to exist (Hutchison 2014; O'Donnell 2017). What this means is that the rivers have been transformed from being considered 'property' into entities with legal standing that can be represented in court when their rights are violated (Hutchison 2014). In New Zealand, the indigenous Whanganui Iwi people are now formally recognised as guardians of the Whanganui river (Hutchison 2014), while in India, guardianship responsibilities for the Yamuna rivers and the Gangotri and Yamunotri glaciers have been conferred on several representatives in the state government of Uttarakhand (O'Donnell 2017). These moves challenge the human-centric view that a 'legal person' is confined to humans (Hutchison 2014), and show that, given sufficient political will, we can change the way we make, live in, manage, design and govern cities. They also show that despite the marginalisation and oppression of indigenous peoples around the world, they could lead the way to show how cities could be conceived, planned and lived in from a more-than-human stance[7] (Porter 2010). This is because they 'have . . .[more] agentic and intentional views of the world of nature' (Plumwood 2009, p. 124). Therefore, 'urban planners and scholars need to think carefully . . . about who speaks for . . . nonhuman[s] in cit[ies] . . . and about whether and how . . . nonhuman[s] might speak for themselves' (Houston et al. 2017, p. 9).

At work in the above scenarios are policies and legislation which enact agency in the protection of non-humans, in this case Mother Earth, rivers and glaciers. However, more correctly, these are examples of more-than-human agencies, where humans and non-humans as collectives or assemblages have intervened and brought about change. This point highlights that just like legal persons, interveners are not necessarily people. In fact, interveners can be 'anyone or anything', including 'physical infrastructures research methods, policies, householders, researchers and politicians', who are all 'potential agents of change' (Maller & Strengers 2015a, p. 197).

Decentring humans and using more open and dynamic methods and types of interventions leads to numerous questions of ethics and politics such that politics becomes 'a more-than-human affair'. Importantly, there i an emphasis on processes and collective efforts to find pathways rather than following standard bureaucratic conventions and the usual human-centric, formalised political processes (Bennett 2010; Hinchliffe & Whatmore 2006). A range of non-humans including animals, plants and minerals, can disrupt and create political acts and events to 'catalyze a public' (Bennett 2010, p. 107). In a nutshell, non-humans like rivers can be and are being elevated to valued members of the political realm (Bennett 2010; Franklin 2017; Houston et al. 2017). Regarding healthy cities as more-than-human habitat, this approach has various benefits. It carves out a political agenda that encourages animals and plants back to urban environments, reduces the environmental impact and damage caused by humans, and makes cities more equitable for disadvantaged human populations and non-human, native and endemic species which also have rights to, and make, city habitats (Houston et al. 2017).

In summary, more-than-human research, policymaking and intervention encourages relational thinking at multiple scales simultaneously, from multi-species assemblages in parks and remnant ecosystems to microbiomes inside human bodies.[8] This transition means embracing different concepts of time and space so that the lives of non-humans, like microbes living life in the fast lane or trees and rivers living life in the slow lane, can be understood outside of our currently limited human conceptions.

Conclusion

In addressing the third aim of the book, this chapter has outlined how inno-vative and inspiring concepts and ideas from more-than-human thinking could be used and experimented with to shift current understandings of urban environments and urban health, and thereby change research, policy-making and intervention practices. I argued that to intervene in cities to benefit both humans and other species, instead of human-centrism, a relational, more-than-human perspective is required. As Plumwood (2009, p. 116) argues, 'human-centredness is not in the interests of either humans or non-humans . . . it is even dangerous and irrational', with one of its consequences 'a failure to understand our embeddedness in and dependency on nature'. Accepting the agency of non-humans in research, policymaking and intervening means we need to overcome the deep-rooted speciesism that says humans are the only 'beings that count' (Whatmore 2002, p. 155) and are always in control. Furthermore, we need to think about understanding, designing, governing and managing cities as *shared* habitats for non-human species as well as humans. Many of the examples provided in this chapter could be brought together to systematically intervene in cities and achieve this goal.

Further implementation of these ideas by researchers and policymakers requires critical reflection on the environmental impacts of cities, both positive and negative, and the need for different sorts of knowledge to understand and attempt to intervene in these impacts in more complex, emergent and more-than-human ways. This epistemological approach is likely to challenge some contemporary research theory and practice. It is difficult to fully grasp or predict the political and ethical consequences of such a move, within and beyond the sphere of research and the academy. However, it is a challenge we must embrace to rethink the notion of healthy cities and healthy urban environments.

Notes

1 As introduced in Chapter 3.
2 As covered in Chapter 3.
3 See, for example, Shove (2017).
4 Acknowledging implications 'that more-than-human approaches [that] . . . absorb all kinds of relational or non-dualist ontology can be construed as a kind of colonising or universalist move' (Head 2016, p. 81).
5 Where Country is recognised as the first author on publications, as discussed in Chapter 3.
6 Acknowledging that 'weeds' is a socially constructed term that frames plants in relation to human-centric values (Houston et al. 2017) and that some non-native plants can be vital habitat of some cities as part of novel ecosystems (Low 2003).
7 It is important to note that seeing urban places in more open, dynamic and relational ways will not make up for or resolve the histories of violence, suppression, invasion and domination towards indigenous peoples that characterises most cities.
8 Mills et al. (2017, p. 2) propose the 'Microbiome Rewilding Hypothesis'. This contends that increasing biodiversity in urban greenspaces 'can rewild the environmental microbiome to a state that benefits human health by primary prevention as an ecosystem service'.

References

Abrahamsson, C 2011, 'Book review forum: *Vibrant Matter: A Political Ecology of Things*', *Dialogues in Human Geography*, vol. 1, no. 3, pp. 399–402.
Barad, K 2003, 'Posthumanist performativity: toward an understanding of how matter comes to matter', *Signs*, vol. 28, no. 3, pp. 801–831.
Barad, K 2007, *Meeting the Universe Halfway: Quantum Physics and the Entanglement of Matter and Meaning*, Duke University Press.
Bawaka Country, Suchet-Pearson, S, Wright, S, Lloyd, K & Burarrwanga, L 2013, 'Caring as Country: towards an ontology of co-becoming in natural resource management', *Asia Pacific Viewpoint*, vol. 54, no. 2, pp. 185–197.
Bawaka Country, Wright, S, Suchet-Pearson, S, Lloyd, K, Burarrwanga, L, Ganambarr, R, Ganambarr-Stubbs, M, Ganambarr, B & Maymuru, D 2015, 'Working with and learning from Country: decentring human author-ity', *Cultural Geographies*, vol. 22, no. 2, pp. 269–283.
Bawaka Country, Wright, S, Suchet-Pearson, S, Lloyd, K, Burarrwanga, L, Ganambarr, R, Ganambarr-Stubbs, M, Ganambarr, B, Maymuru, D & Sweeney, J 2016, 'Co-becoming Bawaka: towards a relational understanding of place/space', *Progress in Human Geography*, vol. 40, no. 4, pp. 455–475.

Bell, SJ, Instone, L & Mee, KJ 2017, 'Engaged witnessing: researching with the more-than-human', *Area*, doi:10.1111/area.12346.

Bennett, J 2007, 'Edible matter', *New Left Review*, vol. 45, pp. 133–145.

Bennett, J 2010, *Vibrant Matter: A Political Ecology of Things*, Duke University Press.

Blue, S, Shove, E, Carmona, C & Kelly, MP 2016, 'Theories of practice and public health: understanding (un)healthy practices', *Critical Public Health*, vol. 26, no. 1, pp. 36–50.

Browne, A, Medd, W, Anderson, B & Pullinger, M 2015, 'Methods as intervention: Intervening in practice through quantitative and mixed method methodologies', in Y Strengers & C Maller (eds), *Social Practices, Intervention and Sustainability: Beyond Behaviour Change*, Routledge, pp. 179–195.

Burghardt, GM 2007, 'Critical anthropomorphism, uncritical anthropocentrism, and naive nominalism', *Comparative Cognition and Behavior Reviews*, vol. 2, pp. 136–138.

Callahuanca, ROM 2017, 'Law of the Rights of Mother Earth', World Future Fund, www.worldfuturefund.org/Projects/Indicators/motherearthbolivia.html, accessed 23 November 2017.

Castree, N 2003, 'Environmental issues: relational ontologies and hybrid politics', *Progress in Human Geography*, vol. 27, no. 2, pp. 203–211.

Cloke, P & Jones, O 2003, 'Grounding ethical mindfulness for/in nature: trees in their places', *Ethics, Place & Environment*, vol. 6, no. 3, pp. 195–213.

Connell, R 2007, *Southern Theory: The Global Dynamics of Knowledge in Social Science*, Allen & Unwin.

Coole, D 2013, 'Agentic capacities and capacious historical materialism: thinking with new materialisms in the political sciences', *Millennium-Journal of International Studies*, vol. 41, no. 3, pp. 451–469.

Coole, D & Frost, S 2010a, 'Introducing the new materialisms', in D Coole, S Frost & J Bennett (eds), *New Materialisms: Ontology, Agency, and Politics*, Duke University Press, pp. 1–43.

Coole, D & Frost, S 2010b, *New Materialisms: Ontology, Agency, and Politics*, Duke University Press.

Department of Environment and Heritage Protection 2017, *Living Near Flying-foxes*, Queensland Government, https://www.ehp.qld.gov.au/wildlife/livingwith/flyingfoxes/living-with-flying-foxes.html, accessed 22 November 2017.

Despret, V 2004, 'The body we care for: figures of anthropo-zoo-genesis', *Body & Society*, vol. 10, nos 2–3, pp. 111–134.

Dickinson, JL, Shirk, J, Bonter, D, Bonney, R, Crain, RL, Martin, J, Phillips, T & Purcell, K 2012, 'The current state of citizen science as a tool for ecological research and public engagement', *Frontiers in Ecology and the Environment*, vol. 10, no. 6, pp. 291–297.

Franklin, A 2017, 'The more-than-human city', *The Sociological Review*, vol. 65, no. 2, pp. 202–217.

Gaver, WW, Boucher, A, Pennington, S & Walker, B 2004, 'Cultural probes and the value of uncertainty', *Interactions*, vol. 11, no. 5, pp. 53–56.

Graham, S & Connell, J 2006, 'Nurturing relationships: the gardens of Greek and Vietnamese migrants in Marrickville, Sydney', *Australian Geographer*, vol. 37, no. 3, pp. 375–393.

Haraway, DJ 1991, *Simians, Cyborgs, and Women: The Reinvention of Nature*, Routledge,.

Haraway, DJ 2008, *When Species Meet*, University of Minnesota Press.

Haraway, DJ 2016, *Staying with the Trouble: Making Kin in the Chthulucene*, Duke University Press.

Head, L 2016, *Hope and Grief in the Anthropocene: Re-conceptualising Human–nature Relations*, Routledge.

Head, L, Muir, P & Hampel, E 2004, 'Australian backyard gardens and the journey of migration', *Geographical Review*, vol. 94, no. 3, pp. 326–347.

Hinchliffe, S & Whatmore, S 2006, 'Living cities: towards a politics of conviviality', *Science as Culture*, vol. 15, no. 2, pp. 123–138.

Hitchings, R & Lee, SJ 2008, 'Air conditioning and the material culture of routine human encasement: the case of young people in contemporary Singapore', *Journal of Material Culture*, vol. 13, no. 3, pp. 251–265.

Houston, D, Hillier, J, MacCallum, D, Steele, W & Byrne, J 2017, 'Make kin, not cities! Multispecies entanglements and "becoming-world" in planning theory', *Planning Theory*, doi:10.1177/1473095216688042.

Hutchison, A 2014, 'The Whanganui River as a legal person', *Alternative Law Journal*, vol. 39, no. 3, pp. 179–182.

Jones, DN & Everding, SE 1991, 'Australian brush-turkeys in a suburban environment: implications for conflict and conservation', *Wildlife Research*, vol. 18, no. 3, pp. 285–297.

Kaika, M 2017, '"Don't call me resilient again!": the New Urban Agenda as immunology . . . or . . . what happens when communities refuse to be vaccinated with "smart cities" and indicators', *Environment and Urbanization*, vol. 29, no. 1, pp. 89–102.

Katterman, SN, Kleinman, BM, Hood, MM, Nackers, LM & Corsica, JA 2014, 'Mindfulness meditation as an intervention for binge eating, emotional eating, and weight loss: a systematic review', *Eating Behaviors*, vol. 15, no. 2, pp. 197–204.

Kimmerer, RW 2013, *Braiding Sweetgrass: Indigenous Wisdom, Scientific Knowledge and the Teachings of Plants*, Milkweed Editions.

Kirkpatrick, JB, Daniels, GD & Zagorski, T 2007, 'Explaining variation in front gardens between suburbs of Hobart, Tasmania, Australia', *Landscape and Urban Planning*, vol. 79, no. 3, pp. 314–322.

Kirksey, SE & Helmreich, S 2010, 'The emergence of multispecies ethnography', *Cultural Anthropology*, vol. 25, no. 4, pp. 545–576.

Law, J 2009, 'Seeing like a survey', *Cultural Sociology*, vol. 3, no. 2, pp. 239–256.

Lemke, T 2015, 'New materialisms: Foucault and the "Government of Things"', *Theory, Culture & Society*, vol. 32, no. 4, pp. 3–25.

Low, T 2003, *The New Nature*, Penguin Books.

Maller, C 2017, 'Epigenetics, theories of social practice and lifestyle disease', in A Hui, TR Schatzki & E Shove (eds), *The Nexus of Practices: Connections, Constellations, Practitioners*, Routledge, pp. 68–80.

Maller, C & Horne, R 2011, 'Living lightly: how does climate change feature in residential home improvements and what are the implications for policy?', *Urban Policy and Research*, vol. 29, no. 1, pp. 59–72.

Maller, C & Strengers, Y 2013, 'The global migration of everyday life: investigating the practice memories of Australian migrants', *Geoforum*, vol. 44, pp. 243–252.

Maller, C & Strengers, Y 2015a, 'Conclusion: transforming practice interventions', in Y Strengers & C Maller (eds), *Social Practices, Intervention and Sustainability: Beyond Behaviour Change*, Routledge, pp. 196–200.

Maller, C & Strengers, Y 2015b, 'Resurrecting sustainable practices: using memories of the past to intervene in the future', in Y Strengers & C Maller (eds), *Social Practices, Intervention and Sustainability: Beyond Behaviour Change*, Routledge, pp. 147–162.

Maller, C & Strengers, Y 2017, 'Studying social practices and global practice change using scrapbooks as a cultural probe', *Area*, doi:10.1111/area.12351.

Miller, CK, Kristeller, JL, Headings, A & Nagaraja, H 2014, 'Comparison of a mindful eating intervention to a diabetes self-management intervention among adults with type 2 diabetes: a randomized controlled trial', *Health Education & Behavior*, vol. 41, no. 2, pp. 145–154.

Mills, JG, Weinstein, P, Gellie, NJC, Weyrich, LS, Lowe, AJ & Breed, MF 2017, 'Urban habitat restoration provides a human health benefit through microbiome rewilding: the Microbiome Rewilding Hypothesis', *Restoration Ecology*, vol. 25, no. 6, pp. 866–872.

Mol, A 1999, 'Ontological politics: a word and some questions', *Sociological Review*, vol. 47, no. S1, pp. 74–89.

Mumaw, L 2017, 'Transforming urban gardeners into land stewards', *Journal of Environmental Psychology*, vol. 52, pp. 92–103.

Mumaw, LM, Maller, C & Bekessy, S 2017, 'Strengthening wellbeing in urban communities through wildlife gardening', *Cities and the Environment (CATE)*, vol. 10, no. 1, pp. 1–18.

O'Donnell, EL 2017, 'At the intersection of the sacred and the legal: rights for nature in Uttarakhand, India', *Journal of Environmental Law*, vol. 30, doi:10.1093/jel/eqx026/4364852.

Pickering, A 1993, 'The mangle of practice: agency and emergence in the sociology of science', *American Journal of Sociology*, vol. 99, no. 3, pp. 559–589.

Pickering, A 2013, 'Being in an environment: a performative perspective', *Natures Sciences Sociétés*, vol. 21, no. 1, pp. 77-83.

Plumwood, V 2009, 'Nature in the active voice', *Australian Humanities Review*, vol. 46, pp. 113–129.

Porter, L 2010, *Unlearning the Colonial Cultures of Planning*, Ashgate.

Puig de la Bellacasa, M 2017, *Matters of Care: Speculative Ethics in More than Human Worlds*, University of Minnesota Press.

Rose, DB 1996, *Nourishing Terrains: Australian Aboriginal Views of Landscape and Wilderness*, Australian Heritage Commission.

Rose, DB 2015, 'Flying foxes in Sydney', in K Gibson, DB Rose & R Fincher (eds), *Manifesto for Living in the Anthropocene*, punctum books, pp. 83–89.

Shove, E 2010, 'Beyond the ABC: climate change policy and theories of social change', *Environment and Planning A*, vol. 42, pp. 1273–1285.

Shove, E 2011, 'On the difference between chalk and cheese – a response to Whitmarsh et al's comments on "Beyond the ABC: climate change policy and theories of social change"', *Environment and Planning A*, vol. 43, no. 2, pp. 262–264.

Shove, E 2014, 'Putting practice into policy: reconfiguring questions of consumption and climate change', *Contemporary Social Science*, vol. 9, no. 4, pp. 415–429.

Shove, E 2015, 'Linking low carbon policy and social practice', in Y Strengers & C Maller (eds), *Social Practices, Intervention and Sustainability: Beyond Behaviour Change*, Routledge, pp. 31–44.

Shove, E 2017, 'Practice theory methodologies do not exist', https://practicetheory methodologies.wordpress.com/2017/02/15/elizabeth-shove-practice-theory-methodologies-do-not-exist/, *Practice Theory Methodologies*, accessed 28 February 2017.

Shove, E & Pantzar, M 2005, 'Fossilisation', *Ethnologia Europaea*, vol. 35, pp. 59–63.

Shove, E, Pantzar, M & Watson, M 2012, *The Dynamics of Social Practice: Everyday Life and How It Changes*, SAGE Publications.

Silvertown, J 2009, 'A new dawn for citizen science', *Trends in Ecology & Evolution*, vol. 24, no. 9, pp. 467–471.

Spurling, N & McMeekin, A 2015, 'Sustainable mobility policies in England', in Y Strengers & C Maller (eds), *Social Practices, Intervention and Sustainability: Beyond Behaviour Change*, Routledge, pp. 78–94.

Stengers, I 2015, *In Catastrophic Times: Resisting the Coming Barbarism*, Open Humanities Press.

Strengers, Y & Maller, C 2015, 'Introduction: social practices, intervention and sustainability, beyond behaviour change', in Y Strengers & C Maller (eds), *Social Practices, Intervention and Sustainability: Beyond Behaviour Change*, Routledge, pp. 1–12.

Strengers, Y, Moloney, S, Maller, C & Horne, R 2015, 'Beyond behaviour change', in Y Strengers & C Maller (eds), *Social Practices, Intervention and Sustainability: Beyond Behaviour Change*, Routledge, pp. 63–77.

Van Dooren, T, Kirksey, E & Münster, U 2016, 'Multispecies studies: cultivating arts of attentiveness', *Environmental Humanities*, vol. 8, no. 1, pp. 1–23.

Walker, G, Shove, E & Brown, S 2014, 'How does air conditioning become "needed"? A case study of routes, rationales and dynamics', *Energy Research & Social Science*, vol. 4, pp. 1–9.

Whatmore, S 2002, *Hybrid Geographies: Natures Cultures Spaces*, SAGE Publications.

Wolch, J 1996, 'Zoöpolis', *Capitalism Nature Socialism*, vol. 7, no. 2, pp. 21–47.

Wolch, J 2002, 'Anima urbis', *Progress in Human Geography*, vol. 26, no. 6, pp. 721–742.

8 More-than-human healthy futures

To briefly recap the book's journey to this point, Part I (Chapters 2, 3 and 4) addressed the first aim of this book, which is to generate a greater appreciation of the non-human publics that make the world more-than-human. It began 'at the theoretical level, with an eye to rethinking urban theory and unsettling its anthropocentric traditions' (Wolch 2002, pp. 734–735). These chapters made a case for dissolving troublesome binary categories in traditional scientific and academic thinking, and thereby decentred humans to better recognise and understand the vibrant living and non-living non-humans comprising everyday life in cities. Furthermore, they emphasised the significance of ongoing processes and performance through everyday practices. This part of the book also argued that the many non-humans that make up what some humans call 'nature' should be conceptualised as part of cities rather than being positioned passively as 'background', or worse, irrelevant to urban life only occurring in imagined 'wilderness' or remote areas (Franklin 2017; Head 2016; Hinchliffe & Whatmore 2006).

Part II (Chapters 5, 6 and 7) argued that we need to understand health differently – get better at seeing and knowing the non-human species already extant in cities, make more room for them, encourage them back, and accept the myriad of ways human and non-human lives are entangled and co-dependent. In tackling the second aim of the book, Chapters 5 and 6 opened new ways of thinking, knowing and understanding cities and urban environments as more-than-human habitat. In conceiving health as more-than-human through theories of social practice, Chapter 5 showed how materials, materialities, living and non-living non-humans and their relations and links across space and time in urban environments determine health outcomes. The chapter also discussed how more-than-human thinking is aligned with health promotion in that it requires multiple policy sectors to work collaboratively together. Chapter 6 illustrated how cities as habitat are made and remade autonomously by non-human animals and plants, as well as through their encounters with humans via practices such as gardening and wildlife feeding. Chapter 6 thereby demonstrated that cities provide, and are made habitat for, a range of species, including but not limited to humans, and can therefore be reconceptualised as more-than-human habitat.

The book's third aim was to encourage experimentation with new concepts and ideas from a more-than-human perspective and thinking about different interventions for change, accepting that, due to the dynamic complexity of cities, there will be unpredictable or unforeseen outcomes. In focusing on this aim, Chapter 7 demonstrated that the perceived 'exclusive' human right to cities, and the human-centrism of planning and other land management decisions, can no longer be justified (Garrard & Bekessy 2014; Houston et al. 2017). Chapter 7 covered a range of methods and approaches that could be used in research, policymaking and practice to think about, know, govern and live in cities as more-than-human habitat. In transforming the way we think about cities, policy and research interventions have the potential to bring to the fore our relations with the many non-humans that share and make cities what they are.

Together with these three aims, I have used more-than-human theories as a foundation to rethink and transform the idea of 'healthy cities'. Current ideas about healthy cities, as reflected in the UN's New Urban Agenda, are underpinned by western-centric, bifurcated theories and knowledge that can only partially transform cities and urban environments into healthier and more equitable places. Reflecting on the persistence of this limited view and the difficulties encountered in thinking differently, Castree (2003, p. 204) observes: 'non-relational thinking . . . evidently dies hard'. Through a more-than-human, relational lens, I argued that problematic binary categories *can* be dissolved, humans *can* be decentred, and we *can* begin the work of not only reanimating cities (Wolch 2002), but getting to know, and care for, the non-human animals and plants that are already present.[1] In this vein, as argued in Chapter 7, Narayanan (2017, p. 488) encourages us to formulate 'new multispecies-inclusive geographies' that 'recognise the agency and personhood of non-humans, as well as the ways in which they claim and occupy space'. In short, to centre living non-humans in cities, we need to decentre humans.

Throughout the chapters, I have therefore developed a vision of healthy cities as places and habitats that acknowledge, invite and encourage some non-humans to flourish and where beneficial more-than-human relations productively co-exist.[2] To do so, the book has drawn on the work of scholars from several disciplines who have traversed, grappled with and provided detailed accounts of a range of associated positions, propositions, arguments and limitations. I have drawn on the collective contributions of these efforts with the purpose of transforming currently accepted ways of understanding cities and how we think about healthy urban environments. I have also sought to translate these contributions in a way that will assist in and encourage experimentation in research and policymaking.[3] More-than-human perspectives are therefore not just academic notions with limited potential for practical application or everyday life. I have shown how they can help policymakers, planners and researchers to reassess and change their practices, to experiment with ways of becoming-with, and to find innovative ways of thinking about the research, planning, design and governance of cities as more-than-human habitat (Houston et al. 2017; Wolch 2002). For example, urban policy and conservation practices could look beyond human-centrism and the protection of individual species or remnant fragments of habitat, to the interwoven webs of non-humans, ecosystems – and humans – that make cities what they are. By better understanding the interdependencies between all the entities that comprise cities, more inclusive, and potentially more effective, interventions could be implemented.

Despite our extensive knowledge about health, and some incredible techno-logical advancements, we're still heading down the path of unprecedented global damage caused by climate change, pollution and habitat destruction, with many places becoming more inequitable and unhealthier. As Haraway (2015, p. 159) explains, 'it's more than climate change; it's also extraordinary burdens of toxic chemistry, mining, depletion of lakes and rivers under and above ground, ecosystem simplification, vast genocides of people and other critters' that threaten multiple, major system collapses. These losses will affect the health and well-being of numerous generations of humans and non-human species alike, and we are unlikely to understand the impacts on our health and the world's ecosystems until it is too late. The reason for this is our myopic, human-centric view of the world, including our understanding of cities, that prevents us from seeing humans as part of ecosystems (Plumwood 2009).

Although not always visible or noticed, vibrant non-humans are very much part of cities and similarly urbanised settings – in the water that flows through drains and pipes; in rock and other ancient substrates under asphalt and concrete – furthermore, insects, animals, birds, trees and other types of vegetation persist, and innumerable microbes are found everywhere. Yet simplified binaries between humans and other species, and cities and 'wild' (or rural) landscapes, for example, persist and continue to be replicated in most urban policy, planning and research. Meanwhile, habitat loss and species extinctions are accelerating as new cities appear globally and urban-isation continues to spread. Commenting on how non-human animals are losing traditional forms of habitat and are marginalised in urban environ-ments, Narayanan (2017, p. 476) argues that they 'face steady eviction from spaces that are increasingly privatised, ghettoised, developed, or otherwise removed from nonhuman access'. Haraway (2015, p. 160) makes a similar claim: 'the earth is full of refugees, human and not, without refuge'. This book has argued that to even begin to understand and divert this destructive trajectory, we need to think about and treat cities as more-than-human. As Haraway (2015, p. 159) argues: 'no species, not even our own arrogant one pretending to be good individuals . . . acts alone'.

Although more-than-human thinking might be regarded by some as challenging, 'fringe' or 'risky', what it achieves is a disruption of the status quo, which is exactly what is needed if the current problems facing cities are to be addressed. In particular, it is urgent to dismantle 'the human-centeredness of planning practices in which humans are unquestionably situated as active knowers, decision-makers and place makers' (Houston et al. 2017, p. 6). However, it is also necessary for policymakers, practitioners and scholars to carefully consider who 'speaks' for non-humans and whether it is possible that they might speak for themselves, if we know how to listen. We also need to learn to think more collectively and relationally regarding human–non-human relations and better understand the multiple relations non-human species have with each other. Therefore, using more-than-human thinking to reconceptualise cities as more-than-human habitat raises numerous questions of politics and ethics. Although some of these issues were touched on in Chapter 7, there are opportunities for further work directed towards the rights, ethics and politics of human–non-human relations in urban environments (e.g., see Castree 2014; Whatmore 2002; 2006; Haraway 1991a; 2008; Singer 2013; Steele et al. 2015; Twine 2010).

I especially encourage further engagement with, and learning from, the enlightening contributions from indigenous scholars and those who work genuinely with indigenous peoples, including Deborah Bird Rose (1996; 2012), Marcia Langton (2006), Bawaka Country et al. (2013; 2015; 2016), Jonathan Yotti Kingsley et al. (2013), Libby Porter (2010; Porter & Barry 2016) and Robin Wall Kimmerer (2013). Relatedly, issues of gender, race, indigenous and environmental justice require detailed focus and attention (see Butler 1993; Connell 2007; Haraway 1989; 1991b; Instone 1998; Massey 1994; Porter 2010; Porter & Barry 2016; Walker 2012; 2015).

As noted at the outset, new ways of thinking and understanding urban problems, and imagining innovative solutions are desperately needed to challenge current paradigms about health and urban environments, and to redress the current suite of serious challenges facing cities throughout the world. I have demonstrated that approaches drawing on more-than-human thinking can fulfil this need because they embrace complexity, emergence and process. Through the book, I have outlined, translated and synthesised the literature that adopts a more-than-human stance to derive some clear paths forward to productively push disciplinary boundaries to more trans-formative, trans-disciplinary ways of thinking and knowing the world. I close with an invitation from the late ecofeminist and philosopher Val Plumwood (2009, p. 128), who wrote: 'the struggle to think differently, to remake our reductionist culture, is a basic survival project . . . I hope you will join it.' The need to change the way we think about cities could not be more urgent, for our own survival and that of the planet.

Notes

1   I acknowledge that, in general, the book's focus has been on macro animals and plants, and there was not the opportunity to give sufficient attention to microbiota. There was also limited space to deal in detail with non-living non-humans such as infrastructures and technologies.

2   By focusing on the positive health outcomes, or what might be termed the 'co-benefits', for humans and non-humans, I do not mean to override or ignore the negative impacts non-humans can have on human health, well-being and quality of life, and vice versa. In addition to being beyond the scope of this book, these negative effects are better covered by disciplines such as ecohealth. For example, see work by McMichael and colleagues (McMichael 2001; 2009; McMichael et al. 2007).

3   Theories have their boundaries, and incommensurability is always a risk (Kuhn 1982).

References

Bawaka Country, Suchet-Pearson, S, Wright, S, Lloyd, K & Burarrwanga, L 2013, 'Caring as Country: towards an ontology of co-becoming in natural resource management', *Asia Pacific Viewpoint*, vol. 54, no. 2, pp. 185–197.

Bawaka Country, Wright, S, Suchet-Pearson, S, Lloyd, K, Burarrwanga, L, Ganambarr, R, Ganambarr-Stubbs, M, Ganambarr, B & Maymuru, D 2015, 'Working with and learning from Country: decentring human author-ity', *Cultural Geographies*, vol. 22, no. 2, pp. 269–283.

Bawaka Country, Wright, S, Suchet-Pearson, S, Lloyd, K, Burarrwanga, L, Ganambarr, R, Ganambarr-Stubbs, M, Ganambarr, B, Maymuru, D & Sweeney, J 2016, 'Co-becoming Bawaka: towards a relational understanding of place/space', *Progress in Human Geography*, vol. 40, no. 4, pp. 455–475.

Butler, J 1993, *Bodies that Matter: On the Discursive Limits of 'Sex'*, Routledge.

Castree, N 2003, 'Environmental issues: relational ontologies and hybrid politics', *Progress in Human Geography*, vol. 27, no. 2, pp. 203–211.

Castree, N 2014, *Making Sense of Nature*, Routledge.

Connell, R 2007, *Southern Theory: The Global Dynamics of Knowledge in Social Science*, Allen & Unwin.

Franklin, A 2017, 'The more-than-human city', *The Sociological Review*, vol. 65, no. 2, pp. 202–217.

Garrard, GE & Bekessy, SA 2014, 'Land use and land management', in J Byrne, N Sipe & J Dodson (eds), *Australian Environmental Planning: Challenges and Future Prospects*, Routledge, pp. 61–72.

Haraway, DJ 1989, *Primate Visions: Gender, Race, and Nature in the World of Modern Science*, Routledge.

Haraway, DJ 1991a, *A Cyborg Manifesto: Science, Technology, and Socialist-feminism in the Late Twentieth Century*, Routledge.

Haraway, DJ 1991b, *Simians, Cyborgs, and Women: The Reinvention of Nature*, Routledge.

Haraway, DJ 2008, *When Species Meet*, University of Minnesota Press.

Haraway, DJ 2015, 'Anthropocene, Capitalocene, Plantationocene, Chthulucene: making kin', *Environmental Humanities*, vol. 6, pp. 159–165.

Head, L 2016, *Hope and Grief in the Anthropocene: Re-conceptualising Human–nature Relations*, Routledge.

Hinchliffe, S & Whatmore, S 2006, 'Living cities: towards a politics of conviviality', *Science as Culture*, vol. 15, no. 2, pp. 123–138.

Houston, D, Hillier, J, MacCallum, D, Steele, W & Byrne, J 2017, 'Make kin, not cities! Multispecies entanglements and "becoming-world" in planning theory', *Planning Theory*, doi:10.1177/1473095216688042.

Instone, L 1998, 'The coyote's at the door: revisioning human–environment relations in the Australian context', *Ecumene*, vol. 5, no. 4, pp. 452–467.

Kimmerer, RW 2013, *Braiding Sweetgrass: Indigenous Wisdom, Scientific Knowledge and the Teachings of Plants*, Milkweed Editions.

Kingsley, JY, Townsend, M & Henderson-Wilson, C 2013, 'Exploring Aboriginal people's connection to Country to strengthen human–nature theoretical perspectives', in MK Gislason (ed.), *Ecological Health: Society, Ecology and Health*, , vol. 15, Emerald Group Publishing, pp. 45–64.

Kuhn, TS 1982, 'Commensurability, comparability, communicability', *PSA: Proceedings of the Biennial Meeting of the Philosophy of Science Association*, pp. 669–688.

Langton, M 2006, 'Earth, wind, fire, water: the social and spiritual construction of water in Aboriginal societies', in B David, B Barker & IJ McNiven (eds), *The Social Archaeology of Australian Indigenous Societies*, AIATSIS – Aboriginal Studies Press, pp. 139–160.

Massey, D 1994, *Space, Place, and Gender*, Polity Press.

McMichael, AJ 2001, *Human Frontiers, Environments and Disease: Past Patterns, Uncertain Futures*, Cambridge University Press.

McMichael, AJ 2009, *Climate Change in Australia: Risks to Human Wellbeing and Health* The Nautilus Institute.

McMichael, AJ, Powles, JW, Butler, CD & Uauy, R 2007, 'Food, livestock production, energy, climate change, and health', *The Lancet*, vol. 370, no. 9594, pp. 1253–1263.

Narayanan, Y 2017, 'Street dogs at the intersection of colonialism and informality: "subaltern animism" as a posthuman critique of Indian cities', *Environment and Planning D: Society and Space*, vol. 35, no. 3, pp. 475–494.

Plumwood, V 2009, 'Nature in the active voice', *Australian Humanities Review*, vol. 46, pp. 113–129.

Porter, L 2010, *Unlearning the Colonial Cultures of Planning*, Ashgate.

Porter, L & Barry, J 2016, *Planning for Coexistence? Recognizing Indigenous Rights through Land-use Planning in Canada and Australia*, Taylor & Francis.

Rose, DB 1996, *Nourishing Terrains: Australian Aboriginal Views of Landscape and Wilderness*, Australian Heritage Commission.

Rose, DB 2012, 'Why I don't speak of wilderness', *EarthSong Journal: Perspectives in Ecology, Spirituality and Education*, vol. 2, no. 4, pp. 9–11.

Singer, P 2013, *In Defense of Animals: The Second Wave*, Wiley.

Steele, W, Mata, L & Fünfgeld, H 2015, 'Urban climate justice: creating sustainable pathways for humans and other species', *Current Opinion in Environmental Sustainability*, vol. 14, pp. 121–126.

Twine, R 2010, *Animals as Biotechnology: Ethics, Sustainability and Critical Animal Studies*, Earthscan.

Walker, G 2012, *Environmental Justice: Concepts, Evidence and Politics*, Routledge.

Walker, G 2015, 'Beyond individual responsibility: social practice, capabilities and the right to environmentally sustainable ways of living', in Y Strengers & C Malle (eds), *Social Practices, Intervention and Sustainability: Beyond Behaviour Change*, Routledge, pp. 45–60.

Whatmore, S 2002, *Hybrid Geographies: Natures Cultures Spaces*, SAGE Publications.

Whatmore, S 2006, 'Materialist returns: practising cultural geography in and for a more-than-human world', *Cultural Geographies*, vol. 13, no. 4, pp. 600–609.

Wolch, J 2002, 'Anima urbis', *Progress in Human Geography*, vol. 26, no. 6, pp. 721–742.

Index

Page numbers in italic refer to boxed material and figures.

ABC approaches to health and well-being 100
Abrahamsson, C. 53, 136
Abram, D. 5
accountability 57
actant 56–7, 59, 64, 65n17
actor-network theory (ANT) 26, 73, 77–8, 80, 81
affect(s) 23, 47, 51, 99; defining 9, 15n14, 30–1, 33; emergence of 33; and emotions 32–40; in neuroscience 34–5; in non-representational thought 9, 29, 30–2; in practice theory in 82; and psychoanalysis 34–5; and psychotherapy 34–5; social practice theories 78, 79; social psychology approach 31–2; three translations of (Anderson) 39; use of term 43n15
affective/affectual geographies 35–8, 39
affective thinking 80–3
Affective Turn 8, 9, 138; affect and emotions 32–40; conclusion 40–1; introduction 23; non-representational thought 25–32; what is representation? 24–5; agents/agency 64; in affect and emotions 82; as distributive and confederate 49, 57; more-than-humans 80–2, 144; new materialisms 56; non-humans 10, 13, 47, 115, 119, 121, 138–9, 145, 152; not predictable 57–8; plants 118–19, 121; in practice theory 82, 83
Albrecht, G. et al. 34
allotments 118
Amazon (company) 135

'analytics of affect' (Anderson) 39
Anderson, B.: affect 33, 34, 39–40; affect-emotion bifurcation 35, 36; 'analytics of affect' 39; *Encountering Affect: Capacities, Apparatuses, Conditions* 34; new materialisms 50, 65n9; non-representational thought 26, 28, 29, 30, 31, 42, 42n1, 42n6, 42n7, 43n11, 43n13; practice theories 80; social constructivism 42n2; three translations of affect 39
animal-assisted therapy 102–3
animal cognition and behaviour 61–2
animals 94, 102, 152
Anthropocene 111–12, 124n5
anthropocentric paradigm 4
anthropology 78
anthropomorphism 61–2, 66n26
Apple 135
Arnhem Land, Northern Australia 60–1, 66n24
artificial intelligence 103, 135
assemblage/assemblage thinking 27, 42n4, 49, 51, 54, 65n18, 76, 81, 82, 84n13, 144
Aussie Backyard Bird Count 139

Barad, K. 24, 26, 49, 51, 52, 136
Baudry, S. 114–15
Bawaka Country 61, 62, 66n24, 135, 139, 154
'becoming with' 49, 54–6, 60, 110, 117, 119, 121, 124, 132, 153
behaviour, and health 96
behaviour change theories 7
'being-for-the-other' 121, 122, 124, 134–5

Bell, S.J. et al 60, 139
Bennett, J. 15n14, 26, 40, 49, 51, 54, 58, 65n20, 136; agency 56; 'artful consumption of food' 132; environmentalism 94; intervention in 'environmental problems' 62–3; new materialisms, political potential 59, 60; North American electricity blackout 56–7; thing power 47, 56; *Vibrant Matter: A Political Ecology of Things* 5–6; vital materialism 53, 62, 94; vitalism 53, 55
Bentley, M. 98
Bergson, H. 9, 10, 53
binaries 12, 39, 100, 104, 111, 153; city/nature divide 109; dissolving 151; eschewing 53; human/nature binary 98, 117; nature/culture divide 48, 99, 121; problematic 152; *see also* dualism
biodiversity 1–2, 5, 61, 120, 133
biophilia hypothesis 48, 65n4, 109, 124n8
bird feeding 111, 121–3, 125n11
Bissell, D. 30
black-legged ticks 113
bluespaces 116–17
bodies: as open systems 55; use of term 84n14
body/mind complex 78
Bolivian Plurinational Legislative Assembly 144
Bondi, L. 35, 37, 38
boundaries, transcending 4, 7, 10, 15n10, 54, 63, 64, 135, 136, 154
Bourdieu, P. 11, 72, 84n15
Brisbane 112–13
Brundtland Report 94, 104
brush turkeys 112–13, 120, 135
Burghardt, G.M. 62

Canada, electricity blackout 56–7
Castree, N. 8, 124n2, 152
change, as dynamic 131–2
changing practices: conclusion 145–6; impacts of 145–6; intervening for 141–5; introduction 131–3; and policymaking 13, 132–45; and research 13, 132–45
chaos theory 58
cities: common problems for residents 5; conceptualised 41; use of term 14n1
cities as more-than-human habitat: cities as habitat for non-human

species 111–15; conclusion 123–4; introduction 109–11; more-than-human encounters and human health and well-being 115–17
citizen science 10, 63, 139
city/nature divide 109
class theory 55
climate change 140
Cloke, P. 62, 121, 123
Clough, P.T. 9, 38
co-presence 94
community gardening 118
competences/competencies 33, 73, 74, 82, *101*, 118, 138, 142
complexity theory 58
connected situationalism 84n12
conviviality 96
Coole, D. 51–2, 54, 58, 65n1, 136; agency 56, 58, 65n18; bodies as open systems 55; new materialisms, political potential 59
Country, Indigenous Australians' notion of 143–4
Coutts, C. et al 98
Cresswell, T. 26, 30
critical anthropomorphism 61–2, 64, 135, 140
Cronon, W. 43n11, 58

Dadirri 60–1, 62, 139
dance 26, 31
Daston, L. 66n26
Davidson, J. 35, 38
DeLanda, M. 51, 76
Deleuze, G. 9, 14n4, 26, 32, 40, 42n3, 42n4, 49, 53
DEMAND Centre, Lancaster University 80, 84n17
DeNicola, A.J. et al 113
desire lines 51
Despret, V. 62, 135
Dewsbury, J.-D. 24, 25, 26, 29–30, 32, 42n6
distributed agency 49
Doel, M. 25
dualism 35, 36, 38, 50, 99
Duhl, L. 2

Earth Charter 96
eating 132
Echo (Alexa: Amazon) 135
ecological models 96–8; limitations to 98–100; Mandala of Health 97–8
ecosystem services, trees 121

ecosystem 153; and gardening 120; humans part of 98; novel 112
emotion 23; and affect 32–40; practice theory in 82; study of 34–5
emotional geographies 35–8
'emotional' versus 'affective/affectual' geographies 35–8
encounters *see* events and encounters
energy consumption 81, 103
engaged witnessing 60, 62
England, transport and mobility 137
environment, as passive 99
Environment Protection and Biodiversity Conservation (EPBC) Act (1999) 15n6
environmental microbiome 120
environmental problems, intervention in 62–3
environmentalism 94
epigenetics 52
epistemological approach 145–6
epistemology 23
'ethical mindfulness' 121, 124
ethics 57, 58, 103, 134–5
events and encounters, non-representational thought 28–9, 30–1
'evolving ecological public health paradigm' 98
experimentation 48
extinction 114, 153
extinction debt 114

feminist approaches 33, 36, 38, 55
Ferguson, K.E. 60
first nations *see* indigenous peoples
flat ontology 76–7, 84n11
'flatness of the social world' 76
flying foxes 135
focused intensity 32
food supplies 114
forest, urban 54–5
Foss, P. 65n7
Foucault, M. 72, 77
Franklin, A. 135
Frigg, R. 24
Frohlich, K.L. et al 96
Frost, S. 51–2, 54, 58, 65n1; bodies as open systems 55; new materialisms, political potential 59

Ganga river 144
Gangotri glacier 144
gardening 13, 103, 110, 112–13, 118–21, 124, 151; complex of practices 118, 122, 142; and

ecosystems 120; health benefits of 120; recrafting 142–3; shifting dynamics of 119; substituting elements 142–3
geography 10, 11, 23; affective/affectual 35–8; and assemblage thinking 49, 54; cultural 8, 78, 117; emotional 35–8; human 9, 13, 14, 26, 34–5, 36, 38, 49, 65n9, 110, 117, 123; and new materialisms 54
Gherardi, S. 84n3
Giaccardi, E. et al 82
Giddens, A. 11, 72, 84n15
Ginn, F. 34
glaciers 144
global damage 153
global responsibility 96
gold bell frogs 111
'grammar of animacy' (Kimmerer) 61
green bell frogs 111
greening initiatives 60–1, 66n24
greenspaces 116–17
Gregg, M. 15n14, 33
Gregson, N. 59
Guattari, F. 9, 14n4, 26, 32, 40, 42n3, 42n4, 49, 53

Habitat III, the *United Nations Conference on Housing and Sustainable Urban Development* 4–5
habitat loss 153
habitat protection and provision 143, 153
habitation 94
Hancock, T. 2, 96, 97–8, 97, 99
Haraway, D.J. 58, 61, 110, 121, 125n10, 132, 135, 136, 139, 153; *Staying with the Troubles: Making Kin in the Chthulucene* 5
Harrison, P.: non-representational thought 26, 28, 29, 30, 31, 42, 42n6, 42n7, 43n11; practice theories 80; social constructivism 42n2
Head, L. 110, 146n5
Head, L. et al 62, 119, 121
health and well-being: ABC approaches to 100; and behaviour 96; ecological models for 96–8; more-than-human approach to 100–4; more-than-human encounters 13, 115–17; and social practices 100–2
health as more than human: conclusion 104–5; current ideas of urban health 95–100; introduction 93–5

health promotion 3, 95–6, 151
healthy cities 2, 4, 152
Healthy Cities Programme 2–3, 4, 94, 105, 133
Heidegger, M. 72
Helmreich, S. 139
Hinchliffe, S. 50
Hitchings, R. 119, 120
Houston, D. et al 143, 144, 154
Hui, A. 72, 75
human-centrism 59, 62, 81, 82, 98–100, 124n5, 145, 153, 154
human exceptionalism 10, 59, 109, 115, 124n5, 143
human movement 26, 31
human/nature binary 98, 117
human-non-human interaction 11, 94, 103, 151, 152, 155n2
human-wildlife conflicts 123
humans: decentring 10, 11, 37, 38, 40, 47–8, 51, 98, 110, 136, 138, 139, 144–5, 151, 152; impact of 58; interaction with non-humans 60; migration 142; need for nature 1; non-humans, equal status with 47–8; part of ecosystem 98; as part of nature 1–2, 116–17; recentring 110–11; sovereignty 57, 64
hyperseparation 2

India 144
Indigenous Australians, Country, notion of 143–4
indigenous peoples 139, 146n7, 154
indigenous scholars 154
'informal' greenspaces 117
International Union for Conservation (IUCN) Red List of Threatened Species 14n6
interveners 144
intervening for change 141–5
Ives, C.D. et al 5

Jones, D.N. 112, 115, 122
Jones, O. 29, 62, 121, 123

Kaika, M. 6, 99
Kant, I. 65n18
Kimmerer, R.W. 61, 154
Kingsley, J.Y. 154
Kirksey, S.E. 139
Kowarik, I. 112
Ku-ringgai Chase National Park, New South Wales 62

Langton, M. 154
language: changing 61; depersonalising 139; overemphasis of 24, 40, 50, 65n10, 99, 138
large-scale phenomena 75–6
Latham, A. 32
Latour, B. 26, 42n6, 51, 56, 58, 81
Law, J. 138
Law of the Rights of Mother Earth (Bolivia) 144
'legal person' status 144
Lemke, T. 65n21, 136
Leys, R. 33, 35
Li, T.M. 49, 81
'life-force' 53
lifestyle drift 96, 99; moving beyond 104
Lorimer, H. 26, 37, 43n11
Low, T. 111, 114
Lulka, D. 1
Lyme disease 113

macro social phenomena 75–6
'making kin' 135
Maller, C. 79, 140
Mandala of Health 97–8, 97
Marx, K. 10–11, 52, 72
Massumi, B. 32
materialism, language and text, overemphasis of 50, 65n10
materialism/materiality 24, 94, 99; interests in 51; interventions 64; matter as dynamic 51; and non-representational thought 27; post-humanist 58; and practice 102–3; surfaces 102, 105n4; use of term 65n1; vital 53, 62
materiality *see* materialism/materiality
materials 94, 101–2, 118, 138, 142; and practice 102–3
matter: as dynamic 51; as vibrant 56–7
McCormack, D.P. 26, 32, 35, 37
McMeekin, A. 137, 141, 142, 143
meanings 101, 118, 138, 142
mediation 39
Melbourne 140
memory, and non-representational 29–30
Merleau-Ponty, M. 78
methods of assessment, different practices 138–41
micro-social phenomena 76
microbes 120
'Microbiome Rewilding Hypothesis' 146n8

162   *Index*

microbiomes 55, 120
microorganisms 120
migration, human 142
Mills, J.G. et al 146n8
mindfulness 121, 132, 134–5
Mitman, G. 66n26
mobility, England 137
Mol, A. 58
monism 51, 65n11
Montpelier 115
moralism 57
more-than-human: agency 80–2, 144;
    encounters 13, 115–17; theories 6–7;
    thinking 5–6, 153–4; use of term
    15n7; *see also* non-humans
more-than-human approach: to change
    131–3, 141–5; to health 100–4; and
    intervening for change 141–5;
    theories and origins 8
Morse, N.B. et al 112
Mother Earth 144
motivation 72–3, 84n2
multispecies ethnography 139–40
mycorrhizal networks 52, 65n12

Narayanan, Y. 153
natural sciences, and social sciences 52,
    54, 65n15, 135
nature 48; conceptualised 151; contact
    with 110; human dependence on 98;
    human need for 1; humans as part of
    1–2, 116–17; as passive 99; use of
    term 115–16, 124n2
nature/culture divide 48, 99, 121
neuroscience: and affect 34–5; and
    bifurcation of body and mind 35
New Materialism 15n15
new materialisms 80–3, 132, 134–5;
    and agency 56; characterising 54–8,
    64; conflict and harm 59–60;
    contexts 63–4; in geography 54;
    material agency not predictable
    57–8; origins of 49–53, 53, 63–4;
    politics of 58–63; processes of
    becoming 60; scholarship in 136
New Materialisms Turn 8, 10–11;
    characterising new materialisms
    54–8, 64; conclusion 63–4;
    introduction 47–9; new politics 10;
    origins of new materialisms 49–53,
    63–4; politics of new materialism
    58–63; relational and democratic
    stance 10
New Urban Agenda 4–5, 6, 98, 105,
    152

New Zealand 144
nest boxes 111
Nguyen, J. 24
Nicolini, D. 7, 73, 76, 77, 84n12,
    84n13
Nielsen Park she-oak 114
non-humans: agency 10, 13, 47, 115,
    119, 121, 123, 138–9, 145, 152;
    equal status with humans 47–8; and
    human interaction 60; perceived to
    go wrong 28, 40–1; use of term 1;
    vibrancy 10, 40, 47, 55, 115,
    118–19, 121, 123, 132, 153; *see also*
    more-than-human; more-than-
    human approach
non-relational thinking 152
non-representational thought 9, 23,
    25–32, 27, 42, 47, 51, 63, 76, 82,
    138; and affect 9, 29, 30–2; events
    and encounters 28–9, 30–1; and
    materialism/materiality 27; and
    memory 29–30; not necessarily
    anti-representational 43n11; and
    performativity and practice 27–30;
    relationality in 65n18; research and
    policymaking 9–10, 32; temporality
    23, 28–9
North America, electricity blackout
    56–7
North London 119
'novel ecosystems' 112

Obama, B. 34
object, use of term 55–6
old materialisms 52–3
ontology 23, 36
Ortner, S.B. 72
Ottawa Charter for Health Promotion
    2–3, 4, 94, 95–6, 98, 104, 133

Pantzar, M. 11, 101
Papay, J. et al 96
Paris 115
parkland 54–5, 102
Parkour 32
pathways 51
Patton, P. 65n7
Pellegrini, P. 114–15
performance arts 31
performativity 28
Perkins, F. 97
pet robots 103
pets/companion animals 102–3,
    124n7; feeding practices 113

Pickering, A. 4, 11, 14n4, 24, 26, 50, 51, 52, 73
Pile, S. 35, 37, 38
Pink, S. 78
plants 94, 102, 103, 114–15, 146n6, 152; agency 118–19, 121; capacities 118–19; uncooperative 119; *see also* gardening
Plumwood, V. 2, 143, 144, 145, 154
policymaking 9, 152, 153; and changing practices 13, 132–45; and non-representational thought 9–10, 32; reframing urban problems 134–7
Porter, L. 154
post-humanism 11, 27; materialism/ materiality 58; and practice theories 11, 71, 79, 80, 81
power, and practice theories 77–8
Power, E.R. 119, 121
practice memory scrapbooks 140–1
Practice Turn 8, 11: comparing social practices to affective and new materialist thinking 80–3; critiques of social practice theories 75–80; history of theories of social practice 72–5; introduction 71–2
practice(s) *see* social practice(s)
practice theories *see* social practice theories
Priest, G. 6
protest marches 39
psychiatry 34
psychoanalysis, and affect 34–5
psychotherapy, and affect 34–5
Puig de la Bellacasa, M. 114, 121, 122, 135, 139

rational choice theory 7
Reckwitz, A. 11, 39, 73–4, 78, 78–9
redefining health urban environments: conclusion 13–14; introduction 1–4; structure and overview 7–14; theories and thinking about healthy urban environments 6–7; urban context 4–6
renewed materialisms 52; *see also* new materialisms
representation 24–5, 38, 40, 42n2, 133, 138; in social sciences 24, 42n3; three prongs of 42n3
research 9, 152; and changing practices 13, 132–45; different practices 138–41; and non-representational thought 9–10, 32; reframing urban problems 134–7

(re)turn to materialism *see* materialism/ materiality
rivers 9, 144
road-kill 111
roads 9
Rose, D.B. 135, 143, 154
Rouse, J. 78
Royal Botanic Gardens, Sydney 135

Schatzki, T.R. 11, 72, 76, 79, 84n3, 84n15
school-age children, and gardening 118
science and technology studies (STS) 8, 10, 11, 73, 80
Seigworth, G.J. 15n14, 33
'shadow of the linguistic turn' 14n4
Shove, E. 11, 73, 74, 75, 101, 136
Shove, E. et al 81, 101, *101*
Simonsen, K. 78
Singapore, 'biophilic city' 109
Siri (Apple) 135
skills *see* competences/competencies
Slow Food Movement 132
smart homes 103
social change, and practice theories 79–80
social constructivism 42n2
social determinants 12; of health and health promotion 95–6; limitations to 98–100
social marketing campaigns 142
social practice theories 28, 80–3, 132; and affects 78, 79; and agency 82, 83; and bodies 78; critiques of 75–80; defining 73–5, 84n5; every practice can change 132; hybrid model 83; and individual experience 77; and intervening for change 141–5; more-than-human agency 80–2; motivation 72–3, 84n2; post-humanist position 11, 71, 79, 80, 81; and power 77–8; and routine 83; sensations and experience 75, 78–9; and social change 79–80; types of action 83–4; unit of enquiry or analysis 136–7; *see also* changing practices; practice
social practice(s) 28, 99, 152: bird feeding 111, 121–3, 125n11; as building blocks 74–5; bundled 141–5; as 'doings and sayings' 74, 84n8, 94n9; elements of 101–2; features of 71–2; gardening 118, 122, 142; and health 100–2;

interlocking 143; as lead theory 12, 71, 80, 83, 95, 131; long working day 101; materials and materiality 102–3; pet feeding 113; and research 138–41; and routine 11, 12, 73–4; and scale 75–8; use of term 11; walking 101, *101* wildlife feeding 13, 110, 117, 123, 124, 151; *see also* changing practices; social practice theories

social psychology, and affect 31–2

social sciences: and natural sciences 52, 54, 65n15, 135; representation in 24, 42n3

socio-ecological models 12

'solastalgia' 34

Spinoza, B. 9, 10, 33, 53, 56

'spontaneous flora' 114–15

Spurling, N. 137, 141, 142, 143

'state apparatus' 14n4

Stengers, I. 51, 58

Strengers, Y. 79, 140

Strengers, Y. et al 81, 136–7

surfaces, materiality of 102, 105n4

surveys 24–5, 138

sustainability 96

Sustainable Development Goals (United Nations, 2016) 93, 105, 117

Swyngedouw, E. 109, 123

Sydney 112–13, 114, 135; gardeners 119–20

Sydney Olympics (2000) 111

technology 10, 82, 83, 94, 103, 133, 135, 139

teleo-affectivities 79, 84n15

temporality 9, 23, 28–9

text: changing 61; depersonalising 139; overemphasis of 24, 25, 32, 40, 50, 65n10, 99, 138

theory, as important 6–7

Thien, D. 35, 36, 37–8

thing, use of term 56

'thing power' 47, 56

threatened species 5; *see also* extinction

Thrift, N. 15n14, 37, 63; affect 33; dance 31; human movement and dancing 26; *Non-Representational Theory: Space, Politics, Affect* 31; non-representational thought 26, 27, 42n1, 42n6, 42n7, 76, 82; performance arts 31; social

sciences 31–2; wild ideas/ thinking 7, 9, 30

thrushes 114

Tolia-Kelly, D. 35, 36, 37, 50, 65n9

traffic-centred intersections 114

transport, England 137

trees 54–5, 64, 94, 114; perform 'ecosystem services' 121; social life of 52, 65n13

turn, use of term 15n11

Turner, B.S. 105n4

uncertainty 11

United Nations: *Habitat III, the United Nations Conference on Housing and Sustainable Urban Development* 4–5; New Urban Agenda 4–5, 6, 98, 105, 152; Sustainable Development Goals (United Nations, 2016) 93, 105, 117

United Nations General Assembly 5

unpredictability 48, 63, 64, 152; of agency 57–8

urban health: current ideas of 95–100; limits to current approaches 98–100

vegetation 114–15; *see also* plants; trees

vibrancy: matter 56–7; non-humans 10, 40, 47, 55, 115, 118–19, 121, 132, 153

viruses 2, 55

vital materialism (Bennett) 53, 62, 94

vitalism 53

Wainwright, S.P. 105n4

walking, practice elements of 101–2, *101*

Warde, A. 73, 84n2

Washick, B. 10, 58–9

water supplies 114

Watson, M. 11, 76, 77–8, 79

weeds 119–20, 142, 146n6

Wetherell, M. 15n14, 31, 78

Whanganui Iwi people 144

Whanganui river 144

Whatmore, S. 4, 52, 58, 145

white-tailed deer 113–14, 120

wild spaces 120–1

'wild' thinking (Thrift) 7, 9, 30

'wilderness areas' 5

wildlife feeding 13, 110, 117, 123, 124, 151
wildlife gardening 118, 120–1, 142–3
winds 120
Wingrove, E. 10, 58–9
Wittgenstein, L. 72

Wohlleben, P. 55
Wolch, J. 114, 135, 139, 151
World Health Organization (WHO) 1, 2

Yamuna river 144
Yamunotri glacier 144
Yolŋu people 61

For Product Safety Concerns and Information please contact our EU
representative GPSR@taylorandfrancis.com
Taylor & Francis Verlag GmbH, Kaufingerstraße 24, 80331 München, Germany

*9 7 8 0 3 6 7 4 5 9 0 3 1 *